Transforming Human Culture

SUNY SERIES IN
CONSTRUCTIVE POSTMODERN THOUGHT
DAVID RAY GRIFFIN, EDITOR

David Ray Griffin, editor. *The Reenchantment of Science: Postmodern Proposals*

David Ray Griffin, editor. *Spirituality and Society: Postmodern Visions*

David Ray Griffin. *God and Religion in the Postmodern World: Essays in Postmodern Theology*

David Ray Griffin, William A. Beardslee, and Joe Holland. *Varieties of Postmodern Theology*

David Ray Griffin and Huston Smith. *Primordial Truth and Postmodern Theology*

David Ray Griffin, editor. *Sacred Interconnections: Postmodern Spirituality, Political Economy, and Art*

Robert Inchausti. *The Ignorant Perfection of Ordinary People*

David W. Orr. *Ecological Literacy: Education and the Transition to a Postmodern World*

David Ray Griffin, John B. Cobb, Jr., Marcus P. Ford, Pete A. Y. Gunter, and Peter Ochs. *Founders of Constructive Postmodern Philosophy: Peirce, James, Bergson, Whitehead, and Hartshorne*

David Ray Griffin and Richard Falk, editors. *Postmodern Politics for a Planet in Crisis: Policy, Process, and Presidential Vision*

Steve Odin. *The Social Self in Zen and American Pragmatism*

Frederick Ferré. *Being and Value: Toward a Constructive Postmodern Metaphysics*

Sandra B. Lubarsky and David Ray Griffin. *Jewish Theology and Process Thought*

J. Baird Callicott and Fernando J. R. da Rocha, eds. *Earth Summit Ethics: Toward a Reconstructive Postmodern Philosophy of Environmental Education*

David Ray Griffin. *Parapsychology, Philosophy, and Spirituality: A Postmodern Exploration*

Jay Earley. *Transforming Human Culture: Social Evolution and the Planetary Crisis*

TRANSFORMING HUMAN CULTURE

Social Evolution and the Planetary Crisis

Jay Earley

State University of New York Press

Published by
State University of New York Press, Albany

Printed in the United States of America

For information, address State University of New York Press
State University Plaza, Albany, NY 12246

Production by Dana Foote
Marketing by Nancy Farrell

Library of Congress Cataloging-in-Publication Data

Earley, Jay, 1944–
Transforming human culture : social evolution and the planetary crisis / Jay Earley.
p. cm. — (SUNY series in constructive postmodern thought)
Includes bibliographical references and index.
ISBN 0–7914–3373–0 (hc : alk. paper). — ISBN 0–7914–3374–9 (pb : alk. paper)
1. Social ecology. 2. Social evolution. I. Title. II. Series.
HM206.E19 1997
303.4—dc 21

97–2331
CIP

This book is dedicated to Bonnie, with all my love.

Contents

Introduction to Suny Series in Constructive Postmodern Thought

The rapid spread of the term *postmodern* in recent years witnesses to a growing dissatisfaction with modernity and to an increasing sense that the modern age not only had a beginning but can have an end as well. Whereas the word *modern* was almost always used until quite recently as a word of praise and as a synonym for *contemporary*, a growing sense is now evidenced that we can and should leave modernity behind—in fact, that we *must* if we are to avoid destroying ourselves and most of the life on our planet.

Modernity, rather than being regarded as the norm for human society toward which all history has been aiming and into which all societies should be ushered—forcibly if necessary—is instead increasingly seen as an aberration. A new respect for the wisdom of of traditional societies is growing as we realize that they have endured for thousands of years and that, by contrast, the existence of modern society for even another century seems doubtful. Likewise, *modernism* as a worldview is less and less seen as The Final Truth, in comparison with which all divergent worldviews are automatically regarded as "superstitious." The modern worldview is increasilyly relativized to the status of one among many, useful for some purposes, inadequate for others.

Although there have been antimodern movements before, beginning perhaps near the outset of the nineteenth century with the Romanticists and the Luddites, the rapidity with which the term *postmodern* has become widespread in our time suggests that the antimodern sentiment is more extensive and intense than before, and also that it includes the sense that modernity can be successfully overcome only by going beyond it, not by trying to return to a premodern form of existence. Insofar as a common element is found in the various ways in which the term is used, *postmodernism* refers to a diffuse sentiment rather than to any common set of doctrines—the sentiment that humanity can and must go beyond the modern.

Beyond connoting this sentiment, the term *postmodern* is used in a confusing variety of ways, some of them contradictory to others. In artistic and literary circles, for example, postmodernism shares in this general sentiment but also involves a specific reaction against "modernism" in the narrow sense of a movement in artistic-literary circles in the late nineteenth and early twentieth centuries. Postmodern architecture is very different from postmodern literary criticism. In some circles, the term *postmodern* is used in reference to that potpourri of ideas and systems sometimes called *new age metaphysics*, although many of these ideas and systems are more premodern than postmodern. Even in philosophical and theological circles, the term *postmodern* refers to two quite different positions, one of which is reflected in this series. Each position seeks to transcend both *modernism* in the sense of the worldview that has developed out of the seventeenth-century Galilean-Cartesian-Baconian-Newtonian science, and *modernity* in the sense of the world order that both conditioned and was conditioned by this worldview. But the two positions seek to transcend the modern in different ways.

Closely related to literary-artistic postmodernism is a philosophical postmodernism inspired variously by pragmatism, physicalism, Ludwig Wittgenstein, Martin Heidegger, and Jacques Derrida and other recent French thinkers. By the use of terms that arise out of particular segments of this movement, it can be called *deconstructive* or *eliminative postmodernism.* It overcomes the modern worldview through an anti-worldview: it deconstructs or eliminates the ingredients necessary for a worldview, such as God, self, purpose, meaning, a real world, and truth as correspondence. While motivated in some cases by the ethical concern to forestall totalitarian systems, this type of postmodern thought issues in relativism, even nihilism. It could also be called *ultramodernism*, in that its eliminations result from carrying modern premises to their logical conclusions.

The postmodernism of this series can, by contrast, be called *constructive* or *revisionary.* It seeks to overcome the modern worldview not by eliminating the possibility of worldviews as such, but by constructing a postmodern worldview through a revision of modern premises and traditional concepts. This constructive or revisionary postmodernism involves a new unity of scientific, ethical, aesthetic, and religious intuitions. It rejects not science as such but only that scientism in which the data of the modern natural sciences are alone allowed to contribute to the construction of our worldview.

The constructive activity of this type of postmodern thought is not limited to a revised worldview; it is equally concerned with a postmodern world that will support and be supported by the new worldview. A postmodern world will involve postmodern persons, with a postmodern spirituality, on the one hand, and a postmodern society, ultimately a postmodern global order, on the other. Going beyond the modern world will involve transcending its individualism, anthropocentrism, patriarchy, mechanization, economism, consumerism, nationalism, and militarism. Constructive postmodern thought provides support for the ecology, peace, feminist and other emancipatory movements of our time, while stressing that the inclusive emancipation must be from moderniy itself. The *postmodern*, however, by contrast with *premodern*, emphasizes that the modern world has produced unparalleled advances that must not be lost in a general revulsion against its negative features.

From the point of view of deconstructive postmodernists, this constructive postmodernism is still hopelessly wedded to outdated concepts, because it wishes to salvage a positive meaning not only for the notions of the human self, historical meaning, and truth as correspondence, which were central to modernity, but also for premodern notions of a divine reality, cosmic meaning, and an enchanted nature. From the point of view of its advocates, however, this revisionary postmodernism is not only more adequate to our experience but also more genuinely postmodern. It does not simply carry the premises of modernity through to their logical conlusions, but criticizes and revises those premises. Through its return to organicism and its acceptance of nonsensory perception, it opens itself to the recovery of truths and values from various forms of premodern thought and practice that had been dogmatically rejected by modernity. This constructive, revisionary postmodernism involves a creative synthesis of modern and premodern truths and values.

This series does not seek to create a movement so much as to help shape and support an already existing movement convinced that modernity can and must be transcended. But those antimodern movements which arose in the past failed to deflect or even retard the onslaught of modernity. What reasons can we have to expect the current movement to be more successful? First, the previous antimodern movements were primarily calls to return to a premodern form of life and thought rather than calls to advance, and the human spirit does not rally to calls to turn back. Second, the previous antimodern movements either rejected modern science, reduced it to a description of mere appearances, or assumed its adequacy in principle; therefore, they could base their calls only on the negative social and spiritual effects of modernity. The current movement draws on natural science itself as a witness against the adequacy of the modern worldview. In the third place, the present movement has even more evidence than did previous movements of the ways in which modernity and its worldview *are* socially and spiritually destructive. The fourth and probably most decisive difference is that the present movement is based on the awareness that *the continuation of modernity threatens the very survival of life on our planet.* This awareness, combined with the growing knowledge of the interdependence of the modern worldview and the militarism, nuclearism, and ecological devastation of the modern world, is providing an unprecedented impetus for people to see the evidence for a postmodern worldview and to envisage postmodern ways of relating to each other, the rest of nature, and the cosmos as a whole. For these reasons, the failure of the previous antimodern movements says little about the possible success of the current movement.

Advocates of this movement do not hold the naively utopian belief that the success of this movement would bring about a global society of universal and lasting peace, harmony, and happiness, in which all spiritual problems, social conflicts, ecological destruction, and hard choices would vanish. There is, after all, surely a deep truth in the testimony of the world's religions to the presence of a transcultural proclivity to evil deep within the human heart, which no new paradigm, combined with a new economic order, new childrearing practices, or any other social arrangements, will suddenly eliminate. Furthermore, it has correctly been said that "life is robbery": a strong element of competition is inherent within finite existence, which no social-political-economic-ecological order can overcome. These two truths, especially when contemplated together, should caution us against unrealistic hopes.

However, no such appeal to "universal constants" should reconcile us to the present order, as if this order were thereby uniquely legitimated. The human proclivity to evil in general, and to conflictual competition and ecological destruction in particular, can be greatly exacerbated or greatly mitigated by a world order and its worldview. Modernity exacerbates it about as much as imaginable. We can therefore envision, without being naively utopian, a far better world order, with a far less dangerous trajectory, than the one we now have.

This series, making no pretense of neutrality, is dedicated to the success of this movement toward a postmodern world.

David Ray Griffin
Series Editor

Acknowledgments

I am especially endebted to Bob Ressler, Tom Atlee, and Florian Lewenstein, who each read the manuscript from beginning to end and provided many useful comments. Jean Houston and Marcia Yudkin also provided helpful suggestions.

INTRODUCTION

The human race is at a turning point in its history, a crossroads in social evolution. We are facing a crisis of planetary proportions, led by our environmental problems. We are confronted with immense dangers and exciting possibilities. On one hand, we are courting ecological disaster. On the other hand, we have the opportunity, as never before, to create a healthy global society, truly dedicated to human betterment. This crisis is not an aberration. Despite our grave danger, our situation can be understood as a natural outgrowth of our evolution. This means that there is a way to surmount the crisis which is also a natural continuation of our historical course.

We have a chance now to fundamentally advance along the path of social evolution, an opportunity to move to a new level of evolution. We have the capacity to take charge of history! In order to do this we need to understand our past and our trajectory. Who are we? Where are we headed? How have we have managed to create, on the one hand, such great humanitarian and cultural accomplishments, and on the other, such massive human misery and ecological destruction. This book offers an answer to these questions and points the way toward a healthy future. When we understand ourselves and our history, we can take charge of our future. We can consciously direct our evolution. We can resolve the crisis and progress toward a world that will truly be dedicated to harmony and fulfillment—for all people, for our descendants, and for the natural world.

In this book I develop a theoretical model of social evolution. It explains how the present crisis emerged through the natural flow of historical trends, and how these trends can shape the transition to a healthier world. In nurturing this transition, if we understand these social forces, we can flow with them and use them to create the future. This will help us understand the personal changes we need to make and how to influence others. We can see how our institutions and social structures must change and how to tell real change from window dressing. This book provides new perspective on today's situation by portraying it in a larger context.

SYNOPSIS

The following is a synopsis of this model of social evolution and its relationship to our current planetary crisis. I will state it very simply here and then provide reasons and evidence for the model and examples of its application throughout the rest of the book.

At the start of social evolution, human beings enjoyed certain qualities, which I call *ground qualities*:

1. connection with nature
2. sense of belonging and richness of experience
3. egalitarian community

As time went by, our population continually grew in a world of limited resources, and groups threatened each other with war. Therefore over the course of history we were forced to develop other qualities in order to survive. These *emergent qualities* gave us more conscious choice and power over our environment and ourselves:

1. technology
2. reflexive consciousness
3. social structure

These qualities helped free us from the vagaries of weather and climate and threats from predators. They allowed us to grow more food and harness more energy, to coordinate increasing numbers of people. They gave us the military power to protect ourselves. They gave us a way of understanding ourselves and the world and the advantages of civilization and higher culture. In time we had the opportunity for education and personal development.

The ground qualities are characterized by vitality and organic wholeness; the emergent qualities are characterized by power and differentiated organization. So far in social evolution the ground and emergent qualities have been opposed to each other, though it is possible to integrate them.

In today's crisis, the emergent qualities have come to dominate and the ground qualities have been suppressed, so we are paying the price of losing our original vitality and wholeness. We are alienated from the natural world, from each other, and from ourselves. Our economic system emphasizes material growth at all costs. Our technical power and our population are so large that we are acting in ways that threaten our ecological well being and perhaps our very survival.

1. We have developed technology and destabilized our environment.
2. We have gained understanding and lost vitality, meaning, and empathy.
3. We have developed social structure and lost equality and community.

Now we are beginning to be aware enough to grasp this. We have an opportunity to consciously redevelop the original ground qualities in harmony with the established emergent qualities. This integration has already been forming for a few hundred years in the realm of power; it is called "democracy." It is just now beginning to transpire in other realms.

It is not enough to focus on regaining the ground qualities. We must recognize that the emergent qualities are also valuable for a healthy society. Our difficulties at this time are not because humanity has too much of the emergent qualities, but rather because we have suppressed the ground qualities. At this time in human history we need integration—integration of conscious power and organic vitality. We must have both sides of our nature now.

We are called on to practice this in our personal lives and to embody it in our institutions and our culture. Then we will have:

1. ecological technology
2. integrated mind and heart
3. social structure that promotes community and equality

As we integrate the ground qualities, the emergent qualities can safely develop even further, to give us greater clarity and consciousness, more intelligent technology, and a global society that is democratic, pluralistic, and dedicated to the good of the all human beings and the earth.

Our social evolution has been driven by the need for societies to survive in war and feed their increasing populations, and so it is not surprising that our achievements have been mixed. We have accomplished much that is admirable and much that is destructive. However, now is our moment! We have enough understanding and power that we can consciously take charge of our evolution, and create a new global society that truly promotes the well-being of humanity and the biosphere.

Human social evolution is part of the larger story of the evolution of the physical world and of life. In all realms, evolution moves toward increasing levels of complexity and autonomy, but so far in social evolution this has happened at the expense of wholeness and therefore has brought us to our current crisis. *We must now consciously choose to regain our wholeness and vitality in conjunction with our complexity and autonomy, as individuals and communities, as organizations, as a world society, and as a living planet.* This will resolve the current crisis and advance us to an entirely new stage of evolution.

REVERSE SPLITTING

In psychotherapy terminology, *splitting* is a defense mechanism where people tend to see things in extreme good or bad terms. They may see one person as an all-loving angel and another person as totally dangerous and evil. Or they may see the same person as all-good at one time and all-bad at another. The most important aspect of splitting is that it prevents a person from seeing shades of gray or recognizing that a person can have both positive and negative characteristics. Prejudice is an example of splitting at the social level, where one cultural group (or religion or race) is seen as all-bad and one's own group is seen as all-good. A prejudiced person can't see that different people of one cultural group have a variety of personal characteristics, and that each cultural group has both positive and negative characteristics.

In this book, I want to broaden the concept of splitting so it can apply to human qualities as well as people. In other words, someone can see a certain human quality as all-good and another quality as all-bad. For example, our culture tends to see logical, analytical thinking as the best form of consciousness and intuition/emotion as inferior and mistaken. By my broadened definition, this can also be considered a form of splitting. There is no recognition that intuition and emotion have positive attributes or that an integration of emotion and intellect might be best, for example.

From this perspective, our Modern society has engaged in splitting the ground and emergent qualities. We believe in the wonderful benefits of technology and science (emergent), and until recently, we denigrated untamed nature and indigenous people (ground) as wild, primitive, and brutish. We have lauded the importance of large-scale social organization and nation-building (emergent) and viewed anything else as backward or dangerously anarchic.

On the other hand, socially conscious people who recognize the dangers of our current social arrangements tend to reverse this. In realizing our overreliance on the emergent qualities and our need for the ground qualities, they often view the ground qualities as all-good and the emergent qualities as all-bad. They praise the wonders of emotions, intuition, and spirituality (ground) and warn of the dangers of rational, linear thinking (emergent). They speak of the beauty of nature (ground) and the evils of technology (emergent), the joy of community (ground) and the dangers of the market and multinational corporations (emergent). While some of this is true, this kind of split thinking throws the baby out with the bath water. Although nature, emotion, and community *are* beautiful, technology can be enormously beneficial, rational thinking is essential for much that we value, and some form of large-scale social structure is necessary to coordinate a world of billions.

In analogy to the terms "reverse racism" and "reverse sexism," I will use the term *reverse splitting* to refer to the attitude of overvaluing the ground qualities and denigrating the emergent qualities. This is a major problem for progressive thinkers and social change agents. Even those who understand the value of both sides often subtly slip into a posture of devaluing the emergent qualities, sometimes without even realizing it. One of the important contributions of this book is to clarify this problem and restore balance and integration to our understanding of the human qualities needed for a healthy resolution of the current crisis.

THE PLANETARY CRISIS

It is becoming increasingly clear that humanity is facing a planetary crisis, so I will just discuss it briefly. Even though our current mode of operation has served us well for the past few centuries, it is no longer working, and we are plagued with one problem after another. We seem to have survived the immediate threat of nuclear war between the superpowers only to be faced with a major ecological crisis. In addition, we are struggling with economic problems, rising crime, drug abuse, homelessness, terrorism, nuclear proliferation, genocide, and many other seemingly unrelated issues.

It is not chance that we are simultaneously afflicted with these multiple crises. We are at one of those few times in human history when profound changes are happening in every aspect of life, and they are happening even faster than in previous crises. The modern worldview, which guided us for hundreds of years, is now outmoded. Based on science and rationality, it treats everything as a machine to be analyzed and controlled. This has brought us tremendous gains in knowledge, freedom, and comfort. It has brought us an enormous expansion of our technical power, our population, and our capacity to control the natural world. But these abilities have created immense problems which cannot be adequately comprehended with our current mentality. When we attempt to solve these problems using approaches that are familiar to us, it only succeeds in making matters worse.

Similarly our current lifestyle is outmoded. Based on material consumption and personal ambition, it once benefited us by fueling our drive toward mastery. But now it, too, is contributing to the dangers at hand. Our desires and our powers have expanded terribly, while our natural vitality and sense of connection have diminished. This imbalance is the true source of our predicament.

Our Task. The stakes are high. We may do irreparable damage to our ecological life-support systems before we realize that we must alter our course. For example, we may cause enormous climatic disruptions or destroy much of our genetic diversity. However, the opportunities are exhilarating. Public awareness and concern about environmental issues are increasing. The ending of the cold war gives humanity an opportunity to cooperate internationally and to redirect resources from military uses to ecological and social betterment. For the first time in human history, we have the knowledge and power to choose our overall direction with foresight. We have the opportunity to construct a planetary society that will provide security, health, and prosperity for everyone, that will foster love, harmony, and creativity. However, we are not yet choosing this path. So far, we haven't developed the global consciousness that would foster cooperation and wisdom. This is our great task at this time in planetary history.

To promote a healthy transformation, we must proceed wisely. We need vision and compassion, strength and understanding. We need to understand how we arrived at such a crisis and the forces that are leading us toward wholeness. We must move quickly while recognizing that our fondest dreams will take some time. We must call for the deepest, most fundamental changes, and also understand the fears of those who are stuck in outmoded attitudes. We must believe passionately in our own visions for the world while realizing that we don't have all the answers. There must be profound changes in our consciousness and way of being, and also in our institutions and social structures. Everyone has a part to play. We need protesters and mainstream translators; we need visionaries and organizers; we need thinkers and doers; we need charismatic leaders and people who make practical changes in their lives.

My Frustration. One of my on-going frustrations is knowing what is happening to our world and not being able to change things right away. When I so clearly see our danger, I want to shout from the rooftops, "Stop! Don't you see what's happening! We have to change." Then I return to sanity and try to understand why change doesn't happen more quickly. Many of us know that change is needed. But few people realize how serious things are, and many don't believe they can do anything about it. Society needs to change in *fundamental* ways, and that level of change doesn't happen easily.

How does change happen? What can we, what can *I* do to encourage it to happen, with the least suffering and destruction. My frustration is knowing roughly where we need to go, but not knowing how to make it happen. But maybe my job isn't to "make it happen," but just to play my part in this transition. So instead of shouting from the rooftops, I wrote this book.

USEFULNESS OF THIS BOOK

The Model. Even though the environmental crisis is the most serious problem humanity is facing right now, it is only a symptom of a much broader social crisis. Therefore the model of social evolution I present in this book is also broad. It deals with material, social, and psychological processes. Even though my academic background is in psychology (and before that computer science), the theory I present is not restricted to the psychological area or even to individual change. It also deals with social, political, and economic issues; with technology and ecology; with science and religion. I draw on psychology, sociology, history, anthropology, archeology, and general systems theory. To understand the situation, we must consider events from as wide a perspective as possible; we must attempt to deal with the whole.

Other Studies. Most other treatments of this problem focus their attention on only one dimension. Some authors recognize that change is happening over many dimensions but believe that it is driven by only one. Some social critics focus on spiritual development (Ferguson 1980; Harman 1988), some on science and knowledge (Capra 1982), some on power (Bookchin 1982; Schmookler 1984; Eisler 1987), or the environment (Anderson 1987; Berry 1990), or community (Bellah et al. 1985; Peck 1987). Many social critics do not have a historical perspective, or they only look at the medieval and modern eras. Those theories that specifically deal with social evolution also tend to focus in one area only—technology (Harris 1978; Harris 1980; Sahlins and Service 1988) or social structure (Parsons 1966; Johnson and Earle 1987) or consciousness (Jaynes 1976; Wilber 1983; Elgin 1993). Most works on social evolution also tend to be heavily academic and not explicitly oriented toward solving today's planetary crisis.

This book is broad in scope, covers the entire course of social evolution, and relates directly to the current crisis. Of course, this means that I can't go into as much detail as other authors. I must paint in broad strokes. I often have to cover in a paragraph or even a sentence a complex topic that talented scholars may have spent their lives studying. I run the risk of skimming over significant controversies, slighting important points of view, missing the depth of certain topics, and being just plain wrong. It isn't possible for me to be thoroughly knowledgeable about everything I discuss in this book. I hope that my overall perspective is valuable even if I am amiss in certain specifics.

Most studies of social evolution focus only on the emerging trends and not on what has been lost or suppressed in the process of evolution. A few take the opposite stance, focusing only on what has gone wrong and not on our advances. I believe that social evolution has produced both pluses and minuses, and that our problems today are because of dissociation and imbalance. Some recent authors are taking a similar perspective (Johnston 1984; Tarnas 1991).

Two excellent books, by Duane Elgin (1993) and Ken Wilber (1995), come closest to my approach. Their ideas were developed independently of mine, and I think, of each other, though both Elgin and I made use of Wilber's previous book on social evolution, *Up from Eden* (1983). I discuss and critique these approaches in chapter 18.

SOCIAL EVOLUTION

Biological and Social Evolution. There are two kinds of evolution that have led the human race from our original state as animals embedded in the world of nature to our current status as intelligent, sophisticated world conquerors. The first is biological evolution, in which our actual physical attributes changed and our minds grew and developed in power and scope. This took place over hundreds of thousands of years, even millions of years. As we became more intelligent, we developed the beginnings of language, art, and culture; we became capable of planning for the future and using abstract thought.

At some point, maybe thirty-five thousand years ago, we developed biological capacities that are very similar to those we have today. In that time, there haven't been many significant genetic changes in humanity.

This is not to say that biological evolution couldn't continue, but left to natural selection, it would go at such a slow rate that it couldn't affect the events that now concern our future. Furthermore, any biological changes in our future are likely to be chosen through biotechnology, not evolved naturally.

The other kind of evolution that has formed us is social evolution. This is the evolution of human culture and social systems, the ways we think, live, and organize ourselves. Social evolution includes the evolution of government, institutions, values, family structure, and worldview, everything except our biological underpinnings. We are so much the products of our culture that with little biological change, the human race has evolved from primitive hunter-gatherers with the most rudimentary language to world conquerors with the power to create masterworks of art and science and to destroy the entire planet. Figure 1.1 shows the relative time scales of biological and social evolution.

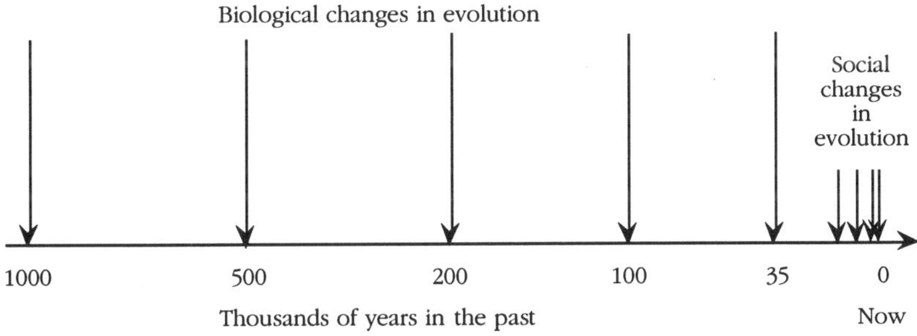

Figure 1.1 Time Scales of Biological and Social Evolution

The Question. All these changes have happened through social evolution, driven by our natural desire to survive and bring more comfort and pleasure into our lives. Let's look at this process from the broadest possible perspective. What has happened? Are we improving or progressing? If so, why are we in such a crisis now? On the other hand, maybe we have fallen from grace. Did we once live in a golden age of peace and harmony and abundance? Did we make a dreadful mistake when we developed technology, oppression, and war?

What is the overall direction and meaning of social evolution? This is a crucial question, because it strongly affects our view of ourselves as a species and our understanding of future directions. Let's consider three possible answers to this question.

1. *Progress.* From this perspective, history and social evolution have produced continual uphill progress toward human betterment. Some see this as coming through the gradually broadening civilization of the world and an improvement in civic virtues. Others see it as coming from our increasing understanding and control of the natural world and ourselves. They believe that in the long run, technology can solve any problem and science can answer any question. Humanity is moving toward a technological wonder world which will bring comfort, power, and happiness. Our current world view is the best possible, and all previous cultures were merely primitive versions of it.

This is the dominant view today in the industrialized world, but belief in it is being increasingly strained as the realities of the planetary crisis become more apparent. There is clearly some truth in this perspective, but it ignores not only the current crisis but also the many evils of civilization and technology—oppression, exploitation, war, environmental destruction.

2. *Wrong Turn.* Some radical social critics have a very different view of our evolution. They believe that at one time humans lived in harmony with the natural world and in relative harmony with one another. Then something happened to cause us to fall on evil ways, and we began to engage in domination and war and environmental destruction. They believe that social evolution took a wrong turn at some point in our history. Some believe this occurred when we left our primitive state as hunter-gatherers (Bookchin 1982). Some see it as happening with the introduction of widespread war (Schmookler 1984) or with the triumph of patriarchy in the Bronze Age (Eisler 1987). Others see it happening in the Ancient Era (Whyte 1948) or more recently with the Industrial Revolution, when we lost our sense of spirituality and accelerated our technological domination of the earth (Berman 1984; Harman 1988).

Whenever they believe we went wrong, these critics agree that we made a mistake in social evolution which must be righted. Our job now is to restore the original harmony that was lost. We must regain our spirituality, or our egalitarian social structure, or the partnership between the sexes, or our connection to the earth, or all of these. There is much truth in these points of view, but they don't provide an explanation for the substantial creative, spiritual, scientific, and humanitarian accomplishments that have occurred since the wrong turn.

3. *Marxism.* Marxism has a historical view that is different from both of these. It believes that history is driven solely by economic considerations, that societies move through a sequence of economic systems—from feudalism to capitalism, to communism. In this view, human society

is moving forward dialectically. That is, Marx believed that a social system would continue to develop until the contradictions or problems within it eventually caused it to change course. Then the new direction would also work for a while, until its internal problems led to another redirection of energy. Thus capitalism grew out of feudalism, and Marx's expectation was that the excesses of capitalism would cause a new system, communism, to grow out of it.

Though Marx was certainly right in many of his criticisms of capitalism, he failed to see its flexibility and potential for improvement. He also focused too narrowly on economic factors as being the only significant cause of historical movement.

My model is also dialectical. It understands our social evolution as a process in which certain qualities and ways of being have been emerging and the original ground qualities have been lost or suppressed. We are now at the point where the suppression is causing such serious consequences that we must reconnect with the abandoned qualities. Thus the model explains both the horrible suffering we have caused and the great beauty we have created.

THE ERAS

I will follow the journey of social evolution according to the major eras in human history, as summarized in Table 1.1.

Table 1.1 Stages of Social Evolution

Stage	Era	Dates	Characterized by
1	Upper Paleolithic	35,000–7000 B.C.	Hunting & gathering, tribes, magic
2	Neolithic	7000–3000 B.C.	Horticulture, villages, mythology
3	Archaic	3000–500 B.C.	Agriculture, first cities, gods and heroes
4	Ancient/Medieval	500 B.C.–1500	Religion, philosophy, historic empires
5	Modern	1500–2000	Science, industry, democracy, individuality
6	Next	2000–	Next?

We will start in approximately 35,000 B.C. because that is when the human race reached its current status in biological evolution. A baby born today has roughly the same endowment as one born 35,000 years ago. All the changes since then have been the result of social evolution, not biological. The Upper Paleolithic era is popularly known as the Stone Age, when people lived in small bands, obtained their food by hunting and gathering, shared freely with each other, and sensed spirit in everything. The Neolithic era was characterized by early agricultural villages and a mythological understanding of the world. Women often played a prominent role in society. The Archaic era introduced the first cities, the emergence of large-scale war, the triumph of male gods, and the beginnings of civilization. The Ancient era marked the beginning of religion, philosophy, and the more organized empires of historical record. (I have included the Medieval era together with the Ancient because the advances of the Medieval were not significant enough to warrant a separate era.) The Modern era of science, industry, and democracy includes roughly the last 500 years, and the next era is being created during the current period of transition.

Each of these eras has been identified by many scholars of history and social evolution, though few recognize them all. Each era marks the beginning of a new stage of social evolution.

Why So Far Back? You may wonder why I think it is valuable to look so far back. In studying historical trends, isn't a couple hundred years sufficient? What can today's crisis have to do with events that happened five or ten thousand years ago?

We certainly need to look back more than a few hundred years. The Modern era began four or five hundred years ago. At the very least we must understand the change from the Medieval to the Modern era. But this is not enough. Many of the social structures that are now in transition began long before the Medieval era. For example, social stratification and wars of conquest emerged for the first time five to seven thousand years ago. If we don't attend to their beginnings, we could mistakenly think they have always existed. Throughout history, social evolution has been driven by powerful historical forces, some of which had their beginnings in distant times, though they are still operating today. If we are to understand these processes, we need to study the full trajectory of social evolution.

The Paleolithic era is also relevant, because it lasted for such a long time and it contains our human roots. We evolved biologically as hunter-gatherers in the wilderness. That is the lifestyle and environment that fit us. We now live in an environment that is radically different from that which we're made for. This has profound implications for our social and psychological health (Glantz and Pearce 1989).

Organization of this Book. Chapter 2 describes the model of social evolution in detail. Part 1 that follows explores the story of social evolution, including a chapter for each era in human history, and further delineates the model. Those of you who aren't interested in history can skim this part. Part 2 deals with the current crisis, devoting a chapter to each of the three primary realms—material, social, and consciousness—and one to the crucial issue of population. Part 3 explores ways to resolve the crisis through integrating the ground and emergent qualities. I look at politics and economics, gender and culture, the environment and population, consciousness, and community. The model is used to elucidate how any person, group, or movement could contribute to resolving the crisis. Part 4 places the model within an inclusive framework for general evolution and explores the possibility of the development of global consciousness.

II

THE MODEL OF SOCIAL EVOLUTION

Good/Bad Models. Let's now look in detail at the model of social evolution I am presenting in this book. This model is designed to accentuate the issue of dissociation versus integration. Too often in works of social theory, our current social arrangement is conceptualized in good/bad terms, often through reverse splitting. Their major concepts explain how the current arrangement is bad and the author's proposed solution is good. For example, technology is bad and ecology is good. "Dominator" is bad and "partnership" is good. These distinctions are useful in alerting us to the problems and dangers of our current way of life and pointing out possibilities for the future, but they tend toward simple-mindedness and divisiveness.

Good/bad schemes can be especially problematical when they encourage a judgmental attitude toward people who find value in our current way of operating. Should people who value and enjoy technology feel bad about that? Should those in power feel guilty even if they are concerned about others? Are men naturally dominators, so only women can contribute to a cooperative world? Of course, these are simplistic notions which the original authors of the ideas would probably not support. Nevertheless, using a good/bad model often encourages this kind of thinking.

Dissociation and Integration. As social change agents, if we approach things through reverse splitting, we alienate many of our potential allies. And we also miss out on a deeper truth—that humanity is in process. There is a flow to history, from our origins to differentiation, and then to dissociation and finally integration. There are social and historical forces underlying even the most destructive social arrangements which we need to understand with compassion if we are to navigate the rapids into a positive future.

I see our problems in terms of dissociation, suppression, and splitting. The emergent and ground qualities are dissociated from each other. For example, our current technology cuts us off from the natural world.

The emergent quality (technology) is *dissociated* from the ground quality (natural living). They are opposed to each other rather than working in harmony. This causes a split in society, where it seems that society must choose between the powerful advantages of technology or the healthy advantages of natural living. Technology also *suppresses* natural living, which means that technology is dominant and natural living is marginalized in today's industrial societies. Similarly, our current social structure (emergent) tends to destroy community (ground).

Sometimes there is also *splitting*, where the ground quality is not only dissociated and suppressed, but also devalued. The emergent quality is seen as good and the ground quality is seen as inferior, bad, or even evil. For example, the ground qualities of emotion, intuition, and spontaneity are often seen as irrational, superstitious, and/or dangerous.

In order to resolve these problems, we don't need to discard technology or social structure. We must achieve an integrated or synergistic relationship, for example, between technological and natural living, between social structure and community.

In working for social change, if we have an understanding of the historical path that led to the current predicament, it allows us to see things from a compassionate perspective, empathizing with the outlook of those who don't yet understand the need for change. It might enable us to understand what role they could play in the transition and how to reach them.

The model is divided into three realms. The material realm deals with physical reality, especially the relationship between nature and technology. The social realm deals with the way people interact, at all levels from interpersonal relationships to the world economy. The consciousness realm deals with our inner world—psychology, religion, meaning, morality, and people's everyday experience of life.

THE MATERIAL REALM

Each realm is characterized by two healthy complementary qualities. In the material realm these are *natural living* and *technological living*. Natural living is known as a *ground* quality because it has been present from the beginnings of human social evolution. Technological living has gradually emerged over time, becoming increasingly prominent and powerful; therefore I call it an *emergent* quality.

Natural living means living in harmony with the biological world, using processes which work *with* the natural flows of the earth. In some cases, this may be due to the virtual absence of technology as in the Stone

Age, when people had no choice but to harmonize with nature. In other cases, it can mean using technology that is aligned with natural process, which follows the existing patterns of biology whenever feasible and disrupts as little as possible, for example, technology designed to minimize consumption of energy and resources and reuse wastes.

Technological living means using both artifacts (especially machines) and specialized techniques in the material aspects of life. Of course, technological living has come to emphasize complex and sophisticated machines. It usually aims to maximize productivity and labor efficiency. It has given us much in the way of power, comfort, and protection, but this has come at the cost of alienating us from our roots in the natural world.

Complementary Qualities. Central to this model is the idea that the ground and emergent qualities are complementary, not opposite. For example, if natural living were defined as living without technology, then the two qualities would be opposites; it would not be possible to integrate them. The most society could aim for would be a good balance between them. We could strive to minimize our technology, but this would overlook the more important goal of creating harmonious technology, eco-technology. In defining these qualities as complements, we can aspire to integrate them, for example, to create technology that is aligned with the earth, such as heating a house with passive solar heat. In this way we achieve not just balance but integration, where the two complementary qualities work together.

Even though integration is possible, it is not easy. It can appear at first that technological and natural living are intrinsically opposed, that society must choose one or the other of these two modes of operation. Indeed, historically they have been antagonistic. The human race began social evolution with pure natural living, and as our technological prowess has expanded, we have become increasingly out of step with the natural world. This has now progressed to the extent that we are threatening it with serious damage. However, this opposition is not necessary, and our mission today must be to integrate the complementary qualities, not just in the material realm, but in all realms.

Graphic Representation. Throughout the book, I will use a form of overlapping ovals to represent the complementary qualities in each realm. This is illustrated in figure 2.1 for the material realm.

Technological living is represented by the oval on the right in figure 2.1. Natural living is represented by the one on the left. When a society is structured so that two qualities are integrated, this is represented by the heavily shaded place where the ovals overlap in the center, which I am

Figure 2.1 Material Living

calling *eco-technological living.* When a society is arranged so that technological living dominates and natural living is suppressed, this is represented by the part of the lightly shaded oval on the right. I call this *artificial living.* When a society has little or no technology, where natural living is the primary mode, this is represented by the part of the shaded oval on the left. I call this *primitive living.*

Artificial living is exemplified by today's industrialized nations, which are so involved in technological pursuits and the material side of life that they diminish people's sense of connection to the earth and threaten the biosphere. Primitive living is illustrated by the material situation of our early ancestors who lived in hunter-gatherer bands. With eco-technological living there is not just a compromise or balance between natural living and technology, the qualities are integrated so that they work together and possibly even enhance each other. For example, we could combine our technological sophistication with our knowledge of ecosystems to preserve and restore the beauty of the natural world. We could use our scientific, medical knowledge about childbirth to create a method of natural childbirth that is safer and more soothing for the child and mother.

I will use this form of graphic to represent the relationship between the ground and emergent qualities in each realm and subrealm. The generic form is shown in figure 2.2.

Figure 2.2 Generic Representation

Building a Model. Any theory or model emphasizes certain aspects of reality that seem most important to the builder of the model. By choosing a model that features complementary qualities rather than opposites, I have accentuated the issue of integration versus dissociation. This then highlights integrative solutions to the current crisis.

In my model, I have chosen the three realms—material, social, and consciousness—primarily for convenience and because of tradition. Later in the book, I divide these realms into subrealms in order to explore them in finer detail. Even though the selection of realms is somewhat arbitrary, within each realm the choice of complementary qualities is crucial. I have picked each pair of qualities to reflect the major social evolutionary trend in that realm and to highlight the current problems we face.

THE SOCIAL REALM

Figure 2.3 shows the complementary qualities in the social realm.

Figure 2.3 Social Realm

Community characterizes a society whose people feel connected to each other and to the whole, where each person is valued and there are shared traditions and mores. Power is relatively equal and the community takes responsibility for the well-being of its members.

This way of defining community is somewhat unusual because I have not included personal contact as part of the definition. Even though personal contact is an important part of local community, I prefer a definition that can apply to any size grouping. My definition is similar to that used by Daly and Cobb in their book *For the Common Good* (1989), where it is possible for any collection of people to be a community, even a nation or the entire world. Of course, it is easier for small groups to enjoy a high degree of community and much more difficult for large ones. However, by defining community in this way, it makes it possible to strive for the integration of community and social structure.

With *social structure*, transactions are organized and mediated primarily through social roles and institutions rather than direct personal contact. This can mean that interactions are influenced by status, rules of conduct, money, vested power structures, or other means, but underlying all these is the primary influence of role. This could be family role (father), status role (elder), financial role (merchant), occupational role (shoemaker), professional role (lawyer), class role (serf), and so on. With social structure, society tends to be differentiated into various sectors with occupational specialization, and coordinated through institutions such as the government and the economy. Social structure can tend toward being impersonal and stratified, though that is not part of its definition.

Social structure also has its positive side. It is absolutely necessary for coordinating larger associations of people; this can't be done through personal contact alone. Social structure also brings together people from different cultures and traditions, thereby enhancing the possibility of intercultural understanding and appreciation. My definition of social structure is not meant to imply that simple communities are without any structure of a social nature. They also have a kind of structure, but it is more organic and personal and therefore outside my definition.

Anthropologist Victor Turner (1974, 131) defines the term "communitas" as opposed to ordinary social structure; this is similar my definition of community.

I can now complete the explanation of figure 2.3 on the social realm. When there is social structure without a sense of community, power tends to be unequal, leading toward stratification and *oppression*. In addition, since community involves a sense of connection between people, a lack of community results in *alienation*. In the opposite situation, where there is community without much social structure, there tends to be prejudice against those outside the community, which I am calling *parochialism*. In addition, except for small, simple societies, a lack of social structure leads to a state of *anarchy*, where there is not enough societal coordination for proper functioning of the economy and protection of its citizens from violence.

As I discussed previously, the complementary qualities are not necessarily opposites. With conscious effort social structure and community can be integrated. For example, in a large society with a high degree of social structure, there can be some sense of shared tradition and values and a feeling of belonging and caring among its people. Community also involves relatively equal sharing of power among the population, which in Modern social structure is achieved by *democracy*. Integration in the social realm is also characterized by tolerance or even appreciation of cultural differences, known as cultural *pluralism*.

THE CONSCIOUSNESS REALM

The complementary qualities in the consciousness realm can be represented as in figure 2.4.

Figure 2.4 Consciousness

Complementary Qualities. *Participation* or *participatory consciousness* is the ground quality. It is characterized by a sense of belonging to the world and an aliveness and immediacy of experience. In this mode, people relate to the world primarily through instinct, emotion, the body, and the immediate present. Reality is experienced as animate, organic, and spiritual. We are fully alive in the present; our experience of life is not dulled or blocked. We experience our senses, our bodies, our emotions, and our spiritual atunement in a full and vibrant way.

Reflexive consciousness is the emergent quality. This means the ability to understand ourselves and the world through the mediation of images and ideas. It means being able to step back from and reflect on how we experience the world. Rather than simply experiencing, we can also conceptualize and analyze our experience as a way of trying to see it more clearly and understand it more deeply. In its more advanced stages, it means using logical operations on abstract concepts, especially "exclusive" concepts, which specify clear boundaries, such as the dictionary definition of a word. This can grant more objective understanding and allow us to make conscious choices about how to act. It enhances our ability to take control of our environment and plan for the future.

When participatory consciousness uses concepts at all, it tends to use "inclusive" concepts, which are looser and more symbolic, such as a dream image which can mean many different things. It tends to use metaphor, art, and story.

This distinction between participatory and reflexive consciousness is similar to recent work in constructivist cognitive psychotherapy theory. Guidano (1991) discusses the interplay between "embedded immediacy" and "abstract distancing" in meaning making. My emphasis on integration of these two modes of consciousness finds confirmation in the work of Greenberg and Pascual-Leone (1994), who "call for a dialectical synthesis between the direct emotional process and the reflective cognitive knowing processes to guide adaptive action" (Fodor 1996).

Dissociation. The ability to reflect on and analyze our experience is the foundation of much that is uniquely human. Our capacity to observe our actions and deduce their consequences has given us conscious choice, and therefore ethics and philosophy. Our ability to objectively comprehend the material world has given us technology and science.

On the other hand, without our aliveness and our emotions, without our passion and our spiritual depth, without our sense of belonging to nature and to the human community, there would be no point in living. Life would be sterile and meaningless. In figure 2.4, having reflexive consciousness at the expense of participatory consciousness is referred to as *detached consciousness.*

And the reverse, if you have only participatory consciousness without much reflexive consciousness, you are unable to step back from your experience and think clearly and critically about it. I call this *immersed consciousness*. You can't make a conscious choice to go against your impulses, even when it would be best for you. It is hard to see through someone who is manipulating you. You just accept the way things are without thinking for yourself.

What Evolves? In this book, I explore the evolution of consciousness from stage 1, which was largely characterized by participatory consciousness, to stage 5 today, which is largely characterized by reflexive consciousness. However, this doesn't mean that the basic cognitive capacity of stage 5 people is any different from that of stage 1. Our basic biological equipment hasn't changed much during the last 35,000 years. A baby born to hunter gatherers in the Upper Paleolithic era who was magically transported to the twentieth century and raised in a Modern urban culture would no doubt exhibit full stage 5 reflexive consciousness. If this is true, then what do I mean by consciousness evolution?

There are cultural and social influences on consciousness that can be as influential as biological changes in brain structure. While a hunter-gatherer might be capable of the reflexive thought of an Einstein, he or she couldn't actually operate that way growing up in a culture that was participation-oriented, with no written word, no tradition of analytic thought, no one to discuss high level abstraction with, and so on. It has taken the entire span of social evolution for our reflexive capacities to develop culturally (and for our participatory capacities to be suppressed) even though they have been part of our biological heritage all along.

What has evolved has been our psychological tendencies and the culturally based actuality of our consciousness, not our underlying cognitive capacity.

Healthy functioning involves an integration of participation and reflexive consciousness, where you experience full aliveness and belonging, and you have the ability to conceptually evaluate your experience and the world and make autonomous choices. I call this *conscious participation.*

Notice that in the material and consciousness realms there are no really good established terms for the integrated qualities. This is because these qualities are just being developed during this historical transition. In the social realm, there are some good terms like "democracy" and "pluralism" because these integrated qualities have been under development for a few hundred years.

THE CREATIVE MODEL

This model has been inspired by Charles Johnston's Creative Model.* In his book *The Creative Imperative* (1984), Johnston takes on the task of developing a model of human process in the broadest sense—a model that can be applied to such disparate things as (1) creating a work of art, (2) a love relationship, (3) an individual's psychological development, and (4) the social evolution of the human race. His model is broad enough and at a high enough level of abstraction that it can be applied to these four very different processes.

His contention is that when trying to understand living process, especially human process, our old mechanistic models are not adequate to deal with the most important aspects of the subject. He is attempting to create a new kind of model, which is clear and rigorous, but capable of dealing with such things as aliveness, relationship, and evolution. In his model, all human process is viewed as an act of creation. There are stages corresponding to the initial unformed, fertile state; the phase of creation when something is beginning to take form; the finished product; and the time when the creation is integrated with its context. Johnston uses this model to describe not only obvious acts of creativity such as sculpting, but seemingly unrelated processes such as social evolution. Since he is a psychotherapist, he also applies his model to understanding the therapy process.

---

* Johnston's *The Creative Imperative* (1984) is a highly theoretical work which explores this model in detail. In his second book, *Necessary Wisdom* (Johnston 1991), he applies the model to various contemporary issues in cultural change.

Figure/Ground Dialectic. My model is not based on creativity, but it has been inspired by Johnston's insights into dissociation and integration and the dynamic relationship between the ground of creation and the emerging figure. My model, of course, deals with social evolution specifically, while his operates at a higher level of generality which applies to all human process. It might be fair to view my model as a particular application of Johnston's meta-model.

In his Creative Model, there is a dialectical relationship between that which is being created or coming into form and the context or background of the creation. My emergent qualities correspond to his created form and my ground qualities to his context. He identifies a creative rhythm that is divided into three general spaces—differentiation, transition, and integration. Within the differentiation space, there are four stages corresponding to different relationships between the emerging form and its context. I have followed his general developmental rhythm but not exactly his four stages.

Other Concepts of Social Evolution. How do my the ground and emergent qualities in each realm relate to existing ideas about social evolution? In the material realm, many theorists have taken technological level as the measure of social evolution (Harris 1978; Lenski and Lenski 1987; Sahlins and Service 1988). In the social realm, sociologists have generally emphasized social differentiation and social roles as the essential aspect of social evolution (Parsons 1966). In the consciousness realm, most theorists agree with my view of evolution as an increasing ability to emerge from and reflect on previous structures of consciousness (Kahler 1956; Gebser 1986; Elgin 1993; Wilber 1995).

Other Complementary Qualities. Let's examine other possible candidates for complementary qualities that I could have used rather than ground and emergent.

At first glance, the ground and emergent qualities look similar to the Taoist concepts of yin and yang, with yang corresponding to the emergent qualities and yin to the ground qualities. However, there is one significant difference which prevents me from using these ancient concepts. Yin and yang are complementary aspects of reality that have always existed, while my ground and emergent concepts are specifically tied to social evolution, where the emergent qualities were largely nonexistent in its early stages and have only emerged over time.

Another pair of complementary qualities that are frequently used in a similar way are masculine and feminine. These have the same problem as yin/yang in that masculinity and femininity have always existed, and in addition, I don't want to contribute to gender role stereotypes by using gender categories for such important qualities that can, in fact, be embodied by either gender. I discuss this further in the chapter on gender.

The political polarity of left and right might at first look like a possible candidate, but this is an even poorer choice. First of all, left and right, as usually conceived, are opposites, not complements. Second, they really refer to more historically specific positions in the social realm as I will discuss later, not general complementary societal qualities.

EMERGENCE THROUGH MEDIATION

Looking more deeply in the model, it is possible to elucidate a comprehensive understanding of social evolution that transcends any single realm.

There is an underlying meaning for emergence that includes the emergent qualities in each realm—technological living, social structure, and reflexive consciousness. Human beings were originally embedded in our biological nature, and we have gradually emerged and separated ourselves from our original environment. This includes not only the emergence from the natural world through technology, but also emergence from the unconscious through reflexive thinking, and emergence from the biological bonds of community through complex social structure.

Emergence has two parts—separation from embeddedness and the development of a new mediated relationship with the biological ground in which we were embedded. Here I mean *mediation* in the broadest sense of the term, being an intermediary between two parties. To mediate between two entities is to join them, to come between them, to facilitate their interaction in some way. Thus a common thread among the emergent qualities is that they all involve a differentiation and organization of reality through mediation.

Existing Meanings of Emergence. In biology and in the study of complexity in general, "emergent properties" are those properties of a system that are apparent when the system is looked at as a whole, but are not properties of the parts of the system. For example, hydrogen and oxygen have certain properties as separate atoms, but when they are combined into a system of H_2O, then an entirely different set of properties emerge, the properties of water. An "emergent domain" is the level of complexity where the behavior and properties of the system as a whole are studied, perhaps in relation to other such systems. In the water example, the emergent domain is the domain of molecules as opposed to that of atoms.

The study of human society is an emergent domain at one level up from the study of human beings as individuals or as purely biological animals, so in a loose sense we can consider social evolution as the process by which society develops its emergent properties. However, this is not strictly true. Even at the beginning of social evolution, there were human societies with properties, such as community, that were emergent at the societal level (didn't exist at the individual level). Therefore this existing meaning of emergence is closely related but somewhat different from my use of the word.

In psychology, the word emergence has been occasionally used in a way that is completely in line with my use. Robert Kegan, in his excellent book on human development (1982), describes how a process of "emergence from embeddedness" is initiated by the maturing of the child in interaction with the world at each stage of development. He shows how this notion is implicit in the work of Jean Piaget, the great developmental psychologist (1977).

This works as follows: At first children are embedded in a certain way of perceiving and living because they do not see it. Therefore they can't understand it or include it in their thinking. There is something about the world or their way of relating to the world that is invisible to them. Then they emerge from this embeddedness and develop a concept for it. The emergent concept mediates between them and their experience of the world. They now see what was once invisible, and this endows them with a wider vision and greater cognitive functioning.

Emergence in Social Evolution. Let's return now to emergence in social evolution. The ground qualities are all part of our biological heritage; it might be fair to say that they are characterized by *organic wholeness*. This is obvious with natural living—it is defined in terms of ecological harmony. Community is also built into our genes. Human beings evolved biologically to our current form under the social conditions of hunter-gatherer bands, so we are biologically adapted to that social arrangement. Community is a way of organizing society based on the organic nature of personal relationship and the wholeness of group connection. Participatory consciousness, the world of direct experience, is also a biological given and has a natural, unitary quality.

The ground and emergent qualities therefore represent two different ways of perceiving and organizing reality. The ground qualities do this in an integrated, organic way. The emergent qualities do it in a differentiated, mediated way. Let's look at how emergence happens in each realm.

Material Emergence. In the material realm, humanity has gradually separated itself from direct contact with the natural world and used technology as a mediator. We could, of course, relate to the physical world directly, unaided, with only our bodies. If we wanted to travel a distance, we could walk. If we needed food, we could gather it in the forest. However, instead we travel using cars or airplanes as mediating instruments. To obtain food, we cultivate, fertilize, plant, and harvest, using a variety of technical procedures and devices. Most of us live in cities where we are radically separated from nature and have to make a special effort to go to a park to experience it directly. We are also separated from our internal nature. We are born in hospitals using pain killers rather than naturally at home. We wear glasses to see and to protect us from bright sunlight. We take antibiotics when we have infections.

In both external and internal ways, we have emerged from being embedded in nature to form a mediated relationship through technology. Has this been good or bad? I think both. We have gained a great deal of protection, comfort, and power through the mediation of technology, and we have also lost our intimate spiritual connection with nature. Consequently we are threatening to destroy our ecological life-support systems. Our task today is to learn to integrate mediation with a direct experience of and harmony with our biological heritage.

Social Emergence. In the social realm we have gradually moved away from the direct biological connections of local community. The original hunter-gatherer bands were largely based on familial relationships, and even the stage 2 villages were oriented toward family and clan. Community has always involved a deep sense of belonging to the land, of inhabiting a place that is sacred to your family and people. Community relations have been largely based on direct personal contact. This is all clearly biological.

As social structure developed, larger associations came into being which needed other ways of relating, which were mediated through mythic traditions, through roles, through money, through organizations with rules and procedures. Gradually people were separated from local community and came together in large cities with others from different religions and cultures. They related as buyers and sellers, as workers and owners, as nobles and serfs, as citizens and consumers. Direct personal contact was largely replaced with mediated relationships. Individuality became strong.

The individual emerged from the close milieu of community and formed role relationships. If you are a teacher of mine in an institutional setting, then we might be able to have a direct personal relationship, but it is more likely that we will treat each other in ways that are consistent with our roles of student and teacher. We will both assume that you are the knowledgeable one and that you are going to judge my performance in some way. I will probably want to please you or impress you. You probably won't share any of your personal concerns with me. This has both advantages and disadvantages.

Emergence in Consciousness. In the consciousness realm emergence means separating yourself psychologically from your immediate experience and using concepts and rational understanding as mediating devices. In pure participatory consciousness, people experience directly without using concepts, but as consciousness evolves, we increasingly emerge from this direct experience and use images, concepts, and our analysis of them to understand the world and to mediate our experience of reality. Of course, even stage 1 people used concepts. You would have to go back to the hypothetical stage zero to find a time when our ancestors didn't use ideas at all. However, stage 1 people used concepts in a metaphoric, inclusive, accepting way rather than the analytic, skeptical way we use them today, which provides a greater degree of mediation.

If I am swimming in the ocean, in pure participation I could directly feel the cool sensation of the water on my body, the exertion of my arms and legs, the action of the waves, the warmth of the sun, the smell of the salt water. Alternatively I might notice the pull of undertow and use that concept to be careful not to be sucked under and drown. I might notice the cold, clammy feeling on my skin and remember that I had better get to shore and get warm. Here my experience is mediated by concepts and my understanding of consequences, so that I can keep alive and well. However, if I get overly concerned with these concepts, I may not be present enough to enjoy being in the water.

Let's explore a specific example of emergence through mediation. Hunter-gatherer tribes had traditions, rituals, and customs that clearly guided their people in how to live. The people followed this lore without realizing that it was a tradition. It was just "the way things are done." Other tribes were considered strange or evil. As social evolution progressed and cities developed where people from different traditions could interact, new concepts developed. If you lived at that time, you began to realize that there were other customary ways of living. You emerged from your heritage.

This didn't mean you would necessarily abandon your tradition. You might even cling to it more strongly than ever. However, if you kept it, you did that by choice. In the past, you would have followed your people's customs without thinking, without realizing there was any alternative. Now you are separate enough from your tradition to realize that it *is* a tradition. You can form a new mediated relationship with your heritage, mediated by the concept of a "tradition." Your new relationship may be one of rejection or embracing, but in either case you are no longer embedded in your tradition. You have emerged.

Therefore in all realms, social evolution advances by emergence from embeddedness through mediation, as shown in figure 2.5.

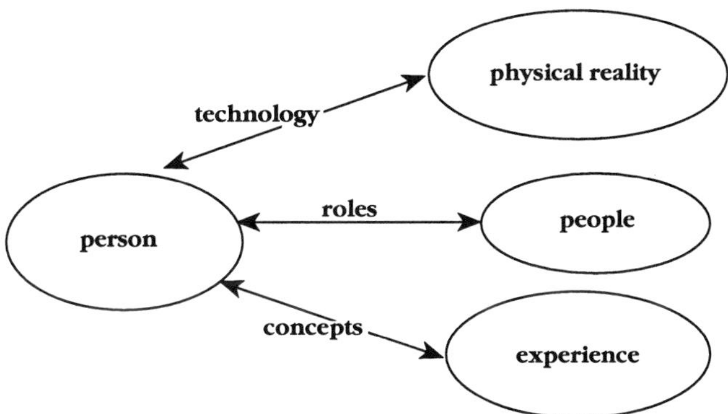

Figure 2.5 Mediation

Power and Vitality. An alternative way of understanding the essence of the emergent qualities is that they have the effect of increasing our *power* in the world. They all give human beings and societies greater ability to make the world the way we want it. Technology gives us power to control the material world. Social structure gives a society greater power to control its own people and to compete with other societies. Reflexive consciousness gives us conscious choice over our own actions and a method of understanding reality that facilitates our ability to control it. This is opposed to participatory consciousness, which allows us to understand reality in a way that encourages communion, not control.

The complement to power for the ground qualities is *vitality*. With participatory consciousness, there is an aliveness to experiencing life directly without our heads getting in the way. There is an unfolding vividness to living in harmony with the earth, and there is an interpersonal vitality to the contact and connection of community.

I can summarize this overall perspective on the model as follows: *Over the course of social evolution, as human beings have emerged from embeddedness in nature and organized ourselves and the physical world through mediation in order to gain power, we have lost vitality and disrupted our organic wholeness. Our great task at this time in history is to integrate these two sides of ourselves.*

Part One

OUR HISTORY

In part 1, I explore human history from the Stone Age to the present and in the process amplify our understanding of the model of social evolution. There is a chapter for each historical era, interspersed with chapters detailing additional aspects of the model as they become relevant to the unfolding story of our evolution.

Chapters 3, 4, and 5 cover the first three stages of social evolution. Chapter 6 studies the driving forces that have propelled social evolution and shaped our current societies. Chapter 7 looks at the subrealm of power and the evolution of oppression. Chapters 8 and 9 complete the historical story with stage 4, beginning in the Ancient era, and stage 5, the Modern era.

III

STAGE 1: TRIBAL HUNTING MAGIC

THE MATERIAL REALM: HUNTING AND GATHERING

In the Upper Paleolithic period, from roughly 35,000 to 8000 B.C. humans lived by hunting and gathering. These Stone Age people lived very close to nature and obtained everything directly as they needed it, in natural form. They hunted animals and gathered roots and berries and other edible plants that were available nearby. When seasonal fluctuations caused animals or plants to become scarce, the people migrated to a place where food was more plentiful. Therefore they were nomadic, moving from place to place in a regular cycle throughout the year in order to inhabit the best areas for obtaining their basic sustenance. They had minimal technology—fire, stone tools, the bow and arrow, hunting techniques, a knowledge of herbs, the domestication of the dog.

They existed in a situation of immediate dependence on the natural world. They lived by its seasons and were susceptible to its droughts, blizzards, and floods. Those who dwelled in lands that were rich and abundant had lives that were comfortable and bountiful with much leisure time. In fact, anthropologist Marshall Sahlins (1972) refers to these primitive groups as the original affluent society. On the other hand, in times of scarcity, stage 1 people had little to fall back on and were prone to starvation. Because of their dependence on untamed nature, people had to be spread sparsely through a region.

Let's review the complementary qualities in the material realm.

Figure 3.1 Material Living

The ground quality in this realm is *natural living,* which means being in harmony with natural processes. There were significant advantages to this. Today we drive hours on a vacation to get to beautiful, unspoiled country so that we can enjoy a hint of the connection with nature that these people experienced daily. Many of them were able to meet all their needs by working only four hours a day.

However, since stage 1 peoples had little technology, it is more accurate to characterize their situation as the dissociated form of natural living, *primitive living*. They had little or no store of provisions against adversity, so that an unusual drought could cause serious difficulties. They had little ability to protect themselves from the hazards of nature, so a chance blizzard or hurricane could produce heavy casualties. They traveled throughout the year, never having a permanent place to settle. They had little in the way of medicine to deal with disease.

In this section for the sake of simplicity, I describe the life of stage 1 peoples as if they were all roughly the same, but this is not really accurate. In fact, there were numerous tribes scattered all over the globe, each with their own way of living. I have given a rough summary of the similarities, but there were undoubtedly many exceptions and a wide degree of variation. This caveat also holds for descriptions of later stages.

THE SOCIAL REALM: COMMUNITY

There were probably three types of social units. The extended *family* was the basic unit. A *band* consisted of a number of families who lived and worked together, twenty to fifty people in all. A *tribe* was a collection of bands with a common language and culture. Families occasionally moved from one band to another within the same tribe. Marriage was often arranged outside the primary band, but always within the same tribe. There was little social contact between tribes, except possibly through warfare in order to defend territory.

Before continuing, let's clarify some terms. By a *society* I mean a group of people that operates as a unit in making political and economic decisions such as warfare, technology, and social structure. A society is frequently a state, although it could also be a band, a village, or an empire. A *culture* is a particular way of living, including worldview, values, and social structures. Sometimes a society and a culture correspond. However, there have been situations where many societies had virtually the same culture, such as when ancient Greek culture was widespread in the Mediterranean. And conversely, many societies contain a variety of subcultures within them. For stage 1 peoples, each band was a society and each tribe was a culture, though some societal decisions were probably made at the tribal level.

Each person lived in intimate contact with everyone in the band. This was their entire social world except for occasional contact with neighboring bands of the same tribe. There was little social complexity or specialization of function except for that based on age and gender. In other words, no one had a unique job as a toolmaker or animal handler or herbalist. Instead, each member of the band was able to personally perform almost all the various necessary tasks. The shaman may have been the one specialist.

Power and Status. The only distinctions in status or power were those due to age and gender, and even these did not result in much power difference. Women and men had different status and power, but the disparities were not great compared to those that resulted from the oppression of women in later stages. Elders usually had greater status, but not necessarily more power. Everyone shared equally in the basic resources of the band. Their economic system was based on sharing according to need and *reciprocity*, which means that things are given when needed or asked for, with the expectation that eventually something roughly equivalent will be returned.

Everyone was free to pursue their lives as they saw fit within the bounds of the tribal norms. No one could command or direct others without their permission. Leadership was temporary and situational rather than based on enduring authority. For example, a man might become a leader because of competence in hunting or canoe construction, and when that job ended, so did his leadership.

Imagine living in a social arrangement like this. There was no need to work like a slave in order to afford a house or to save for a comfortable retirement. No one was rich and no one was poor because people didn't accumulate things or withhold them from others. If things were tough, they were tough on everyone. There were no bosses and no servants, no bored secretaries or line workers, no nobles and no peasants. No one was lonely or isolated; everyone had a place.

Parochialism. There was a certain amount of prejudice, however. People from other tribes with different customs and worldviews were often considered evil, strange, or not quite human. The word that many tribes used as a tribal name, in their own language simply meant "the people," implying a powerful ethnocentrism. This parochialism is not limited to stage 1, of course. There is still much of it today, but we moderns are leaving it behind. We are starting to realize that there are many ways to live and many views of reality. Luckily, in stage 1, the prejudice against outsiders didn't cause a great deal of trouble because people had limited contact with other tribes.

Figure 3.2 Social Realm

The ground quality in the social realm is *community*, which means that a society is cohesive, has common traditions and values, distributes power equally, and cares about the well-being of all its members. Stage 1 peoples indeed had community without much social structure, and because of their small size, they had a form of local community, which included an intimate sharing of daily life. These societies were simple enough that they needed little social structure to avoid falling into anarchy.

THE CONSCIOUSNESS REALM: PARTICIPATION

The consciousness of stage 1 is less clearly known because it can only be inferred from archeological artifacts and from anthropological studies of current-day hunter-gatherers. There are a number of problems with this. It is very difficult to interpret artifacts in a way that guarantees accurate inferences about the consciousness of their makers. Modern-day studies of tribal peoples by anthropologists during this century give us more reliable information, but these peoples may not be completely representative of stage 1. Many of them are actually stage 2 societies, and almost all had contact with later-stage societies before they were studied, which may have influenced them in significant ways.

In addition, it is easy for bias to creep into studies of consciousness because it is so much less tangible than other topics anthropologists study, such as kinship or technology. The early anthropological studies of "primitives" were based on the assumption that their consciousness was inferior to our modern Western consciousness. Then later studies were biased in the opposite direction by anthropologists who sought evidence for "cultural relativism," the belief that all cultures are equally valid and incomparable. It is quite difficult to study the consciousness of a radically different culture without some prejudice. These warnings also apply to our attempts to understand the consciousness of stages 2 and 3.

Keeping this in mind, let's explore what is known or guessed about early consciousness.

The best word to describe the consciousness of stage 1 seems to be *participation,* and thus I use this term for the ground quality. Participation means a deep feeling of belonging—to the tribe and to the natural world. It also implies the sense of being fully alive to sensual and spiritual reality in a way that most of us have lost.

> What Levy-Bruhl calls "a mist of unity" embraces the whole world, material and immaterial, visible and invisible . . . a unity which is . . . felt and lived and therefore purely emotional and mystical. . . . In the primitive world, everything and everybody participates with everything and everybody. Such participation functions as a continuous cycle. One form slips into another and still retains the same substance. Man can be or become an animal, plant, mineral and vice versa, in order to carry out some deed or effect. (Kahler 1956, 34–35)

The consciousness of tribal peoples may have been so different from ours that it is extremely difficult for us to truly comprehend their experience of the world. Morris Berman (1984) suggests that it is hard for us moderns (stage 5) to imagine what medieval consciousness (stage 4) was like. How much harder must it be for us to empathize with stage 1.

Animism. Tribal people were alive to the subtle nuances of nature, from impending rain to the meaning of the track of a jackal. They experienced themselves as an integral part of the natural world, and in many ways they felt closer to neighboring animals than to tribes that were culturally different. Their spiritual life was characterized by *animism,* the impression that everything was alive with spirit—animals, birds, trees, rocks, sacred places, and even their artifacts, such as drums or tools. They felt a kinship with everything, including the animals they killed for food. They had certain totem animals with whom they communed for spiritual guidance. Erich Kahler describes totemism:

> A personified essence of the species . . . takes shape as a First Ancestor, who represents both the origin and the substance of the species. [This] need not always be a human being. He may be an animal or a plant, a rock or a star. . . . Even his descendants may be not merely human beings, but leopards, aras, or crocodiles. (Kahler 1956, 42, 43)

Magic. Their sense of mastery was permeated with *magic,* and they often tried to influence the weather or the hunt through symbolic activities and rituals such as the rain dance. Their primary mode of understanding was vastly different from ours. They didn't step back and logically analyze the world to calculate linear cause and effect relationships. Instead, they related to reality in an inclusive and metaphoric way, through story and symbol. They believed that things could affect each other through contagion and similarity (Rozin and Nemeroff 1990).

Belonging. Stage 1 people also felt a deep sense of belonging to the band and tribe. They knew where they stood and felt at home in their community. They felt little separation from their tribal culture. They could certainly make their own choices about how to live, but these choices were strongly circumscribed by their traditions. A person wouldn't even consider living in a way that violated tribal customs or believing anything different from the tribal world view. However, this description doesn't capture their consciousness, because they didn't see things as "customs" or "worldviews." Those are modern ideas. Customs were simply "the way things are done" and their worldview was simply "the way things are."

Vitality. It seems that there was an immediacy and vitality to their experience of life that we rarely attain even in glimpses. They were not split as we are between thinking and feeling, between observing and experiencing, between doing and being. This is because they didn't engage in nearly as much reflexive thinking or objective observing or long range planning as we do. These early people were open to the beauty of a sunset and the richness of a forest glen. They experienced the vitality of their bodies and enjoyed the closeness of their relationships. Art and religion were not special activities set apart from life. Everything they made was a work of art as well as of practical value, and every ritual was simultaneously an artistic performance and a religious ceremony.

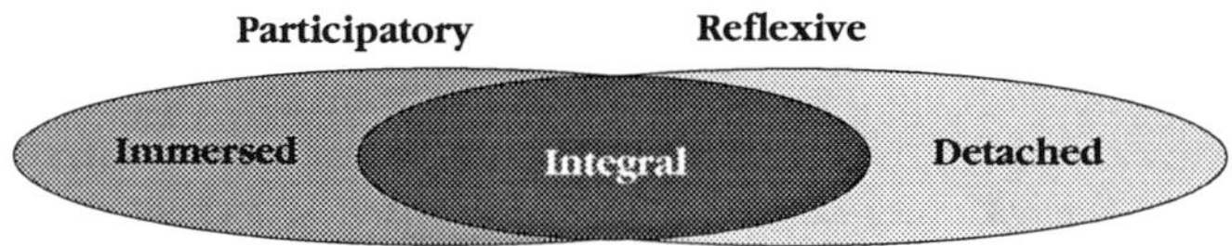

Figure 3.3 Consciousness

The ground quality in this realm is *participatory consciousness* or *participation.* However, since stage 1 people had little reflexive consciousness, I will characterize their consciousness as the dissociated ground quality, *immersed consciousness.*

Imagining Stage 1 Consciousness. What must it have been like to live this way? It's hard to know for sure. I imagine it might be a little like meditation. The object of meditation is to focus on something so consistently that your thinking process slows or stops for a while and you become more present. For anyone except advanced meditators, quieting the the mind in this way is almost impossible for more than a few seconds. The thinking process goes on and on despite our best efforts to focus on our breath or our body sensations. The mind is like a wild monkey, dancing with a life of its own. I suspect that stage 1 people would have a very different experience if they tried meditating. It might be natural for them.

Can you remember being engaged in some activity that was so absorbing that you were totally present, with no distractions, no doubts, when things just flowed, when you and the activity were one? This may have happened when you were dancing or making love or walking in a beautiful forest. It happens on psychedelic trips and in reliving childhood experiences in psychotherapy. This quality of total absorption is probably similar to stage 1 consciousness. When in such a state, it is difficult to use your normal reflexive abilities, to step back and figure things out without losing the intensity and depth of your experience.

Perhaps the best-known depiction of stage 1 in our popular literature is Jean Auel's *The Clan of the Cave Bear,* which describes life in a band in early Upper Paleolithic times. This novel gives a pretty good sense of stage 1 existence, except that the author may have modernized certain aspects of consciousness so that we could better relate to the characters. Table 3.1 summarizes the ground qualities as they existed in stage 1:

Table 3.1 Stage 1

Realm	Ground Quality	Description
Material	Primitive living	Harmony with natural process, minimal technology
Social	Simple community	Closeness, common traditions & values, egalitarianism, little social complexity, parochialism
Consciousness	Immersed consciousness	Belonging, animism, totemism, magic, vitality

REPRESENTING THE RELATIONSHIP BETWEEN THE QUALITIES

At any given stage, I can graphically represent the relative amounts of each complementary quality by the relative sizes of the ovals, and the amount of integration of the qualities by the degree of overlap. So in stage 1, where there is a great deal of the ground quality and little of the emergent quality, this can be depicted as in figure 3.4.

Figure 3.4

The larger oval represents the ground quality (e.g., natural living) and the smaller oval represents the emergent quality (e.g., technological living). Notice that the little bit of the emergent quality is contained within the ground quality. This indicates that they are integrated and not in conflict at this stage.

In stage 5, the Modern era, the emergent quality has grown to the point where it dominates the arena, and the ground quality has been suppressed to the point where it has little influence. In addition, the two qualities are opposed. This is represented in figure 3.5.

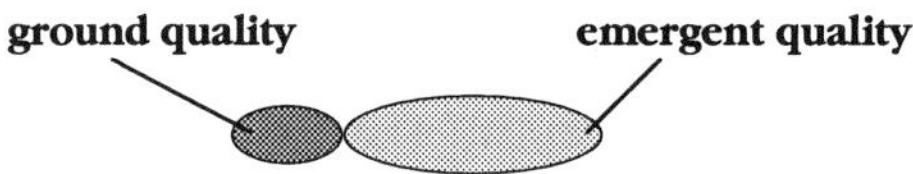

Figure 3.5

Here the ovals are not overlapping, indicating that there is no integration of the qualities.

Stage 0. Notice that even in stage 1, some of the emergent quality has already begun to make itself known. Thus even stage 1 peoples had some technology (e.g., fire, stone tools, the bow and arrow, hunting techniques), some reflexive consciousness (e.g., detailed knowledge of local plants and animals, herb lore, stories), and some social structure (e.g., gender roles, age status, the shaman role). So to be fully complete, the model would have to include a stage zero, when the emergent qualities didn't exist at all. This would fall in the Lower Paleolithic era, when humanity was at an earlier stage of biological evolution and little is known about the consciousness or social life. I will not explore this era in this book.

Table 3.2 depicts the changes in the ground and emergent qualities in the material realm. Look over the succession of ovals to see the evolution of the relationship between natural and technological living.

Table 3.2 Ground and Emergent Qualities in the Material Realm

Stage	Era	Dates	Qualities	Material Realm
0	Lower Paleolithic	?–35,000 B.C.		Hunting & gathering
1	Upper Paleolithic	35,000–8000 B.C.		Hunting & gathering
2	Neolithic	8000–3000 B.C.		Horticulture, herding
3	Archaic	3000–500 B.C.		Agriculture, bronze
4	Ancient/Medieval	500 B.C.–1500		Iron, gradual advance
5	Modern	1500–2000		Fossil fuels, industry
6	Next	2000–		Eco-technology

Note: I have represented the next era graphically as a complete integration of the ground and emerging qualities. This is only to show the ideal situation. We cannot know what form will actually arise as the ground qualities are integrated.

IV

STAGE 2: MYTHOLOGY AND THE FARMING VILLAGE

Life in many stage 1 societies was quite good, except for the occasional ravages of nature and the dangers of disease. Consequently this societal configuration was very stable, lasting for nearly thirty thousand years, and much longer if the Lower Paleolithic era is included. Stage 1 came to an end only when it was forced to, when mounting population made it imperative that new ways of extracting food be used.

Our best reference point in popular culture for understanding stage 2 is Native American tribes. Some of them were horticulturists with a stage 2 consciousness; others were hunter-gatherers. Chronologically, they remained in stages 1 and 2 much later than most cultures in the Old World because they were isolated from contact with the evolving societies of the Middle East and Europe. They are, however, a good reference point for gaining insight into what life was like in stage 2.

THE MATERIAL REALM: HORTICULTURE

The Need for Horticulture. It was possible to live as hunter-gatherers as long as the human population was very sparse, less than one person per square mile. However, by about 7000 B.C. the world's population had grown large enough that something else was required. It was hard to find enough food to keep everyone alive. Migration was no longer a solution because all the land was occupied. In addition, many of the large game animals had been hunted to extinction. In order to deal with this crisis, people gradually began to grow their own plants instead of relying on what nature provided. They used horticulture, a simple form of plant cultivation in which a digging stick or hoe is used to cultivate small gardens. Thus the move into stage 2 was driven by problems in the material realm.

There has been some question about which came first, the invention of horticulture or the need for it. At one time it was assumed that horticultural technique originated around 7000 B.C. at this time of food shortage. However, now there is compelling evidence that horticulture was devised thousands of years earlier but never became widespread until the food crisis, when population pressures made it necessary.

> A growing body of archaeological research indicates that the members of many hunting and gathering societies understood the basic principles of plant cultivation thousands of years before horticulture was adopted as the primary mode of subsistence. . . . Most scholars now doubt that hunters and gatherers abandoned hunting and gathering and adopted horticulture unless they were compelled to do so by circumstances beyond their control. (Lenski and Lenski 1987, 131)

It was the need for horticulture that caused its use to skyrocket, as show in figure 4.1.

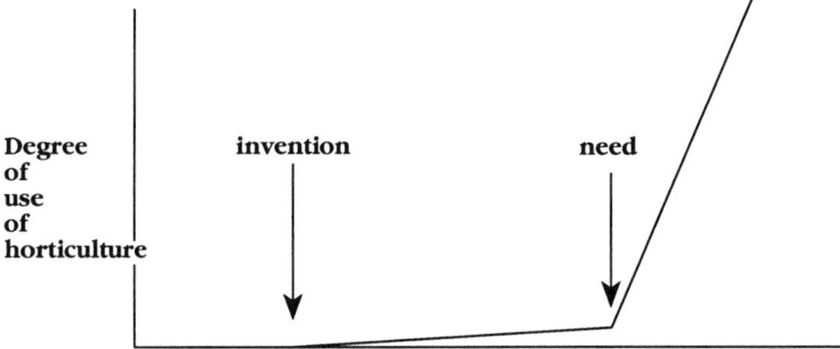

Figure 4.1

Why Then. The horticultural transition can be seen as the beginning of social evolution—the first significant change in humanity through social rather than biological means. If it was caused by population growth and our human technical ability, why did it happen at this time? The populations of animals other than humans are limited by natural ecological constraints. What happened to change that for us?

There are two main ways that an animal population is restrained—being killed off by predators or reaching the limits of its food supply. My guess is that by the Upper Paleolithic era we humans had evolved biologically to the point where we had the intelligence and toolmaking capacity to avoid significant losses to predators and to find food in increasingly ingenious ways. This allowed our population to grow steadily if slowly until we filled the planet and exceeded the limits of its carrying capacity. We were then able to overcome this constraint through the exercise of our biologically evolved intelligence in developing and using horticulture. Thus the advances in biological evolution set the stage for the beginning of social evolution.

Why did this happen about 7000 B.C.? This may simply be the time at which the available space on the planet became saturated. In addition, scholars identify several other factors. As previously mentioned, improvements in hunting weapons allowed many of the important game animals to be hunted to extinction. The Ice Age had come to an end sometime before 7000 B.C., causing massive climatic changes which may have disrupted people's ability to feed themselves. Another factor is that horticulture itself tends to increase population because larger numbers of people can be fed. So as this method began to be used in small ways, it would tend to increase the population, thus leading to a time when it would be need to be used extensively.

Notice the interesting link between population growth and the adoption of horticulture. There is a causal relationship in both directions. Population growth caused the adoption of horticulture as the only way to feed the increased numbers of people. However, the adoption of horticulture also caused more population growth, since population tends to grow as large as the food supply will allow. Therefore there is a circular causal relationship between these two factors. This is also true of the connection between population growth and other major technological advances, as illustrated in figure 4.2. In fact this dynamic is one of the main driving forces behind social evolution, as I will show in more detail later.

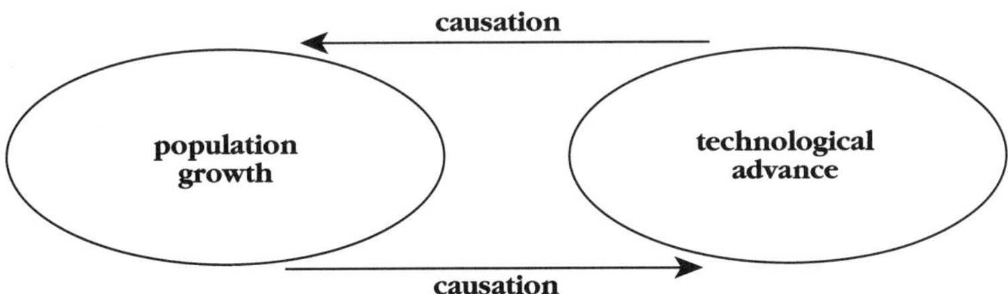

Figure 4.2

Furthermore this kind of circular causality is not unusual. General systems theory (von Bertalanffy 1968) has shown that it is frequently the case that variables exist in such circular, systemic relationships. The old linear cause and effect model has limited usefulness, especially in the biological and social sciences. I will explore this further as we proceed.

A Gradual Transition. The transition to horticulture did not happen suddenly; it was very gradual. Horticultural was first used to supplement hunting and gathering and was only a primary food source in regions where the other methods were not feasible. Only over many generations and thousands of years did horticulture come to replace hunting and gathering.

The transition was so gradual that people noticed only very slight changes during their lifetimes. The actual extent of change was largely invisible, especially given the lack of written records. It is only when we look at the situation from the perspective of thousands of years that we realize what a monumental transformation it was. This also applies to the transitions to stages 3 and 4. Only the transition to stage 5 a few centuries ago and our current transition are happening rapidly enough for the participants to realize that they are in a time of important change.

Ramifications of Horticulture. As horticulture became the major means of subsistence, this technological advance brought marked changes in people's way of life. Instead of migrating with the seasons to find food as was done during the Paleolithic period, people lived in settled communities because their food sources were now fixed. They also lived in larger groups than hunter-gatherers because horticulture could support denser settlements. Food sources were better controlled and grains could be stored more reliably, so there was better insulation against droughts, floods, and other natural calamities. Hunting continued, but it provided a much smaller portion of the food supply. More work was involved in horticulture for the amount of food extracted, so people worked longer hours. Life was more secure, but also involved more drudgery.

Technological progress continued during this entire period (7000–3000 B.C.). Pottery and weaving were invented. Later metal working began to be understood, and metal replaced stone in tools and weapons. Another major technical development during this period was the domestication of animals. Some societies depended on herding as their primary means of subsistence rather than horticulture.

Though there was a substantial increase in technology, it was still fairly primitive and therefore operated in relative harmony with the natural processes of the earth. In terms of the model, technological living was growing but was still largely integrated with natural living. This can be represented as in figure 4.3.

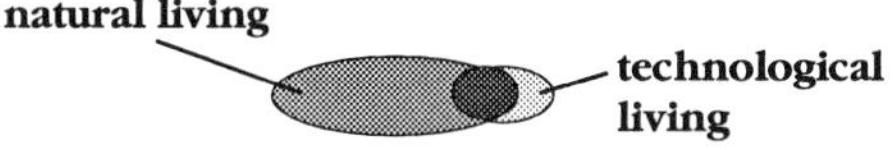

Figure 4.3

THE SOCIAL REALM: VILLAGES AND CHIEFS

The changes in the social realm during the Neolithic era were enormous. The most fundamental change was the size of social groupings. Early horticultural villages contained populations of 100 to 200 people, four times the size of stage 1 bands, and some later communities probably contained two to three thousand or even more. In addition to this, because of the permanence of settlements and improved technology, it was possible to have more substantial possessions, such as bowls, tools, and weapons. This led to a growing importance of trade and commerce.

Toward the later part of the Neolithic era, there was also a gradual increase in warfare. This was probably due to a number of factors—the increase in wealth that could be stolen, men's need to find a substitute activity for hunting, and the scarcity of new land for the expanding population.

All these changes required more social structure than the direct personal contact of a hunter gatherer band. Food surpluses had to be gathered and distributed. They had to be stored against times of drought or famine. Trade had to be arranged and negotiated between groups. Warfare had to be planned and coordinated. This first led to social groups organized around kinship and then later to groups dominated by "big men."

Stages of Social Structure. Morton Fried (1967), in his study of the evolution of political structures, delineates four stages: egalitarian societies, rank societies, stratified societies, and states. As previously mentioned, egalitarian societies are characteristic of stage 1. Both rank and stratified societies appear in stage 2, in that order. The first states emerge in stage 3, to be covered in the next chapter. These relationships are shown in Table 4.1.

A *rank* society is one in which gradations in status exist but do not determine economic power. That is, people's status doesn't determine how much access they have to basic life resources. A high ranking person gets the same amount of food as everyone else. Where reciprocity was the basic economic arrangement in stage 1, rank societies were characterized by "redistribution." This means that food or other resources are gathered centrally and then redistributed to the people.

Table 4.1 Stages of Political Evolution

Stage	Era	Fried's Political Stages
Stage 1	Upper Paleolithic	Egalitarian
Stage 2	Early Neolithic	Rank
	Late Neolithic	Stratified
Stage 3	Archaic	State

Big Men. This gathering of resources was usually done by a "big man," although he was usually more the manager than the owner of the goods.

> The [big man] could summon the community's labor on his own behalf, or on behalf of someone else who requested it, or for general purposes. . . . Besides his right to summon labor he accumulated the greater proportion of the first fruits of the yam crop . . . and he benefited from other forms of food presentation, or by the acquisition of special shares in ordinary village redistribution. . . . Thus the [big man] would collect a significant part of the surplus production of the community and redistribute it in the general welfare. (Sahlins 1962, 293, quoted in Fried 1967)

The power and status of big men were granted to them voluntarily and were easily revocable by the people. One of the main ways in which a big man maintained his position was by the amount of resources he was able to distribute. So even though big men had status and power, they usually didn't use it for personal advantage. However, over the centuries as social groupings became larger, there were greater opportunities to control the resources for personal gain. Leaders who gathered resources garnered the power to keep a disproportionate share, and frequently they developed a political or religious rationale that justified their right to do this. Power became structured and inherited. Big men became chiefs, and a ruling hierarchy and aristocracy developed. Fried calls these *stratified* societies.

Other Social Structures. Ceremony and ritual were important means for holding the larger social groups together and ensuring that the social functions were performed. There were ceremonies for planting and harvesting, gathering and distributing food surpluses, legitimating the power of leaders, preparing for war, and so on. Stage 2 contained the beginnings of occupational specialization. Where in hunter-gatherer bands most tasks could be performed by anyone, in Neolithic villages, specialists gradually took over crafts, leadership, and religious functions.

Women were responsible for the majority of the work involved in horticulture, and vegetation and the earth were seen as feminine. Therefore the primary subsistence activity was female-oriented. Some Neolithic societies were matrilineal, meaning that descent was determined by the line of the mother. Goddess worship was a major part of the spiritual life in some stage 2 cultures. Thus in certain of these societies, women may have had status and power equal to that of men. In general, stage 2 women had relatively higher status than before or since, higher than in some stage 1 societies and much higher than they have enjoyed in subsequent stages.

Notice that there is much more diversity in social structure in this stage than in stage 1. There were rank and stratified societies; matrilineal, patrilineal, and other orders; cultures in which women had status and those in which they didn't; and many other variations.

Relating all this to the model, there was a considerable increase in social structure because of all the mediated social relationships necessary for trade, war, and the coordination of larger communities of people. There was, however, little loss of community; people retained their close ties and common traditions and values. However, one aspect of community, the sharing of power, was beginning to erode. Except for some gender equality, vested power structures were forming which were beginning to significantly undermine the egalitarian relationships of stage 1.

THE CONSCIOUSNESS REALM: MYTH

With the advent of horticulture, more reflexive consciousness was required. Food-producing activities had to be planned and coordinated on a yearly basis. While hunter gatherers were able to live hand to mouth, horticulturists had to plan ahead. Even more than this, the social complexity of stage 2 demanded much more in the way of conceptual understanding. People were no longer just people—there were complex kinship relationships and status gradations. Trade and commerce required a more refined ability to calculate the worth of goods and keep account of transactions. Warfare became more frequent and more complex, requiring a greater capacity to train, plan, and outsmart opponents.

Stage 1 people lived in small bands, and their loyalties and beliefs were strongly organized around blood ties—family and extended family. In moving to stage 2, people emerged from an exclusive family orientation and became members of larger societies which were held together by their mythic beliefs.

Time. The time sense of this period was cyclic—oriented to the yearly cycle of the cultivation of plants on which the livelihood of the people depended. This also applies to stage 3. There was little sense of history or of society changing over time. Each year was seen largely as a repetition of past years.

Mythic Consciousness. Jean Gebser, in his seminal study of the evolution of consciousness (Gebser 1986), identifies the *mythical* structure of consciousness as the dominant structure during what I call stages 2 and 3. He defines *imagination* as the essential subjective medium of this era, where by this he means "making ideational pictures or models of the world" (Feuerstein 1987, 77). Imagination gave people the ability to form more accurate and detailed models of the world. It also enabled them to form more complex, coherent, and delineated mythologies with which to understand the meaning of the world and their place in it. Stage 1 people had myths, too, but theirs were simpler and more immediately connected to their physical surroundings. With stage 2, myths became richer as reflexive consciousness began to grow.

Erich Kahler describes the gradual transition from magical to mythical consciousness:

> There was, then, in the earliest stages, no clear distinction, no gap between primitive man and these creative and life-giving forces [of animism and totemism]. A state of perfect participation existed. The life-giving forces were present always and everywhere. . . . But [in stage 2] in order to shift . . . the totemistic essence of life to a distinct sphere of existence, to make a clear cut between eternity, the past and the present—for this a further development was necessary, a process of objectification which transformed participation into [mythic] religion. . . .
>
> This began with the institution of restricted magical spheres where spiritual forces dwell and work. . . . In fixing . . . the taboo of human ancestors, totems or places where spirits dwell, in conjuring these spirits into holy images . . . through special ceremonies of sacrifice and pleading, worship and religion gradually developed. . . . Myths arose as a first form of history. (Kahler 1956, 43–46)

Notice how the transition from stage 1 to 2 involved drawing boundaries in time and space, making what was immediate into something conceptualized, objectified, and organized, in a word reflexive.

In keeping with the feminine orientation of this period, many of the myths of this period were myths of the Goddess or the Great Mother, emphasizing fertility, creation and destruction, the yearly cycle of vegetation, and humanity's embeddedness within nature.

Referring to the model, even though reflexive consciousness was growing, it was still largely contained within the ground quality of participatory consciousness. Thus in all three realms, the relationship between the qualities can be represented as shown in figure 4.4.

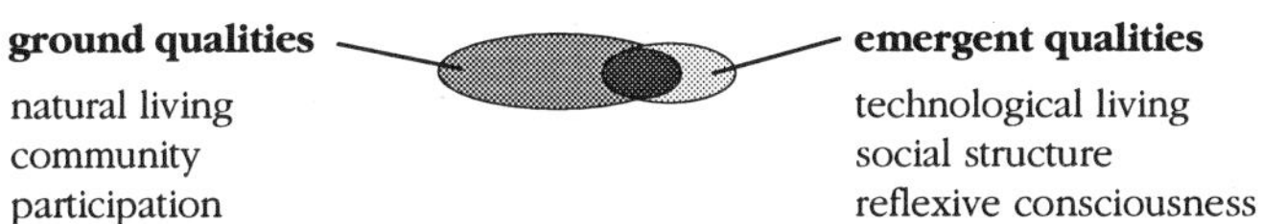

Figure 4.4

SAGAN'S VIEW

In *At the Dawn of Tyranny* (1985), Eli Sagan studies the emergence of individuality during stage 2. He examines stratified societies in order to learn about the psychological underpinnings of the evolution of social structure and oppression. Remember that stratified societies (which he calls "complex societies") are a late stage 2 form of political organization, which are transitional between the tribes and villages of stage 1 and early stage 2, and the states of stage 3. Sagan theorizes that the evolution of political structures is directly related to the evolution of individuality, with primitive societies having little in the way of individuality, Archaic states having a significant amount, and stratified societies forming the transition. He correlates this with the emergence of individuality in children as studied by the influential child psychoanalyst Margaret Mahler.

Mahler (1975) proposed a widely accepted theory in which child development during the first three years is characterized by a process of "separation-individuation." During this time, the child gradually emerges from a psychological symbiosis with the mother to become a separate individual. The child goes through a number of stages in this process, including a pivotal one that she calls "rapprochement," in which the child is caught between the desire to individuate and the urge to reunite with the mother.

Sagan speculates that the major driving force in social evolution is the drive toward individuality. He speculates that tribal and village societies suppressed the development of individuality in their children, thereby preserving the communal character of their societies. He imagines stage 3 states as allowing their children to complete separation-individuation, while stratified societies kept them in the rapprochement phase, giving these societies their transitional nature. He employs a psychoanalytic understanding of these early childhood stages to explain some of the features of stratified societies, such as human sacrifice and veneration of kings. Table 4.2 illustrates these correspondences between theorists.

Table 4.2 Correlations between Social Evolution and Psychological Development

Stage	Political (M. Fried)	Sagan	Psychological (Mahler)
1 & early 2	Egalitarian, rank	Primitive	Symbiosis
Late 2	Stratified	Complex	Rapprochement
3	State	Archaic	Individuation

I think there is some merit to his ideas, especially in understanding how societies in different stages of evolution can have such dissimilar consciousness. We will see that stage 4 consciousness marked the beginning of the superego and sense of guilt. This correlates well with Sagan's ideas, since according to psychoanalytic theory the superego develops during the oedipal stage, after the completion of separation-individuation.

However, I also see some problems with Sagan's ideas. First is his adherence to the rigidly stage-specific developmental ideas of psychoanalysis. If tribal and village people really kept their children at an arrested stage of development so that they didn't complete separation-individuation, these societies wouldn't be able to operate at all. Clearly their people were not functioning like young children as I'm sure Sagan knows. I think that a more accurate picture of child development is that each psychological issue (such as individuality) has a developmental trajectory during all ages though it may be stronger at one particular stage (Stern 1985). In addition, I don't believe that separation-individuation is the only major developmental task for infants. There is evidence that they must develop the ability to *connect* interpersonally as well as to separate (Stern 1985).

Sagan also assumes that research done by Mahler and others on stage 5 infants is valid universally for humans at all evolutionary stages, and therefore that stage 1 and 2 child rearing was deficient. While I have no doubt that their child rearing practices were deficient in significant ways with respect to ours, I don't think it is valid to measure other stages according to our patterns. After all, we stage 5 people have a poorly developed ability to be in community. This probably reflects a deficiency in our child rearing relative to theirs because of our suppression of the ground qualities.

Sagan also seems to define individuality as the tendency to seek, not just selfhood and autonomy, but also power, status, and material gain. (I call this "individualism," and view it as a distortion that results from the suppression of participation.) Using this notion, he claims that earlier societies were lacking individuality. They certainly were lacking in individualism, and the kings and heroes of stage 3 certainly were individualistic, but what this has to say about real individuality is less clear. I will present my views on the evolution of individuality in detail later.

GROUND QUALITY REPRESENTATIVES

During the Neolithic era, stage 2 was the leading edge of social evolution, but many stage 1 societies still existed. In lands that were less desirable or further from the expanding centers of horticultural development, hunting and gathering continued as a way of life. Of course, over time with population expansion and conquest, many remaining stage 1 people were forced into stage 2. However, some retained their stage 1 societies into later eras, and even in the twentieth century some isolated hunter-gatherer tribes have been discovered.

In addition to this, herding societies developed, which were neither stage 1 nor 2, but a mixture. They gained their subsistence from the domestication of animals, occupying lands that were not suitable for horticulture. They resembled stage 1 peoples in being nomadic and living in small bands, close to the earth. However, they were not just a carry-over from stage 1; the wholesale domestication of animals was a new development in the Neolithic. We can view them as stage 2 *representatives* of the ground quality.

Let me explain what I mean by this. In each stage there are some societies or groups that represent the emergent quality and some that represent the ground quality. Furthermore, as the emergent quality develops, the ground quality also changes in response to it, so some ground quality representatives in each stage are different from those of previous stages. They represent the ground quality in its own unique unfolding for that stage. Herding societies can be seen as stage 2 representatives of the ground quality.

Table 4.3 summarizes the developments for stage 2 and charts each realm for stages 1 and 2.

Table 4.3 Stage 2

Realm	Description
Material	Horticulture, herding, weaving, pottery, possessions
Social	Villages, kinship groupings, relatively equal status of women, trade, big men, beginnings of warfare, stratification, chiefs
Consciousness	Myth: Goddess, imagination, beginnings of planning, cyclic time

Stage	Era	Qualities	Material	Social	Consciousness
1	Paleolithic		Hunting & gathering	Family, band	Magic, animism
2	Neolithic		Horticulture, herding	Village, chiefdom	Myth: Goddess

V

STAGE 3: THE WARRIOR STATE

By roughly 3000 B.C., certain areas of the world had changed their way of living so much that it is fair to say they had moved to a new stage of social evolution, characterized by agriculture, the use of bronze, the first cities, and the first political units that could be called *states.* For want of a widely accepted term, I will call this period from about 3000 B.C. to 500 B.C. the Archaic era.

The major Archaic empires were Mesopotamia, Egypt, Babylon, and Persia. Ancient Egypt is the best known of these today, so you might use it in your imagination to visualize what stage 3 life was like. The Inkas and Aztecs created stage 3 urban civilizations in the Western Hemisphere. However, I won't discuss them in this chapter because they occurred much later chronologically, during the late Medieval era.

THE MATERIAL REALM: AGRICULTURE

The animal-driven plow allowed people to use a radically different method of growing plants, agriculture, in which entire fields were kept in constant cultivation, thus greatly increasing productivity. This allowed substantial numbers of people to engage in activities other than those necessary for subsistence. Between roughly 4000 and 3000 B.C. there was a rapid technological advance, including the discovery of metallurgy and irrigation for agriculture.

> The innovations of that period included the invention of the wheel and its application both to wagons and the manufacture of pottery, the invention of the plow, the harnessing of wind power for use in sailboats, the invention of writing and numerical notation, and the invention of the calendar. Collectively these innovations substantially transformed the conditions of life for societies in the Middle East, and eventually for societies throughout the world. With these new cultural resources, societies expanded their populations, in-

creased their material wealth, and developed social organizations for more complex than anything known before. (Lenski and Lenski 1987, 164)

During this period, for the first time a significant number of people were freed from the necessity of producing their own food, and therefore were also removed from such a close connection to the earth. Large cities were built, some housing up to 100,000 people, where the immediate environment was more artificial than natural.

The technology of agriculture in the large river valley civilizations of the Middle East involved methods of irrigation that were not in harmony with natural processes, at least not in the long run. Eventually the heavy agricultural use of these lands turned them from lush, fertile valleys into the deserts they are today. For the first time, technology began to seriously clash with natural living. This can be represented graphically as in figure 5.1.

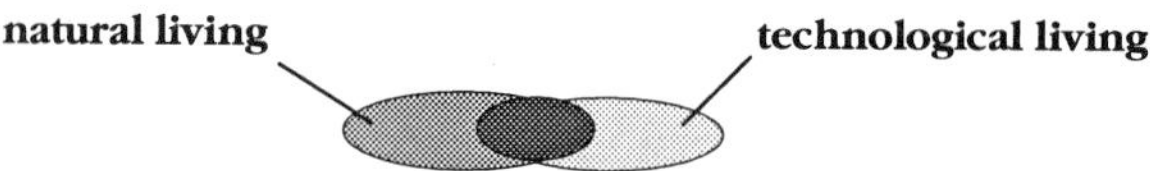

Figure 5.1

Here technological living has grown to approximately the same size as natural living, and the overlap is now smaller than the areas of dissociation.

THE SOCIAL REALM: THE STATE

Large social changes came about in this period, caused by the huge growth in population size and density, the food surpluses that allowed greater occupational specialization, and the need to coordinate the large states and empires that developed. Fried defines a *state* as follows: "The state, then, is a collection of specialized institutions and agencies, some formal and others informal, that maintains an order of stratification . . . [based on] hierarchy, differential degrees of access to basic resources, obedience to officials, and defense of the area" (Fried 1967, 235).

War. Warfare continued to increase, especially now that the victor could gain great reward. As hunter-gatherers, the only possible benefit from warfare was to protect your territory or to take over someone else's. There were few possessions to win, and taking prisoners or slaves wasn't advantageous. Slaves couldn't produce a food surplus for their masters since food supply was limited by population density, not by labor. In stage 2, warfare began to be more lucrative for the victors, and this escalated in stage 3. There were more worthwhile possessions to be taken as booty. Slaves could be made to work the fields, thus producing a surplus to increase the wealth of their masters. Territory could be taken and held, populations could be subjected and governed, thereby increasing one's resources and power.

To make successful use of these rewards, social structures had to be invented to organize increasingly large associations of people and territory. Since size provided an important advantage in war, those societies that could conquer and hold the largest territory and population could field the greatest armies, thus becoming even more successful militarily. Those societies that were not successful in war—that weren't warlike or didn't develop the social complexity and technological sophistication to be successful—were swallowed up by those that were. Once war became moderately widespread, no society could afford to avoid developing its military capacity. Every society that was not geographically isolated had to learn warfare in order to protect its very existence. In this way, the tendency toward war spread rapidly, along with the social inventions that fostered it. This is one of the main driving forces behind social evolution, as described by Schmookler (1984). I will discuss it in greater detail in the next chapter.

In the Archaic era warfare was often initiated by mobile invaders, nomadic herdsmen who survived on less hospitable land and developed military cultures at odds with the gentler farming cultures of the Neolithic era. Once the nomads began to invade, the older cultures were either defeated and taken over, or they learned warfare, too. Those who became warlike discovered that the best defense is often a good offense, and so they became invaders as well. This process escalated, eventually culminating in large warlike states and empires. It seems to have been driven both by technological advances and by the increasing military competition for survival.

Social Differentiation. One of the main areas of increasing social complexity was in occupational specialties. In order to fight most successfully, states required highly trained professional soldiers. In order to govern, they needed administrators and bureaucrats. Scribes handled the complexities of writing and calculating. As commerce and monetary exchange grew, a merchant class developed.

However the increase in complexity went beyond occupation. Societies were becoming more differentiated. Thus there was an army, a governmental bureaucracy, a priesthood, a commercial sector, and even the beginnings of codes of law. In earlier societies all these functions were performed by the same ruling group, or in primitive societies by all the people. Now these tasks were parceled out according to societal sector. A society that is differentiated in this way must find methods of coordinating and integrating the actions of the various sectors. In less evolved societies the coordination was automatic because the tasks were all performed by the same group, but in stage 3, societies had to evolve ways for the sectors to communicate and work together. Therefore along with differentiation the Archaic empires had to create new mechanisms of coordination.

Sociologist Talcott Parsons sees social differentiation (and the accompanying coordination) as the essence of social evolution (Parsons 1966). This is not an unreasonable position if you look exclusively at the social realm, but it doesn't take into account the evolution of technology and consciousness. In addition, it doesn't recognize what is lost in this process—community and power distribution—and so it doesn't understand the dialectical nature of social evolution, where at some point the ground quality must be integrated with the emergent quality.

In the cities, there was some mixing of different traditions and cultures. Community was beginning to be supplanted by the less personal relations of bureaucracy and commerce and by more tolerant interactions between traditions. Societies were much less interested in caring for all their members. However, community was still strong in some ways, especially within classes and ethnic groups, so it would be fair to characterize the relationship between the ground and emergent qualities as one of almost equal strength, as in the material realm (see figure 5.2).

Figure 5.2

Power Inequity. The most extreme changes came in the area of power. Stratification became entrenched and thoroughly rationalized through religious and moral value systems. A small urban, literate elite wielded considerable power over the rural, illiterate peasants. Men gained dominance over women. Slavery and serfdom became widespread. I consider power to be such an important topic that I explore it as a special subset of the social realm in a later chapter.

In describing what life was like in this era, for the first time I must speak separately of the ruling class and the peasant class. For the peasant class, it was increasingly difficult and unpleasant. They were often made to toil long hours for the barest subsistence. The quality of their lives was considerably reduced from that of previous eras. The ruling class, on the other hand, had a much improved situation. They had interesting occupations to pursue, leisure for education and pleasure, and a wider variety of amenities such as crafts and foodstuffs—in other words, the beginnings of civilization.

Population. Population increased dramatically in the Archaic era, even more than in the Neolithic. This was partly due to the enhanced food producing capacity of agriculture and partly due to the greatly increased social stratification. In an egalitarian society, if population increases to the point where it is difficult to feed everyone, all people are affected because food is shared equally. In a stratified society or state, only the lower classes are affected because the ruling class has the power to take what it needs. The poor and powerless will be the ones to starve. This means that in a stratified society those in power aren't nearly as threatened by overpopulation, so they don't have as much motivation to prevent it. Of course, if it gets bad enough there may be social unrest, but this threat is not as severe as that of starvation.

THE CONSCIOUSNESS REALM: GODS AND HEROES

With the increase in technological sophistication and social complexity, greater advances in reflexive consciousness were, of course, needed. But the more significant change in the Archaic era was an emergence from embeddedness and belonging. While this was still an era of mythology, the type of myth changed. The myths of the Neolithic era were myths of embeddedness. Humanity was embedded within the circle of nature and the annual cycle of growth and decay. Persons were embedded within the community and the culture. The Goddess or Great Mother was supreme.

Mythology of Gods and Heroes. The mythology of the Archaic era was very different. Let's listen to Ken Wilber:

> The easiest way to introduce this new myth is by recalling the typical structure of the old Great Mother myths. In those myths . . . the individual . . . involved with Great Mother, usually comes to a tragic end—killed, mutilated, castrated, sacrificed. The Great Mother is always the victor—the self never triumphs over the Great Mother, but is always reduced to one of her mere satellites. . . . But in the new myths, we find an extraordinary occurrence: the individual triumphs over the Great Mother—breaks free from her, transforms

her, defeats her, or transcends her. And this is the "Hero Myth," the myth that *is* this period of history. (Wilber 1983, 183)

Joseph Campbell adds:

The old cosmologies and mythologies of the goddess mother were radically transformed . . . and set aside in favor of those male-oriented, patriarchal mythologies of thunder-hurling gods that by . . . 1500 B.C. had become the dominant divinities of the Near East. (Campbell 1964)

These myths, of course, reflect the change in consciousness of the period. As reflexive consciousness increased, people (specifically men) began to experience themselves as actors in the world who could change things to suit themselves. They could emerge from their embeddedness in nature and community, and take over.

The new myths also represented the triumph of order over chaos. From the point of view of the emergent reflexive consciousness, participatory consciousness meant unconsciousness, chaos, and disorder. It was reviled and suppressed. For example in Babylonian mythology, Tiamat, the goddess of chaos, was conquered and supplanted by Marduk, a god of order. This change happened about 2000 B.C., coinciding with the triumph of patriarchy (Abraham, McKenna, et al. 1992). Of course, the goddesses of the earth don't really represent disorder; there is an exquisite order to nature, as ecologists and chaos theorists have been discovering recently. However, the order of the new male gods was a human order designed and executed from the top of the social structure. It represented the order of an advancing and somewhat dissociated reflexive consciousness.

The Kings. When you reflect on your experience and your situation, it can give you the power to change things. You need not fatalistically accept your position in life and in the cosmos. You can make things to your liking. You can build irrigation systems and cities. You can enjoy art and culture. You can create an empire. Of course, these things were only available to the male ruling classes, and especially the monarchs, but their consciousness dominated and defined the psychology of the times.

Societies were often ruled by kings, usually god-kings, who were frequently also military commanders and/or war heroes. In the social realm, these monarchs were at the top of the power hierarchy. Like the mythic heroes and gods of the time, they took power into their own hands and attempted to subdue the natural world and surrounding peoples. People looked up to them and identified with them, participating vicariously in their triumphs and glories.

The transition from stages 2 to 3 involved replacing a predominantly feminine mode of consciousness with a masculine one, and this went hand in hand with the subjugation of women. The feminine was no longer valued in society. Women lost status and power. They no longer had any say in social and political decisions and were subjected to the rule of their fathers or husbands.

The Model. Returning to the model, reflexive consciousness (in the form of masculine emergence and order) was growing, partly at the expense of participatory consciousness (belonging). Despite the mythic triumph of the new male gods, this stage did not represent the full flowering of reflexive consciousness or the suppression of participation. This drama continues to unfold in stages 4 and 5. At this stage the two qualities were fairly evenly matched, and somewhat dissociated. The dissociation is apparent in how the qualities were split between groups in the population, with the male ruling class exhibiting the emergent quality and the oppressed classes and women the ground quality. This will frequently be the case as our exploration continues.

This is the same relationship between qualities that obtains in the material and social realms, as shown in Figure 5.3. Table 5.1 summarizes the Archaic era developments and depicts the first three stages graphically.

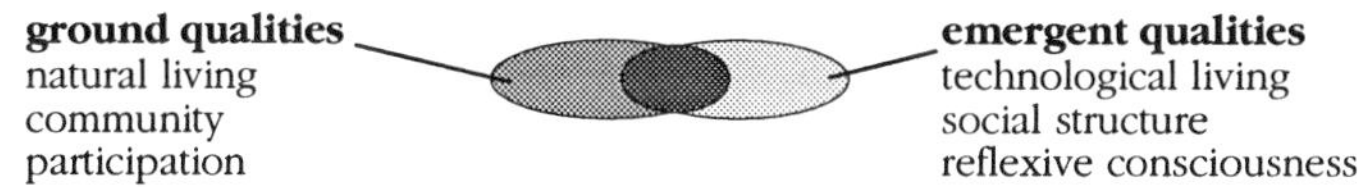

Figure 5.3

Table 5.1 Stage 3

Realm	Description
Material	Agriculture, bronze, irrigation, written language
Social	Cities, early states & empires, occupational specialization, societal sectors, civilization, stratification, widespread warfare, subjugation of women
Consciousness	Myth: gods & heroes, male emergence

Stage	Era	Qualities	Material	Social	Consciousness
1	Paleolithic		Hunting & gathering	Family, band	Magic, animism
2	Neolithic		Horticulture, herding	Village, chiefdom	Myth: Goddess
3	Archaic		Agriculture, bronze	City, early state	Myth: gods & heroes

STAGES AND ERAS

It's time now to make clear the distinction between stages and eras. Notice that even though stage 3 began in the Archaic era, much of the world during this time was still in stage 2 horticultural villages or even in stage 1 bands. The Archaic era represents stage 3 only in the sense that it is the historical era in which stage 3 first became a significant social evolutionary force. It may be that the majority of societies during the Archaic era weren't in stage 3. However, the stage 3 societies were the leading edge of social evolution, and that's what is significant for our purposes.

Today as we witness the transition from the Modern era, stage 5, to whatever comes next, the great majority of the world's population is still in stages 3 or 4. One of the great challenges the industrialized world faces is how to enable them move to stage 6 without making all the mistakes we made in stage 5.

In summary, an era represents a historical time period; a stage represents a point along the path of social evolution. When a stage and era correspond in a chart, it means that the stage started in that era.

VI

EVOLUTIONARY DRIVING FORCES

Now let's discuss a crucial question in social evolution which has only been mentioned so far. What drives the course of social evolution? What forces have caused humanity to move through the progression of historical stages?

The most obvious answer to this question is that social evolution is driven by a desire to better human welfare. A naive view of social evolution would be that over the years, people and societies have chosen those social innovations that work best to foster human well-being and happiness. One could think that we tried different things and retained those that worked best, and in this way made progress. Unfortunately, this isn't the way it has worked. Though some social choices and trends in our history have come from a desire for human betterment, this process has been overshadowed by more powerful forces.

Some authors propose that psychology or consciousness provides the main driving force in social evolution (Wilber 1983; Sagan 1985; Elgin 1993). They observe a progression of modes of consciousness during the course of social evolution and assume that this is the main driving force. The problem with this view is that it provides no explanation for why consciousness evolved as it did, especially why it moved from one stage to another at the times it did.

Others propose that technological invention is the main driving force (Parsons 1966; Lenski and Lenski 1987; Sahlins and Service 1988). However, this thesis is contradicted by the fact that in some cases technical knowledge was known long before it was widely used, and thus there must have been some deeper reason why the technology came into use when it did.

I believe there are two specific evolutionary forces at work driving both consciousness and technology along with the rest of social evolution. These are population/environment constraints and the selection for power. Let's explore them.

POPULATION/ENVIRONMENT CONSTRAINTS

The *carrying capacity* of an environmental region for a given species is the maximum number of individuals of that species that can be supported by the resources of that region. With human beings, the carrying capacity will depend on the level of technology and the accompanying methods of food and energy extraction. At many times in history, the population of an area began to exceed its carrying capacity. When migration was not an option, this caused a crisis. In each case, either the society invented new means for procuring more food and energy or it stagnated and eventually collapsed.

If a society succeeds in inventing or using a new method of production, this means that it also needs new social structures, institutions, modes of relating, and modes of consciousness to support the new mode of production. Most of these new social arrangements don't follow the new means of production, they arrive with it as an integral part of the change-over. The society evolves on all levels, and this is driven by the need to survive with a growing population and a constant or shrinking resource base.

An Example. For example, I discussed earlier the change-over from hunting and gathering to horticulture. This was driven by the fact the world population had grown to the point where it exceeded the carrying capacity of the available land given the existing mode of production (hunting and gathering). This was probably humanity's first population/environment crisis. As a result, a new mode of production (horticulture) was needed which increased the carrying capacity. With this new mode came the host of other social and consciousness changes that characterized the Neolithic era. Thus this major move in social evolution was ultimately driven by population/environment constraints.

Energy. This pattern has been repeated throughout human history right up to the present. Since food production can be seen as just another way to harness energy, this whole process can be conceptualized in energy terms. As a population grows and energy resources shrink, societies try to adapt by discovering new ways to extract and use energy, and this drives social evolution.

Leslie White and his students, pioneering evolutionary anthropologists in the 1950s, went so far as to define evolutionary progress according to the amount of energy a culture uses.

> It seems to us that progress is the total transformation of energy involved in the creation and perpetuation of a cultural organization. A culture harnesses and delivers energy; it extracts energy from

> nature and transforms it into people, material goods, and work, into political systems and the generation of ideas, into social customs and into adherence to them. The total energy so transformed from the free to the cultural state, in combination perhaps with the degree to which it is raised in the transformation (the loss of entropy), may represent a culture's general standing, a measure of its achievement. (Sahlins and Service 1988, 35)

In the past, it may have seemed reasonable to use energy as a measure of social evolution, but today this is reversing itself, and the successful societies of the future will minimize energy throughput. Previously anthropologists such as White conceptualized social evolution as being driven primarily by technological innovation. Now most see it differently. Necessity *is* the mother of invention, or at least the mother of the widespread use of an invention. And the necessity is to increase output or to acquire new resources. Therefore the need is the driving force, not the invention.

> We are used to thinking of great leaps forward in history occurring because someone came up with a better way of doing things. Actually, these so-called better ways are in reality only different ways of doing things occasioned by the need to readjust to harsher, less easily exploitable energy environments. (Rifkin 1981, 75)

The Need for Production. Anthropologist Marvin Harris looks at it this way:

> I think there is an intelligible process that governs the maintenance of common cultural forms, initiates changes, and determines their transformations along parallel or divergent paths. The heart of this process is the tendency to intensify production. Intensification—the investment of more soil, water, minerals, or energy per unit of time or area—is in turn a recurrent response to threats against living standards. . . . In the absence of technological change, it leads inevitably to the depletion of the environment [which paradoxically] in turn leads to low living standards. As living standards decline, successful cultures invent new and more efficient means of production. (Harris 1978, 5)

The key point here is that, until recently, people didn't spend their time trying to invent better subsistence technology unless it was really needed. The population/environment driving force has such potency because it is directly concerned with survival. When such a crisis occurs, there is tremendous pressure to discover a new method of production because the alternative is death and decay. When a new mode of production is not discovered and it isn't possible to migrate to a new location, the result is usually famine, epidemic, and ultimately social disorder. Therefore even the ruling classes have a vested interest in finding a solution to the crisis.

Population. Of course, there is another option besides technological innovation—finding a way to limit population. And indeed, societies have attempted this, too, and even succeeded for a while. But the price has been high. Without our current birth control technology, people had to use methods that were either violent (infanticide, crude abortion) or untrustworthy (withdrawal, abstinence). You can imagine why these would be either unacceptable or ineffective.

Like most creatures, we have "excess reproductive capacity." This means that we are capable of producing far more children than is necessary in order to maintain our numbers. The population of other animals is kept in check by environmental constraints—predators or the available food supply. We are the first animal with the ability to increase our productive capacity by the use of technology and therefore exceed the constraints built in by nature. We have done this repeatedly throughout our history, and it has been one of the major driving forces behind social evolution.

We are used to thinking of our history in terms of progress and the triumph of the human spirit. We like to think that we have evolved by becoming better—smarter, more noble, more capable, more civilized. And in some ways this is true. But our social evolution has been driven by a baser motive—survival—and it hasn't always led to better or more humane ways of being.

Later in the book I will discuss how population/environment constraints relate to the environmental crisis today.

THE SELECTION FOR POWER

For more than 5,000 years, warfare has been widespread across the globe. As a result, every society has eventually been faced with bellicose neighbors and therefore a choice: Develop its power in order to defend itself or be conquered. This process has shaped all societies toward maximizing military power. As described so eloquently by Andrew Bard Schmookler in *The Parable of the Tribes* (1984), this is a social evolutionary process of selection similar to Darwin's biological evolution. The difference is that where biological evolution selects through genes for survival and reproductive capacity, this process selects through culture for war-making power.

The Parable. Schmookler's parable of the tribes goes as follows:

> Imagine a group of tribes living within reach of one another. If all choose the way of peace, then all may live in peace. But what if all but one choose peace, and that one is ambitious for expansion and conquest? Perhaps one tribe is attacked and defeated, its people destroyed and its lands seized for the use of the victors. Another is . . . subjugated and transformed to serve the conqueror. A third . . . flees from the area . . . and its former homeland becomes part of the growing empire of the power-seeking tribe. Let us suppose that others observing these developments decide to defend themselves. . . . But the irony is that successful defense against a power-maximizing aggressor requires a society to become more like the society that threatens it . . . through innovation in organization or technology (or whatever). . . . *In every one of these* [four] *outcomes the ways of power are spread throughout the system.* (Schmookler 1984, 21–22, emphasis in original)

Long-Term Selection. Like population/environmental constraints, this driving force derives its potency from its connection with survival. Again, it's not just individual survival, but societal survival which is at stake. Therefore each society has a strong motivation to develop as much military power as possible. However, the driving force goes far beyond motivation. Even under these competitive circumstances, not all societies will choose to, or be able to, develop their war-making powers. Some have indeed chosen the ways of peace. But they haven't survived, or if they have, it has been a marginal existence.

In the long run, those societies that don't choose the way of war will not survive. So irresistibly the world moves toward war. Regardless of the choices or desires of individual societies, this unfortunate selection process continues, propelling us toward the maximization of military power.

You may suggest that some societies might develop war-making power in order to defend themselves, but not use it aggressively. And in certain isolated cases this might even be true. But this is rare. In most cases the best defense is a good offense. If a society waits too long, only using its power for defense, its neighbors might become too strong. In order to maintain or build its strength, it may need to control nearby resources or access to shipping, and this involves aggression. Furthermore, once a society has the power to conquer, it is all too easy for leaders to become power hungry. Therefore the selection for power rolls on.

The Driving Force. This process didn't just happen in our early history and then stop when all societies were war-oriented. The means for being successful in war can always be improved, and so there has been a continual escalation of military capacity, right up to today. Therefore the selection process has been unending. No society has been able to rest on its laurels for long. There has always been the danger that it might be conquered by an upstart state with more centralized organization or better technology or a horde of more daring barbarians. Thus the selection for military power has been a persistent driving force in social evolution.

The Shaping of Society. The obvious consequence of this selection for power is that all states are war-mongers (despite propaganda to the contrary). However, it goes far beyond that. All aspects of society are related to military capacity, so all are affected by this evolutionary selection process—political organization, the economic system, the level of technological development, psychology, population size, control of natural resources, and so forth. All these have been shaped by the need for military prowess. Whenever a social innovation was adopted by one society that gave it a military advantage, its immediate neighbors would eventually have to adopt it too, or risk defeat. And so the innovation would gradually spread around the world.

What are the qualities of society that promote military might? Among the most important are technology, reflexive consciousness, and social structure—the emergent qualities in our model. Thus the selection for power drives social evolution.

Therefore it becomes clear that there has been a mindless process of social evolution shaping every aspect of our societies toward maximizing power in war. This shaping has not been all bad. Some of the developments have also aided human well-being. But this selection process has not had human welfare in mind, only military power.

A Potential Resolution. As Schmookler points out, there are two conditions needed for this selection process to proceed.

1. Society must have evolved to the point where wars of conquest give significant benefits to the conqueror. This was not so during the Paleolithic era, but it began to be with the introduction of horticulture and reached full influence by the beginning of the Archaic era. Of course it continues to be true today.

2. There must be no intersocietal authority for the settling of conflicts. Notice that the selection for power usually operates only *between* societies, not *within* societies. Within a society, there is normally government, law, and police so that violence isn't the main determinant of who survives and prospers. Only in the intersocietal arena does raw violence rule.

Because of this second condition, humanity will not be burdened with the selection for power forever. It will come to an end when we have a world government or at least a world governing institution that has the military power to enforce its decisions and prevent wars between its member nations. More on this later.

Are Humans Inherently Violent? This driving force, even more than the first, is not pretty to behold. It is not pleasant to think that our world has been so thoroughly shaped by something as destructive as war. This insight makes it evident that in some ways we are really infants when it comes to social development. However, on the positive side, the parable of the tribes makes it apparent that we aren't necessarily very violent and destructive by nature. Some people, viewing our bloodthirsty and oppressive history, imagine that we may be genetically flawed, with an innate bias toward violence.

Schmookler sees it differently. Remember the parable. If all tribes choose peace, then all can have peace, but if one tribe chooses violence, then violence will spread throughout the system. For this to happen we only need to have the genetic *potential* for violence and domination, it need not be strong in us. The selection for power will take over, assuring that this potential for violence spreads throughout the world and shapes our societies. We may not be particularly violent by nature. We are only caught in an unfortunate selection process. The way out is through world order.

INTERACTION OF THE DRIVING FORCES

Synergy of the Forces. These two driving forces are not independent; there has been a constant interaction between them throughout social evolution. They have driven social evolution in virtually the same direction. Both have encouraged the growth of technology. Both have encouraged the growth of population. Increased food-producing technology allows the population to grow, and a larger population gives a military advantage. Similarly, under most circumstances both have encouraged more centralized control and social inequity. Both driving forces have moved societies in exactly the direction represented by the emergent qualities in our model.

Looking at what happens to societies that face a population/environment crisis demonstrates how closely the two driving forces interact. When the population of a particular society grows to the point where it cannot support all its people with its current technology, it must either invent new technology that supports the growing population or it will decay and eventually collapse. Marvin Harris describes a decay scenario in the Archaic centers of civilization during a time when new technology was not invented:

> Century after century the standard of living in China, northern India, Mesopotamia, and Egypt hovered slightly above or below what might be called the threshold of pauperization. When population density in a particular region climbed too high, standards of living dipped below the threshold. This led to wars, famines, and population decline. (Harris 1978, 234–35)

Notice that war is one of the consequences of failing to adapt to population/environment constraints. These weakened societies were often overthrown from inside or conquered from outside, or some combination of the two. Of course, the conquering society or group might not solve the food production problem either, but if they didn't, they probably wouldn't last very long. They would be selected against, by the combination of production failure and war. So there has not only been a strong pressure for societies to solve their population/environment problems, there has been a selection process in favor of those who did. The two driving forces worked together.

Selection for Survival. The first driving force, population/environment constraints, can also be thought of as a selection process, where the selection is for the productive capacity of subsistence technology. Therefore we can think of the two forces as the selection for power and for technology. Remember that these driving forces do not determine the shape of any particular society. They do not even constrain all societies, only those that survive in the long term. In the short term, any society can go against these forces. In the long term, it won't survive.

Lenski and Lenski describes this combined selection process in their macrosociology text:

> The key to the major changes that have occurred in the world system of societies in the last ten thousand years is the process of

> intersocietal selection that has drastically reduced the number of societies. . . . Societies that have grown in size, and developed in complexity, wealth, and power, have been much more likely to survive and transmit their cultures and institutional patterns than societies that have preserved traditional social and cultural patterns and minimized innovation. . . . Because technologically advanced societies have had the advantage in this process of intersocietal selection, their characteristics have increasingly come to be the characteristics of the world system as a whole. (Lenski and Lenski 1987, 72–74)

Causes of the Archaic Transition. Let's now investigate the causes of the transition to the Archaic era based on these insights. I suspect that both driving forces contributed. Population growth during the Neolithic era was enormous compared to that of the Upper Paleolithic era. This led to the need for a technology of food production that was even more advanced than horticulture. The development of metallurgy made this possible in plow-based agriculture, since metal was needed for the blade of a plow. There isn't enough evidence to prove that metallurgy and agriculture were developed in response to this need, but it seems likely. This is the contribution of population/environmental constraints.

Warfare also became widespread and much more aggressive by the latter part of the Neolithic era. This set the stage for the first serious operation of the parable of the tribes and the selection for power. According to Lenski, "The speedup in the rate of intersocietal selection . . . was one of the most critical developments of the horticultural era." Therefore the selection for power led to the emergence of societies dedicated to war and its requirements, "the emergence of urban communities, the greater accumulation of weapons, a greater division of labor, . . . expansion of societal size as a result of conquest, development of the cult of the warrior, increased female infanticide" (Lenski and Lenski 1987, 161), and especially the formation of early states. Therefore the selection for power also played an important part in the Archaic transition.

OTHER FORCES

Let's consider for a moment whether there are other driving forces. What about other factors that are crucial to the survival of a society? These might also shape our social arrangements and therefore be selected for in societal competition. Two factors come immediately to mind—political stability and economic prosperity. Certainly these two have a crucial influence on the survival of any society and therefore they must have affected the shape of our surviving societies.

Certainly they have shaped our societies. All successful societies must be oriented toward political stability, since this is directly related to the survival of a society. Any society that is not very stable politically will likely be overthrown by its own people or conquered by an aggressor. Economic prosperity is also crucial to both political stability and war-making capacity.

Shaping versus Driving Forces. The difference is that shaping society is not the same as driving social evolution. A force such as political stability may be a shaping force but not a driving force. A *shaping force* is a factor that is crucial to the survival of societies and therefore will be selected for in the intersocietal competition. A *driving force* not only shapes society but keeps driving it to evolve. It exerts a continual pressure pushing society in a certain direction. I think that war and technology are driving forces, while political stability is only a shaping force. Once a society has become politically stable it is not compelled to continue evolving politically. It will only become actively oriented toward politically stability if it becomes unstable again and needs to right itself.

War, however, is a driving force. A society is always under pressure to develop better war making capacity because its neighbors might develop better capacity and therefore conquer. A society can never rest secure in its military power for too long. Subsistence technology is also a driving force because of the inevitable increases in population. In the long run, a society can't rest on its technological laurels forever because its population will eventually outstrip its productive capacity, thus causing another crisis and the need for even more productive technology.

Economic prosperity is a more complex issue because it is closely related to the two driving forces. It is enhanced by improvements in subsistence technology, and it contributes to military power. In addition, in the Modern era it has become a major source of societal power, overtaking even the importance of military might. I will discuss this more in a later chapter.

Social Evolution versus Development. The driving forces discussed in this chapter influence long-term social evolutionary directions. They do not necessarily drive or shape every specific change in a society, even changes that are in an evolutionary direction. There are many other forces that may cause particular societal changes, and the dynamics of these changes may be very different from that of the long-term dynamics I am studying in this book. For example, the study of the dynamics of the rise of the Roman Empire is much more specific than the study of the overall evolution of law in society. In biology this distinction is very clear cut. There are shorter-term, specific processes such as the maturation of an organism or the succession of an ecosystem, and there is the long-term process of biological evolution.

In the social area, the distinction is not quite so obvious, but just as important. An influential article in anthropology (Sahlins and Service 1988) defines "specific evolution" as the study of how particular societies change and "general evolution" as the study of how the characteristics of societies as a whole change over the long term. I prefer to reserve the term "evolution" for the long-term dynamics, and to use some other word, such as "development," for the specific, short-term dynamics.

In this book I look at long-term evolution only. It would be very valuable to study the dynamics of the development of specific societies and relate it to the current world situation, but that would require another book entirely.

IMPLICATIONS FOR HUMAN NATURE

These driving forces have propelled social evolution throughout, not just in the early stages. This means that though human beings have accomplished much of great worth and beauty, the primary dynamism behind our evolution has revolved around societal survival. People often assume without thinking that the primary force behind human history and progress has been a desire to improve our lot. We may recognize that this was often done selfishly by a ruling elite, causing misery along the way, but we assume that the human race was at least trying to become stronger, smarter, better, happier. In the process of studying this subject, I have been amazed to realize that the real force behind human progress has been the struggle to survive, the selection of those characteristics that most contributed to societal survival.

If humanity had not been faced with expanding population and the threat of starvation, we would probably have been content to stay hunters and gatherers. If we had not been faced with fierce military competition, we would likely have remained simple village people. Perhaps our great achievements, in technology and science, in social institutions, even in philosophy, religion, and the arts, are somehow related to the struggle to preserve ourselves and our societies in the face of want and danger. Has our evolution been propelled only by the need to solve survival problems? It is humbling to consider this possibility.

If this is true, does this mean that there isn't an internally generated unfolding of our potential as a species? I strongly experience a drive within me toward personal growth and evolution, and I would like to think that we have a similar urge as a species. One possibility is that we do have a built-in evolutionary tendency, but it must be fueled by adversity. That has certainly been the case so far. Another possibility is that we have a self-generating drive to evolve, but this has been overshadowed by survival concerns so far. In this case, our evolution need not continue to be driven by adversity. If we solve the problems of population and war, we can find other reasons to continue evolving, such as expanding our potential and creativity, guiding us on a healthier evolutionary path.

In any case, it is important to know the truth about what has driven our evolution so far. This knowledge can help us with the current crisis. Now the survival of the species is at stake, not just the survival of individual societies. This compels us at this time in human history to make a major change. Not only must we take the next step in social evolution, but we have the opportunity to change the basic driving forces of social evolution. If we can stabilize our population in harmony with the earth and create a world government, the two great driving forces of the past will lose their potency. For the first time we will be able to elevate human betterment to its appropriate position as the most compelling force, as the primary determiner of our future evolution. We can create a world that truly is dedicated to human well-being, creativity, and unfoldment!

VII

THE EVOLUTION OF OPPRESSION

I have separated out power as a subset of the social realm. It seems to be important enough to be studied in its own right for a number of reasons. One is that it has been the most significant area of political and social strife in human history. Most debates about how to structure society have revolved around the question of how power should be distributed. I suspect that this is because the evolution of power has moved more quickly than the other realms and therefore became problematic sooner. This means humanity has been struggling with the problem of power for thousands of years. The difficulties in the material and consciousness realms and in other aspects of the social realm are quite recent.

Factoring out just those aspects of the social realm having to do with power, I create a new pair of complementary qualities (figure 7.1).

Figure 7.1 Power

By *power* I mean the ability to get what one wants in any area of life, especially materially and interpersonally. The ground quality is *power distribution*, the degree to which power is evenly distributed among the people of the society. A large degree of power distribution is known as egalitarianism. Of course, power will never by completely equal, because people have personal qualities such as intelligence, charisma, and assertiveness, which influence how successfully they can get what they want. However, an egalitarian society is structured so that everyone has roughly the same access to the things considered important in that society. The emergent quality, *social structure*, is that which was defined previously for the entire social realm. It refers to the degree that social transactions are structured and mediated.

If a society has social structure without power distribution, then most of its members will be *oppressed* or exploited by those in power. If a society has power distribution without much social structure then there are two possibilities: (1) It may be a very *simple society* such as in stage 1, which has little need for social structure. (2) The lack of social structure may lead to a situation of *anarchy,* where there is too little coordination for the well-being of the society, where people cannot cooperate for their mutual good, such as in trade. This can even result in uncontrolled aggression and violence. When there is social structure *with* power distribution, this is a healthy circumstance generally known in the modern world as *democracy.* An even more evolved society would not only be egalitarian, but also fully *cooperative.* These possibilities will be discussed in detail later in the book.

ARCHAIC OPPRESSION

Already by the Archaic era, the emergent quality, social structure, had developed in opposition to the ground quality, power distribution, to such an extent that power distribution was thoroughly suppressed. *Oppression* was widespread. Society was split.

> The small and often literate urban governing class lived in a strikingly different world from that of the illiterate, rural, peasant majority. . . . The subculture of the governing class . . . included a contempt for physical labor of any kind (except warfare) and for those engaged in it. . . . The scribes of ancient Egypt were fond of saying that the lower classes lacked intelligence and had to be driven like cattle, with a stick. (Lenski and Lenski 1987, 172)

Women were subject to the domination of men. Feminine values and deities were relegated to second place. Masculine and warlike values and gods took over. Women were seen primarily as the property of the male, fit only for reproduction and the care of the home. They had no say in community decisions and probably little power over their own lives.

Serfdom and slavery were widespread. Many serfs and slaves were under the complete power of their masters, who could punish or even execute them on a whim. Most peasants were kept at a bare subsistence level of existence, while the ruling class lived in luxury. Thus for most of the human race, the transition to the Archaic era was a huge step backward in quality of life, and for humanity as a whole it constituted a moral regression.

Why? How did this happen? Why would people who were originally free and in charge of their lives be willing to hand over their power so completely to a ruling class. How could they agree to such domination and misery? These are misleading questions. Though the evolution of power may have been speedy in evolutionary terms, it was very gradual in terms that any one generation could perceive.

People originally gave over some power to the "big men" because there was a need for coordination in war, trade, and other village activities. At first this power was revocable and not oppressive. It was used only for the good of the group. But in some cases, the big men were able to control the resources they managed, and then gradually use them for their own benefit. Over the span of many lifetimes, their power became entrenched and institutionalized. They were able to pass it on to their descendants, who became chiefs.

More lifetimes passed. The size of societies grew. There was greater need for coordination, which brought with it greater possibility for control. Other lands and peoples were subjugated, and their chiefs were ruled over by a superchief. Eventually he became a king and in some cases a god. Prisoners were taken in war; they became slaves. All these changes happened gradually over centuries as power became increasingly unbalanced.

People didn't really choose to give their power away. It was taken from them—sometimes so gradually they didn't really notice, sometimes so violently they had no choice.

Centralization. Many of the great civilizations of the Archaic era were river valley kingdoms which depended for their agricultural productivity on immense irrigation systems tied to the flow of great rivers. This promoted the concentration of power because the irrigation systems were large centralized arrangements that had to be managed and controlled as a whole. This concentrated great power into the hands of the monarchs, which was often used to create social inequity and build empire. The principle is this: The more need there is for centralized coordination, the more opportunity there is for centralized control and therefore oppression.

MALE AND FEMALE

In *The Chalice and the Blade* (1987), Riane Eisler discusses power relations between men and women and the Archaic transition. She defines two types of societies with respect to power. A *partnership* society is one with equal power distribution; a *dominator* society is one based on oppression, not only oppression of women by men, but power hierarchy in general.

Early Partnership Societies. She suggests that the Neolithic horticultural societies of Europe were primarily partnership societies with equal power between the genders, little warfare, reverence for nature, and Goddess worship. In the transition to the Archaic era, these gentle societies were conquered by nomadic herding cultures, which were male-dominated and violent, worshipping warrior sky gods. They created dominator societies to replace the Neolithic partnership cultures.

She presents evidence that one society, Crete, was an even more advanced partnership culture which lasted almost to the end of the Archaic. Crete seems to have had a society with all the positive achievements of civilization associated with the Archaic period, but without war and oppression. This was a high urban civilization with advanced art and architecture. However, unlike the other urban societies of the Archaic, there is evidence of equality between the sexes, relative distribution of power, Goddess worship, and reverence for nature. Crete may have been able to hold out as long as it did because of its protected position as an island, but it was finally conquered by military invaders around 1000 B.C.

Eisler's ideas are largely based on the work of archaeologist Marija Gimbutas, whose research has provoked controversy within her field. I can't present her conclusions as accepted facts, and I don't have enough expertise to evaluate them myself. However, her notions seem reasonable, and I think it is important to include a theory that breaks new ground by stepping outside the male-dominated paradigm in any field.

The Selection for Power. These insights from Eisler are a perfect illustration of the operation of the parable of the tribes: If some societies become warlike, then the rest must either perish or become warlike, too. These Neolithic Goddess cultures eventually had to come up against warlike neighbors, and then they would either be subjugated or learn warfare.

It is not surprising that the initiation of military-oriented culture in Europe would come from herding societies. In these societies during stage 2, men tended to take over herding in place of the hunting they had done in stage 1. Since these cultures didn't emphasize horticulture, they probably didn't develop the same reverence for women and the vegetative cycle. Herding societies also tended to develop on poorer land, which was suitable for grazing but not for farming. So it is not surprising that when things became environmentally difficult and their people were in danger of starving, some herding societies would try to conquer and control the more productive land for themselves. Thus it is likely that population/environment constraints triggered the selection for power.

Are Men Inherently Violent? Does this mean that men are naturally violent and warlike and women naturally cooperative and peaceful? I don't think it is that simple. Since men are naturally bigger and stronger and not directly burdened with children, the primitive division of labor by gender gave men the job of hunting and protecting the band. And it is sometimes only a small step from protecting to aggressing. Therefore any groups that did move in an aggressive direction would certainly do so under male leadership. Remember what the parable of the tribes says: Human beings may not be intrinsically very violent; we only need the capacity for violence to ensure that the selection for power will proceed. Then all surviving societies will have to become warlike.

The same goes for men. Once there are some men who are warlike and lead their societies into aggression, men in other societies will either become warlike in order to protect their people or they will be conquered and killed. From my own personal experience, I don't believe that men in general are innately very violent. I am suggesting that the amount of male violence evident today and for the last 5,000 years may not be intrinsic to our nature. Clearly the capacity for violence is intrinsic to us, but under better social circumstances violence might occur rarely and be resolved more easily. Allan Chinen (1993) suggests that the original masculine archetype in stage 1 wasn't the warrior, but rather the trickster, who was peaceful and egalitarian.

I think the male tendency toward protectiveness and occasional anger has been perverted by the selection for power. Schmookler, in his second book (1988), analyses how warrior psychology developed out of a societal need to deal with the parable of the tribes. Chinen describes this situation:

> Where their nomadic ancestors kept only a few objects which could be carried from camp to camp, farmers began to amass stores of grain and pottery, herds of animals and buildings. . . . Social tensions increased, aggravated by an ever-increasing population. . . . When their crops failed, farmers could not move on to richer lands . . . because all territory was now claimed and occupied. Land could only be taken by force, and the stage was set for a frightening new invention—warfare. . . . Battle became organized, planned, and cold-blooded. The intent was to take land, herds of animals, or hoards of precious goods.

> To survive, farmers moved into fortified villages, and men became warriors. Male instincts, honed by millennia of hunting and neglected in the [horticultural] era, were bent toward a new use: to kill people rather than reindeer, and to seize wealth and power instead of food. . . . In these perilous times, the warrior became an ideal of man-hood. . . . Boys from an early age were taught to be fearless, aggressive, and merciless in battle. Boys were now favored over girls for simple reasons of survival: boys became warriors, warriors were lost in battles, and new warriors were constantly needed. Slowly and insidiously, women lost ground to men. In times of siege, fighting men were fed, not women. Warriors also began treating their own women like the slaves captured in war. The patriarchy took shape, replacing the feminine culture of early farmers. . . . From this time on, being a man meant being a warrior, killing without fear or remorse, dominating women, and aspiring to be a ruling chief. (Chinen 1993)

Notice that the male psychology of violence began to be taught out of a societal need for protection. Our task as men today is to reclaim our masculine vitality without violence. I will return to gender-related power issues later in dealing with the current transition.

GROUND QUALITY REPRESENTATIVES

Every era has a wide variety of societies. There were undoubtedly many stage 2 societies still in existence during the Archaic era. These societies could continue in their relatively peaceful ways until conquered by one of the expanding stage 3 states.

In addition, remember that in each stage some groups represent the emergent quality and others the ground quality. In stage 3 the rural peasant villages represented the ground quality in the social realm. In some ways they lived as their stage 2 ancestors had lived, except for using agricultural techniques rather than horticulture. However, they were subservient to the ruling groups in the cities and this gave their lives a very different quality.

In the consciousness realm, the stage 3 ground quality representatives were the surviving groups studying women's mysteries and worshipping the Goddess. Though our knowledge of them is mostly lost, Riane Eisler discusses evidence of their influence on ancient Greek culture (1987, 111–19). According to Eisler, Crete also seems to be a stage 3 ground quality representative in that it possessed some aspects of stage 3 (urban, civilized) without others (war, oppression).

The Lesson of Crete. Eisler's ideas suggest the interesting notion that the positive aspects of our social evolution are not intrinsically tied to war and oppression. If a society such as Crete existed, there may have been others. If the selection for power had not been operating, maybe the majority of our civilized societies would have been partnership societies. Maybe our world would have had a very different path of social evolution. I discuss later the possibility that some Native American tribes also followed a trajectory that didn't include widespread stage 3 oppression. The relevance of this today is that if humanity can now end the selection for power (through some sort of world order), perhaps it will not be so difficult to create sophisticated partnership societies.

THE SPEEDUP IN THE EVOLUTION OF POWER

The worse abuses of power that exist today were already in full bloom four to five thousand years ago. Thus the timing of evolution has been speedy in the power realm (Table 7.1).

Table 7.1 Social Evolution and Power

Era	Overall Social	Qualities	Power	Qualities
Upper Paleolithic	Family, band		Egalitarian	
Neolithic	Village, chiefdom		Rank, stratified	
Archaic	City, early state, empire		Oppression	

Here in the second and third columns, the relationship between the ground and emergent qualities, community and social structure, is moving slowly from the dominance of community to a relatively equal balance between them. But in the last two columns, the relationship between power distribution and social structure is moving much more quickly. By the Archaic era, their relationship has already moved from one extreme to the other, from egalitarianism to oppression.

In the social realm as a whole and in the material and consciousness realms, it has taken until the present day for evolution to advance to the dangerous point where the emergent quality is suppressing the ground quality so completely. That is why the world is in such a crisis today. However, in the power realm this happened thousands of years ago in the Archaic era. *Power became a serious problem in human affairs long before ecology or consciousness did.* This is why historically most social struggles and most ideological debates have centered on power. Of course, power is still a problem today, and many social critics still see it as the main problem, but now we have reached the problematic stage in all realms. More on this later in exploring the Modern era.

Why the Speedup for Power? Why has the power realm moved so much faster than the others? I suspect that this is because of the parable of the tribes and the selection for power. Let's analyze our two driving forces. Population/environment constraints is a driving force because the inevitable rise in population eventually causes the need for more productive subsistence technology. However, it often takes a long time to invent the new technology. It may require an infrastructure or way of thinking that hasn't yet been developed. Therefore this driving force, though relentless, is not necessarily fast.

The selection for power operates more quickly. No matter how militarily secure a society is, one of its neighbors can always come up with something new—technology, social structure, warrior psychology, resources—which gives it an edge in battle. There is always the possibility of improving your fighting capabilities, and you're not limited to technological improvements. This driving force seems to escalate continuously. So already by the Archaic era, the large societies were completely war-oriented.

This led to a fast evolution of power toward oppression. In those days the more centralized, oppressive regimes were the most successful militarily, so they were favored in the selection for power. In addition, many states and empires gained much of their territory and population through conquest, and they tended to oppress the conquered people, turning them into slaves or serfs. The population of the original conquering society would then become the ruling class in the new larger empire.

Therefore, because of the parable of the tribes, the subrealm of power evolved much faster than other realms and became a serious problem early in our history. Consequently, we have studied it and experimented with it, trying to find solutions. There has been some progress toward integration in the power area, especially in the Modern era with the spread of democracy.

EMERGENCE, INTEGRATION, AND EVOLUTIONARY PROGRESS

Let's look at the relationship between the ground and emergent qualities in the model using power as an example. The qualities are social structure and power distribution. Remember that they are not opposites; it is possible to have an integration of the two. If I had chosen true opposites, such as "dominator" and "partnership" as qualities, then they couldn't be integrated. In my model, it is possible to have both social structure and power distribution. It is possible to have a society that is large and sophisticated, which has organized, mediated power relationships, and which is also egalitarian.

Opposition or Integration. However, this is not easy. Even though the complementary qualities *can* be integrated, they tend to be opposed to each other. The complementary qualities in the model tend to be opposed unless there is a conscious effort by society to create a way of integrating them. Thus, as social structure has emerged and become prominent, there has been a natural tendency toward stratification and eventually oppression. The easiest way to achieve social structure leads to power imbalance. The natural tendency is for the emergent quality in time to become dissociated from the ground quality and to suppress it.

It takes a more mature, educated, thoughtful society to achieve the integration of the two qualities. In the power area it is only in the Modern era that society has been able to achieve some integration of the complementary qualities. We call it democracy. Even now we are far from a full integration. There is still considerable oppression and exploitation, even within the most advanced democracies, and even more when considering the relationship between the industrialized and preindustrialized nations. However, we have made some progress toward integration of the qualities.

This tendency applies to all the realms. The complementary qualities tend to be opposed until society achieves enough maturity to make a conscious effort to create a structure that promotes their integration. This is our most important task in the current planetary crisis.

Evolution and Morality. It should be obvious from examining the power realm that as a society evolves, it doesn't necessarily become better or more moral. It doesn't necessarily become more conducive to the health and happiness of its people. In the power area, the evolution from stage 2 to 3 was actually a step backward morally. This can be confusing because it is common to think of evolution as a movement toward the good.

This dilemma is even more baffling today in trying to understand our current crisis. In many ways humanity seems to be progressing—scientifically, technologically, in some ways socially and psychologically. Yet in other important ways we seem to be regressing. After all, we have frequent wars, massive poverty, and ecological destruction. This can't be a sign of moral progress. What is going on? If we are evolving, what does evolution mean?

Evolutionary Progress. My perspective is that evolution involves a very specific kind of progress. Evolution in general seems to mean that things grow in complexity and autonomy. They become more differentiated into parts, more articulated, and in some cases the parts become better coordinated with each other. Systems also develop greater autonomy and ability to respond creatively to each situation. This is true of all levels of evolution—physical, biological, and social.

In social evolution, our technology, our societies, and our consciousness all become more complex. There is an emergence and an increase in mediation in all realms. In addition, the ground qualities are suppressed and then return. I believe that social evolution is a dialectical movement between mediated organization and organic vitality. At a more general level, this is a movement between differentiation/autonomy and wholeness. Later in the book I will show how this conception of social evolution fits into a unified conception of evolution as it has been studied by general systems theory. Social evolution involves a dialectical kind of progress which doesn't always immediately lead toward a better society. I believe that in the long run social evolution will produce healthier societies, especially when the dialectic turns, and now is that time.

Therefore, in my understanding there is a clear progression in social evolution, but one that is complex morally. I believe that it is crucial today to comprehend exactly what form our history has taken, especially since it has produced massive suffering as well as much that is beneficial.

Vision and Compassion. I must admit that this sometimes makes it hard for me to know how to relate emotionally to our history, especially the chronicle of our oppression. Because of the tremendous increase in oppression in the Archaic era and its perpetuation over five thousand years, untold people have suffered enormous pain and had their lives stunted. The horrors of war, the degradation of slavery, the insidious blighting of human potential—how can I feel anything but outrage at these abominations?

And yet I feel compelled to view these events from a larger perspective. While not excusing the moral transgressions involved, I can also appreciate that much of the oppression was ingrained and systemic. In many cases it would have taken a Herculean effort for someone to transcend their cultural conditioning and refuse to take part in the exploitation that surrounded them. I certainly can't claim that I would have been capable of this had I been born into an oppressor class. Most of us still participate in subtle, less visible forms of exploitation today.

I can also see that the growth in our technical capacity and social structure was a necessary part in our evolution as a species, and we simply didn't have the maturity to do it in a more humane way. This would have required a level of consciousness and cooperation that was beyond us. I can only hope that we are capable of it now.

From this larger perspective I feel compassion for all—oppressor and oppressed, in the past and the present—and I hope that everyone can work together to resolve the current crisis.

In today's industrialized societies we have made considerable evolutionary progress, the emergent qualities are highly developed, but at the expense of the ground qualities. This has led us to the point where we are now in serious danger. At this point continued evolution must mean integration of those ground qualities that have been overthrown. The kind of integration that has begun in the power realm with democracy must now happen in the other realms as well. This will become clearer as we go.

VIII

STAGE 4: UNIVERSAL RELIGION AND PHILOSOPHY

The next great transition in social evolution happened at about 500 B.C. and seems to have been driven primarily by changes in consciousness. It leads us into the next stage, which covers both the Ancient and Medieval eras, continuing until about 1500 A.D.

CONSCIOUSNESS: RELIGION AND PHILOSOPHY

I will explore the consciousness realm first, because that realm led the way into the Ancient era. In stage 4, reflexive consciousness grew to the point where people began to think rationally about the nature of reality and what it meant to be human. Especially in Greek philosophy, they developed their own ideas about life, presented them publicly, and debated them. This was an immense step forward from simply accepting the traditional or tribal views of reality which were developed unconsciously over long periods of time. There was a growth in the complexity of concepts, a first use of rational analysis to understand the world, and an appreciation of the individual mind. Remember that these changes were the result of cultural evolution, not because of any biological improvement in our capacity for reflexive thought.

The Cosmopolitan Outlook. The social changes of the Archaic era—war, trade, and travel—produced a considerable mixing of peoples and traditions. As a result, large numbers of people were exposed to a variety of religious and cultural traditions. It became much more difficult for a person to simply dismiss all other traditions as barbaric. There was an emergence from embeddedness in the mythic traditions and the adoption of a more cosmopolitan attitude of tolerance of other cultures and religions. The idea developed that all people were of value regardless of background and shared a common human bond. This led naturally to the concept of a universal God. Some people, at least, realized that there were other valid ways of living and that they could even choose their culture or religion.

World Religion. The mythic consciousness of the Neolithic and Archaic eras was replaced by world religion. These new religions were monotheistic, universal, moral, personal and largely dualistic. In the West, this began with Judaism and came to fruition with Christianity and later Islam. In China, it was represented by Taoism and Confucianism; in India by Hinduism and Buddhism.

These religions believed in a single supreme God or universal essence. The old mythic religions were each tied to a specific people, a certain tribe or tradition. The Gods of the new world religions were seen as universal and the religions were open to anyone who believed in them. The old mythic religions were not based on faith or belief, but rather on membership in the tribe or the group. The world religions allowed anyone to join who believed in their God (or equivalent) and accepted their traditions and rituals, even women, slaves, foreigners. Everyone was equal in God's eyes. This was the first recognition of the universal value of all human beings.

Some of the Eastern religions, such as Buddhism and Taoism, went so far as to eliminate the concept of God altogether. They preached primarily a spiritual way of being in harmony with the Tao or Dharma. They valued not only all human beings, but all life.

Dualism. The new religions, especially in the West, were dualistic in the sense that they clearly separated heaven and earth, the spiritual and the secular. Stage 1 consciousness made little separation of this sort—everything was both material and spiritual simultaneously. The world was alive with spirit, and existing deities were directly related to material entities, usually spirits of animals, plants, or ancestors. Stages 2 and 3 brought in some separation, as special times and places were set aside for the spiritual, and gods and goddesses were conceptualized as somewhat separate from the human and natural realms. In stage 4 this process culminated in a fully separate and more abstract spiritual realm and a much more secular human world.

> The cult and worship of a tribal source of life [stages 2 & 3] was the first form of detaching and distinguishing a non-self from a self. . . . At this stage, the non-self, the divine source of life, was still in partial physical connection with the self, although cult and worship were already initiating a spiritual connection between man and god. The development [from stage 3 to 4] meant a gradual preponderance of this spiritual connection, a progressive spiritualization of

> a more universal god, and the increasing worldliness and individualization of man. (Kahler 1956, 111)

It is questionable to attribute dualism to all the stage 4 religions, especially since some of the Eastern religions explicitly preached nondualism. Taoism may indeed have been nondualistic. However the Hinduism and Buddhism of this stage show subtle signs of dualism through their denigration of material life and this world in favor of escaping the wheel of karma through enlightenment.

This difference between East and West is an example of a larger disparity that arose during stage 4. The West began to emphasize the emergent qualities in social evolution and the East began to emphasize the ground qualities. L. L. Whyte goes so far as to characterize the emergence of stage 4 consciousness, with its split between instinct and rationality, as the "European dissociation" (Whyte 1948). This geographical disjunction became even more pronounced in stage 5 when the West clearly took the lead in social evolution.

Ethics. The new religions were also for the first time concerned with morality. Their God was the God of love, and they expected humans to be concerned about ethical conduct in the world and the well-being of their neighbors. The deities of stage 3 had been no more ethical in their behavior than humans; they had their lusts and their power intrigues, their greeds and revenges. The God or supreme essence of stage 4 represented the ideal of moral possibility—all-encompassing love and wisdom. For the first time, people begin to observe and reflect on themselves, to examine their behavior and decide on the morally right course of action, to perceive the behavior of others according to standards of good and evil.

Philosophy, of course, was also concerned with good and evil and how to live a moral life. In fact, philosophy and religion were not nearly so separate as they are today. The Greek philosophies were strongly spiritual, and in China, Confucianism was really more a philosophy than a religion. It was especially concerned with how a leader should rule so as to best promote the well-being of the people.

Individuality. The large empires tended to cut people loose from their native communities and traditions and replace these with guilds, trade, law, citizenship, and other mediated social structures. These more abstract associations were not enough to compensate for the vitality and meaning of community, so people were often cut loose, adrift, with nothing substantial to guide them except their personal choices. So, in this way, the empires promoted individuality.

The new world religions were more oriented toward the individual. The mythic religions had been primarily religions of the group. The new world religions, because they were open to everyone and were based on belief rather than ancestry, were necessarily involved with the individual. The individual was responsible for having faith in God, for acting like a good Christian (Buddhist, etc.) in the world, for developing a personal relationship with God (or working toward enlightenment). There was still a community of believers and a church to mediate between the individual and the spiritual, but the emphasis had shifted from the group to the individual.

In *The Heart of History* (1987), John Perry analyzes the process of the democratization of individuality during the transition to the Ancient era for four societies—Egypt, China, India, and Israel. By analyzing the psychology of their myths, he suggests that in stage 3 only the sacred kings were true individuals, with a sense of personal pride, conscious choice, and responsibility to their peoples. By stage 4 this had become democratized to the point where many citizens experienced themselves that way.

> What is most significant about the sacral kings in the evolutionary perspective is that they embodied the psychic image representing the full potential of unique individuality in its nascence, awaiting its realization eventually among the many. . . . [After a while] the prerogative of kings was coveted and then mimicked by the aristocracy, and thus diffused out from the strong central monarchy into the hands of petty princes and barons. . . . The sacrality of the governing office dropped away . . . the ceremonial forms of the sacral kingship . . . underwent a sequence of metamorphoses from era to era representing not only the maturation of cultures but at the same time the differentiation of the human psyche. . . . While the actual rulership was becoming secularized, the sacred royal figure was being internalized; that is, what he had represented in ceremony was increasingly being perceived as happening within the individual member of society. (Perry 1987, 8–9)

Conscious Choice. The central underlying change in stage 4 was the emergence of consciousness out of the instinctual and traditional and into the realm of conscious choice. L. L. Whyte, in his superb analysis of the transition to stage 4, describes this process of advancing reflexive consciousness:

> The circumstances of human life demanded that individual choice, based on personal consideration of the problems of behavior,

> should to an increasing degree dominate behavior. The attention of the individual was drawn more and more to his own thought . . . and he became aware of himself as a thinking and feeling person with the faculty of choice.
>
> In the instinctive or traditional life of [Archaic] man, response followed stimulus along established paths . . . but now that the old traditions were inadequate, situations arose in which this flow . . . was arrested, and no adequate action was possible until the extended processes of thought had worked out the appropriate solution. . . . Each person had increasingly . . . to develop his own personality in his own actions. (Whyte 1948, 87–88)

Rational Study. Reflexive consciousness began to seriously study not only the external world but also the internal world of consciousness itself. The Greeks made rudimentary beginnings in science by attempting to analyze and understand the nature and behavior of matter. India made a serious study of consciousness and developed detailed psychologies of the process of spiritual development in Hinduism and Buddhism.

The time sense in stage 4 became historical. For the first time written records were kept of historical events, and people began to have a sense of progressive change over time, rather than simply a repetition of a yearly cycle.

Many of the stage 4 religions and philosophies began in a participatory way. Their early adherents had profoundly moving spiritual experiences or passionate debates. However, as time went on, churches and dogma sprang up. Ritual which had once been deeply meaningful became a comfortable repetition without real participation. Philosophies were studied for their abstract ideas but without the original keen sense of dialogue and creativity. The advance of reflexive consciousness now began to eclipse participatory consciousness. At this stage their relationship can be represented as in figure 8.1.

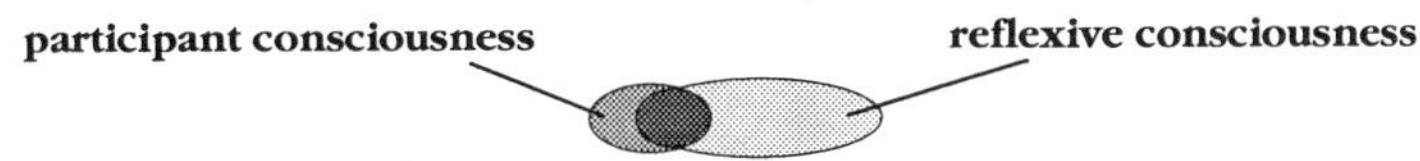

Figure 8.1

Other Consciousness Trajectories. This description of stage 4 consciousness may not tell the whole story. There is evidence that perhaps some Native American tribes had a higher level of consciousness than would have been consistent with their technological attainments (Deloria

1993). In the material realm, they were in stage 1 or 2, but in the consciousness realm, they might be characterized as stage 4 or even higher. Some tribes seem to have had a highly developed sense of ethics and individuality, a historical sense, and a generally more developed reflexive consciousness than would be expected in stage 2. Much of this evidence is based on the writings of current-day Native American scholars, and thus it may be biased or it may reflect a subtle European influence during the last couple hundred years. However, if true, it suggests an interesting addition to the model of social evolution I am developing.

The sequence of stages that I have concentrated on is not the only possible trajectory for a society. If left to their own devices, not all societies will necessarily develop in this way. The sequence I describe is the way the leading edge of social evolution has developed, but there is no reason why some societies couldn't have a different trajectory. For example, a society might not go through the stage 3 development of a large oppressive state and therefore might evolve a different consciousness as well.

However, because of the parable of the tribes, the leading edge of social evolution eventually became every society's path because alternative societies were conquered by the societies that were more advanced militarily and technologically. Therefore different trajectories were only possible for societies that were isolated enough geographically to avoid being conquered.

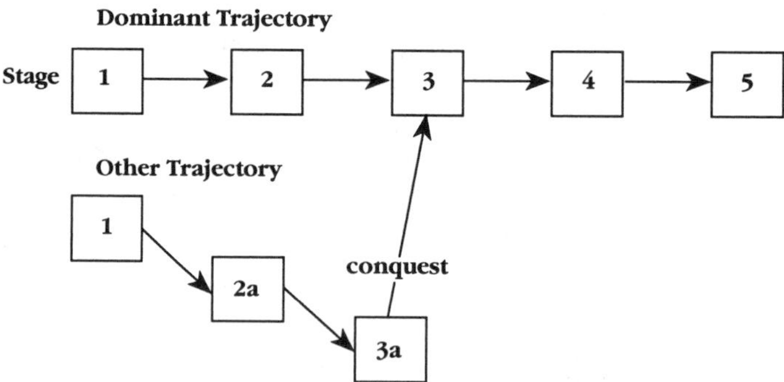

Figure 8.2

As I discussed in the last chapter, Riane Eisler suggests that Crete had a different pathway until the first century B.C. This may have held true even longer for some Native American tribes, since there were no really large stage 3 empires in North America. This may account for the more advanced Native American consciousness. Of course, they were eventually conquered by stage 5 Europeans, but they had longer to develop along their own unique course.

This is only speculation. It would be interesting to study in detail social evolutionary tracks other than main one our world has taken.

MATERIAL: GRADUAL TECHNICAL ADVANCE

The Ancient era is sometimes known as the "Iron Age" because the use of iron became widespread at this time. Even though this did have considerable impact, it wasn't significant enough to characterize the entire era. No technological advance was.

There was a gradual improvement in agricultural, military, and sailing technology. Specific inventions through the centuries were paper, the water mill, porcelain, printing, and gunpowder. Technical advances continued to be driven by the need to increase agricultural output. These came in a continuing array of minor improvements. For example, in Europe between the ninth and eleventh centuries agricultural techniques were gradually improved—first by the introduction of the cross plow, then the three-field rotation system, and finally the use of horse teams in tandem to pull the plows.

SOCIAL: HISTORIC EMPIRES

The social equivalent of world religion in this era was world empire. Vast empires were created which reached far beyond any one cultural or religious tradition. There was a substantial increase in trade and travel; people's horizons widened.

Social differentiation and complexity continued to increase. One of the major advances of this era was Roman law, "the first systematic and elaborate worldly law in history" (Kahler 1956, 108). Citizenship in the Roman Empire was eventually extended to all free peoples within its borders, compelling the law to become increasingly sophisticated to handle such a diverse and far flung association of peoples.

Oppression was still widespread, but there were small beginnings of an integration of power distribution into social structure. For a time Athens had a full-fledged democracy, at least for those of its people who were considered citizens. The Roman Empire had periods of being a republic, in which there was some improvement in the distribution of power. The increasing importance of individuality also provided an impetus toward greater power distribution. After all, if a society begins to value the worth of each individual, regardless of ethnic background or social standing, it lays the groundwork for equalizing power. These were primarily seeds, setting the stage for an egalitarian world view, even if its implementation had to wait until the Modern era.

REASONS FOR THE TRANSITION

Let's now consider the reasons for the transition to stage 4. Since this era seems to have been led by consciousness, it is important to understand how this happened. Unlike some theorists, I don't believe that consciousness spontaneously evolves at certain times in history. I believe that it is driven by social and environmental forces.

The stage 4 consciousness transition seems to have been largely a delayed reaction to the social changes that happened in the Archaic era—the growth of war, trade, travel, and oppression. I speculate that these changes took so long to develop and spread that the response to them happened a couple thousand years later, initiating the Ancient era.

Whyte's View. L. L. Whyte (1948) provides an analysis of the transition to stage 4 as a reaction to some of the excesses of stage 3. In that stage, the ruling classes had command of a virtually unlimited degree of sense comfort and pleasure. For the first time in human history, some people could satisfy their instinctive needs without limit, and this undoubtedly led to excess and decadence. At some point there had to be a reaction to this, a way of internally limiting one's indulgence, since there were no longer external limits. This involved a splitting of the psyche into a spontaneous instinctive part and a deliberate moral part, leading to ethics and dualism. The evidence indicates that before stage 4, people did not have a conscience or superego, at least in the way we have today. This part of the psyche was probably developed during the Ancient era.

Human society had emerged sufficiently from its ground that the natural biological controls were no longer adequate to ensure healthy behavior. However, humanity was not advanced enough to understand our true nature as integrated and evolving beings. So our stage 4 religions and philosophies developed concepts of right and wrong that were static and rigid. (This is apparent today in the abortion debate.) We then tried to control ourselves through guilt and repression, and this developed into a profound split in our nature, a split between reflexive and participatory consciousness. I see these developments as a social evolutionary advance at the time, and Whyte probably does, too, but he emphasizes their negative aspects, which are very apparent today.

According to Whyte's analysis, this split happened primarily in Europe rather than the East, and was propagated in European and Western culture, which has come to dominate the world, becoming even more extreme in the Modern era. He called it the "European dissociation." Whyte's solution was to introduce an integrated, process perspective from which to understand humanity; this was an early predecessor of general systems theory.

In addition, the large discrepancies between the resources and well-being of the rich and poor could not be wholly rationalized on class or religious grounds. Some people were undoubtedly appalled at the widespread human misery resulting from these imbalances, and they must have searched for a way of understanding this situation, evolving a new awareness involving concepts of good and evil and moral injunctions.

In summary, stage 3 societies were split in such a way that the ruling classes were engaging in behavior that was destructive for their societies and sometimes even for themselves. This eventually resulted in societal changes in consciousness that paved the way for stage 4. Some of the social advances of the Ancient era, such as Athenian democracy and Roman law, were also attempts to deal with these disturbing imbalances.

Driving Forces. How is this related to the driving forces? This transition, unlike the previous ones, was not directly driven by population/environment constraints or the selection for military power. Instead it seems that it was a reaction to the changes of the previous era. You may wonder, how can there be a major transition that is not caused by the driving forces? Remember that the driving forces don't necessarily produce each significant social change. Instead, they constrain the direction of long-term social evolutionary changes. Even as important a change as a stage transition can have other causes.

It is interesting to contemplate the similarity between stage 4 and today's circumstances. The stage 4 transition seems to have been caused by a reaction to the problems of the previous stage. The driving forces produced stage 3 (as well as 2), but after some time it became apparent that there were serious difficulties with the stage 3 way of life. This led to a cultural response resulting in the religions and philosophies of the time. Similarly in today's crisis, society is facing the overwhelming problems caused by the advances of the previous stage, and we need a transition that is a creative response to them. It is encouraging to realize that this type of stage transition has occurred before in human history.

GROUND QUALITY MOVEMENTS

The Medieval Era. There were few additional advances during the Medieval era until a few centuries before the transition to the Modern era. Consequently I have included the Medieval era and the Ancient era together. However, there were a number of interesting ground quality responses during the Medieval era.

During every era, as the emergent quality comes to prominence, there are countermovements that emphasize the ground quality that is being suppressed. These may simply be anachronisms from a previous era, or they may be vital attempts by the ground quality to assert itself against the encroaching emergent quality.

Possible Outcomes. In *Coming to Our Senses*, Morris Berman undertakes a study of ground-quality movements in the consciousness realm throughout history. He suggests that there are at least four different outcomes possible in the struggle between the ground and emergent qualities, and he gives an example of each (Berman 1990).

1. The first possibility is success of the ground-quality movement followed by a gradual loss of the ground quality. He points to evidence that the early Christian movement emphasized participatory consciousness in a way that was quite different from the practices the Church ultimately adopted. Despite the success and extraordinary influence of this movement, its participatory quality was gradually assimilated to the emergent reflexive consciousness and social structure of the Church and partially lost.
2. The second possibility is that the movement will be repressed and co-opted. He illustrates this with the Cathar movement of romantic and courtly love in the 12th and 13th centuries in France. This was a major movement emphasizing participatory consciousness that developed enough influence to seriously threaten the established Church. It was violently repressed and certain elements of its lore were incorporated into Church practices.
3. Berman suggests that the practice of magic at the beginning of the Modern period was actually one of the precursors of modern science. This illustrates the third possibility, which is that the movement will be transformed and incorporated into the continued development of the emergent quality.

4. The fourth possibility, represented by Nazism, is that a participatory movement may turn to evil.

I might add that a fifth possibility is that the movement may remain intact without having a decisive impact on society. It serves as a protest against the emergent quality and as a precursor to future developments. The modern Romantic movement is an example of this.

Berman's most provocative assertion is that much of history is driven by the continual eruption of the ground quality in its attempt to undo its suppression and the various ways this is handled by the emergent quality. He, of course, doesn't use the terms ground and emergent quality, but there is no mistaking what he means.

Overall, the Ancient/Medieval era saw an increase in the emergent qualities in all realms at the expense of the now dwindling ground qualities. Table 8.1 summarizes these advances and highlights the qualities of the first four stages.

Table 8.1 Stage 4

Realm	Description
Material	Iron, gradual technical advance
Social	Historic empires, law, cosmopolitanism, seeds of democracy
Consciousness	World religion, personal religion, philosophy, morality, beginnings of rationality, history, universality, dualism

	Era	Qualities	Material	Social	Consciousness
1	Paleolithic		Hunting & gathering	Family, band	Magic, animism
2	Neolithic		Horticulture, herding	Village, chiefdom	Myth: Goddess
3	Archaic		Agriculture, bronze	City, early state	Myth: gods & heroes
4	Ancient/ Medieval		Gradual advance	Historic empire	Religion, philosophy

IX

STAGE 5: THE MODERN ERA

During the period from the 1500s to the 1700s humanity went through a complex transition from the Medieval to the Modern era, leading us to the world of today.

Regional Leadership. The leading edge of social evolution, which in the Ancient era had shifted from the Middle East to southern Europe, in the Modern era moved into northern and western Europe and the United States. However, the Modern Era seems to be the first era to be dominated by one geographical region. In other eras, a specific region may have led the way into the new stage, but then shared the limelight with other areas.

For example, the first stage 3 civilizations were in the Middle East, but during the Archaic era comparable stage 3 civilizations developed independently in India and China. In the Ancient/Medieval era, stage 4 cultures developed more or less simultaneously in southern Europe, the Middle East, and the Orient, and none dominated the era. The characteristics of the European empires (Greece and Rome) had a greater influence on later developments, but during the Ancient/Medieval era, there were times when China and some Muslim societies were more culturally advanced than Europe. So before the Modern era, the leading edge of social evolution was reasonably distributed over the globe, with no region assuming clear leadership.

Then Europe took over and the pattern changed. Because societies had evolved to the point where empires could span the globe, once Europe developed its lead, it proceeded to colonize most of the rest of the world. This brought stage 5 culture to other societies, under the domination of the European powers. Only the United States and much later Japan were able to establish autonomous stage 5 cultures that rivaled or surpassed those of Europe.

Perspective. In exploring the Modern era, keep in mind the extra difficulty we moderns have in understanding it. Because we inhabit the era, it is tempting to unconsciously see our Modern view of reality as the right one and others as primitive versions of ours. It helps to remember that our world view is just one choice along the road of social evolution, with its strengths and weaknesses. The trick is to step back and emerge from our own culture, to see it clearly.

On the other hand, for those of you who see our destructiveness, it is tempting to dismiss everything in the Modern era as fundamentally flawed. It is easy to overlook the positive aspects of our culture and worldview. At the beginning of our era, 400–500 years ago, the entire Modern worldview was exciting and revolutionary and very much needed to overcome the inadequacies of the Medieval worldview. It is tempting to view the Modern era in either all-good or all-bad terms, but this obscures the path of our evolution.

THE MATERIAL REALM: INDUSTRY

From the late twelfth century on, increasing technological advance accelerated the pace of social evolution. In the 1500s the invention of the compass and new shipbuilding techniques enabled worldwide navigation and the settlement of the New World. This greatly increased the importance of trade and undermined the feudal economy, preparing the way for capitalism and the widespread power of the merchant class. The use of gunpowder in ship-based cannons permitted European navies to dominate the world.

Driving Forces. The transition to the Modern era seems to have been initiated by worldwide navigation and the commercial revolution encouraged by it. These prepared the way for much that followed. How does this square with our understanding of driving forces? Morris Berman suggests that it was partly population/environment constraints that provoked these early developments:

> It was, however, in the economic sphere that the feudal system became increasingly nonviable. . . . The limits of feudalism had been reached as early as the thirteenth century. . . . [There was] an upper limit to productivity. . . . This in turn caused a strain that was starting to transform peasant rebellions . . . into a class war. . . . In response to this threat, there emerged an enormous pressure to expand the geographical base of economic operations . . . [which] contributed to the rapid ascendancy of the imperial program of expansion and . . . a host of inventions that made such a program possible. (Berman 1984, 41)

In addition, the parable of the tribes was clearly a strong influence. Once one European power began sailing the world, improving its economic standing, and threatening to dominate the high seas and establish colonies, it became a major military menace to the rest of the continent. Its neighbors had to follow quickly with their own parallel developments or risk defeat. Therefore both of the driving forces were in full sway at this transition.

The Industrial Revolution. The printing press revolutionized the spread of information, education, and literacy. The growth of science was enabled by the invention of various scientific instruments and the elucidation of the scientific method. These advances were accompanied by a whole host of social developments—the Renaissance, the Protestant Reformation, the growth of market economies, the Enlightenment. These all set the stage for the Industrial Revolution, which introduced not only a continuing array of technological innovations but a complete change in our relationship to technology and to the natural world.

Before then, despite a gradual growth in city life, most people were farmers (or peasants or slaves working farms) and therefore spent the large portion of their work lives growing food. Now this was no longer the case. Using the new technology, each farmer was able to produce much more food, so many people were forced off the land and into the cities. They became workers in the new industries and factories.

An Energy Crisis. There was also a radical change in the amount of energy used and its sources. Where before, energy had come from human and animal power and from burning wood, now it came primarily from burning coal (and later oil) for use in the new machines. The switch to coal, like so many other technical advances, was provoked by a population/environment crisis. This time it was a crisis in energy production:

> Many parts of Northwestern Europe had achieved a kind of saturation with humankind by the 14th century. . . . In the most densely inhabited regions, scant forests remained. Since woodlands were vital for fuel and as a source of building materials, mounting shortages created severe problems for human occupancy. (McNeill 1976, 147, quoted in Rifkin 1981)
>
> The economic problem was greatly magnified by the expanding population in cities that needed to be fed. . . . It was the quickened pace of commercial activity that led to a timber famine. . . . By the sixteenth and early seventeenth centuries, the timber crisis was so acute in England that royal commissions were set up to regulate

> the cutting down of forests. The regulations proved ineffective. . . . The answer to the wood crisis was coal. But it was not just a simple matter of replacing one energy base with another. The cultures of Europe had been thoroughly integrated into a wood-based existence. The changeover necessitated the radical uprooting of an entire way of life. (Rifkin 1981, 73–74)

This illustrates the continuing importance of population/environment constraints as a driving force.

The Twentieth Century. This century has seen only an acceleration of the growth of industry. Technical advances began to be based on scientific discoveries, not just the inventions of creative individuals, and this increased the pace of change. The rapid growth of industry was also spurred by the introduction of new methods of mass production and by the tremendous leap forward in our communication and transportation technologies. With the hegemony of capitalism, all these developments were spurred by the race for profits.

The latest developments have been nuclear energy, the computer, space exploration, and biotechnology. Even now computer technology is in the process of changing virtually everything, and soon biotechnology may have as great an impact.

Advantages and Disadvantages. The material advances of the Modern era enabled our food and energy production to keep up with our expanding population, and also brought other important advantages. Sanitation, improved diet, and medicine made great strides in lengthening the life span and improving health. In fact, the short life span of stage 1 (approximately 30 years) improved only slightly through all the subsequent stages before it leapt forward in stage 5. The enormous growth in communication and transportation encouraged humanity to become acquainted with itself. People traveled, read, watched television, and the world opened up before them. For the first time masses of people had an opportunity to learn about distant lands, foreign cultures, different traditions.

The Industrial Revolution has completely altered our relationship with nature. Most people now live in cities or suburbs and have little if any direct relationship with the natural world except as recreation. Almost our entire existence is lived in an artificial environment—houses, cars, office buildings, factories. Our technology has been designed for labor efficiency, power, comfort, and pleasure—not for ecological harmony. Because of this and because of the sheer extent and power of our technology, the ground quality, natural living, has been suppressed.

This is represented in the model in figure 9.1.

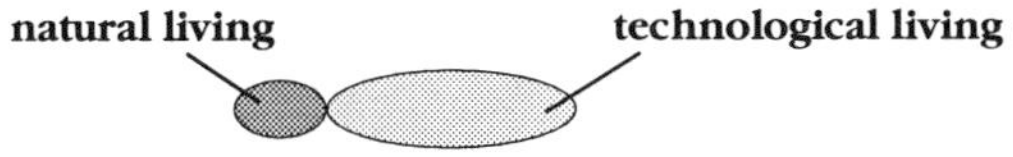

Figure 9.1

The relative sizes of the ovals indicate how much technological living has taken over, and the lack of overlap indicates how much they are opposed. This combination results in the suppression of natural living, the ground quality.

THE SOCIAL REALM: CAPITALISM

In the Modern era, the march of social structure continued at the expense of community. This happened primarily in the economic area, with the full development of capitalism and the market economy.

The Market. Many areas of human life that were handled personally and privately under feudalism and previous social systems, now came under the power of the market. Where before, most of people's daily food and tools were produced at home, now almost everything was purchased. In the twentieth century this has expanded to include many services. Now food preparation has shifted to the restaurant, care of children and elders has shifted to the daycare center and nursing home. Increasingly, our lives are taken up with economically organized transactions rather than family- or community-oriented interactions. This has bought us personal freedom and economic efficiency at the cost of interpersonal relatedness.

The Modern era has seen a profound shift in moral attitudes toward work, consumption, and wealth. In previous eras it was often considered strange or immoral to strive for money and possessions. Even the upper classes based their self-esteem on status and breeding rather than on money. In the Modern era, the Protestant work ethic changed this, making hard work and material success the mark of a successful and honorable person. This value shift supported the expansion of capitalism.

In the Modern era there has been a shift away from local or regional economic transactions toward global ones. Whereas before food or crafts might have been produced for local barter or sale, now whole regional economies are oriented toward production of single products for international export. This requires even an even higher degree of social structure.

Loss of Community. Mobility has increased enormously as a result of the market economy and greatly improved transportation and communication. People now feel free to move at will and are often forced to move to preserve or increase their economic standing. This has been a prime contributor to the further breakdown of local community and family ties. As community has been lost, many of the social problems that were previously handled through personal connection now must be handled by the market or the government. A rudimentary sense of community has developed at a national level, where people often have shared traditions and values. There is even some feeling of caring for others, especially for the people of one's own nation. However, this is weak and forms a poor substitute for the vitality of the community that has been lost.

Government. Government now plays a much larger role in people's lives. Where before government was mainly concerned with war, security, law, trade, and religion, now it also takes responsibility for transportation and communication, education, health, social welfare, and other aspects of our personal and social lives. This is partly because of real concern about people's welfare and partly because of the need to take over the functions previously handled at the local community level.

Specialization. Social differentiation has also increased substantially. In the Modern era, separate societal sectors have developed for education, science and scholarship, finance, law, entertainment, communication, construction, and much else. And each sector has become divided and subdivided into smaller and smaller areas of concern. It's remarkable to realize that in academia alone, many of the hundreds of separate study areas of today were all contained under philosophy only 150 years ago. If you go further back to the Medieval era, academia itself was not separate from religion.

Effectiveness of Social Structure. In the Modern era, along with the increase in the amount of social structure, there has been an improvement in the effectiveness of social structure. The market is a much more effective way to organize an economy than feudalism. A democratic republic is not only more humane than a monarchy, it is probably a more effective way to govern. Insofar as the population is educated and involved in governing decisions, those decisions are likely to be wiser, more relevant to the people's needs, and more readily acceptable to the people than in a monarchy or dictatorship.

In this model of social evolution, the growth of the emergent quality is quantitative and qualitative. Over time it becomes more pervasive *and* more effective. As society has evolved, social structure has become more effective; so has technology and reflexive consciousness. Overall we have become increasingly effective at organizing and controlling the world, and at achieving our goals. This still leaves open the question of our goals, where we have gotten off track in the Modern era. We have become very effective at what we do, but we have lost track of what we are doing because of the suppression of the ground qualities.

In summary, in the Modern era society has grown ever more complex, social mediation has increasingly taken over our lives, and social structure has become more effective, at the expense of community. In the model in figure 9.2, this produces a situation similar to that of the material realm.

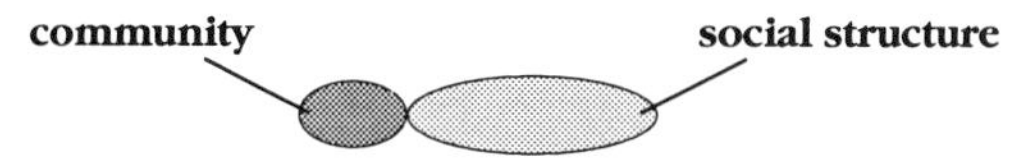

Figure 9.2

POWER: DEMOCRACY AND CAPITALISM

Power is a subrealm of the social realm (figure 9.3).

Figure 9.3 Power

Remember that power evolved more quickly than other realms, so that already by the Archaic era there was a destructive suppression of the ground quality (power distribution). In the Ancient/Medieval era there was a small resurgence of power distribution, and in the Modern era there was a serious step toward the integration of power distribution with social structure. Thus power has had a different trajectory than the other realms, as illustrated in figure 9.4.

Lenski (1987, 313) remarks on the phenomenon in social evolution that inequality has risen and then fallen. He presents indirect evidence for this in the form of a graph of income inequality (power imbalance) versus economic development (a very rough indicator of social evolution) in contemporary societies. His graph has the same trajectory as our power graph in figure 9.4.

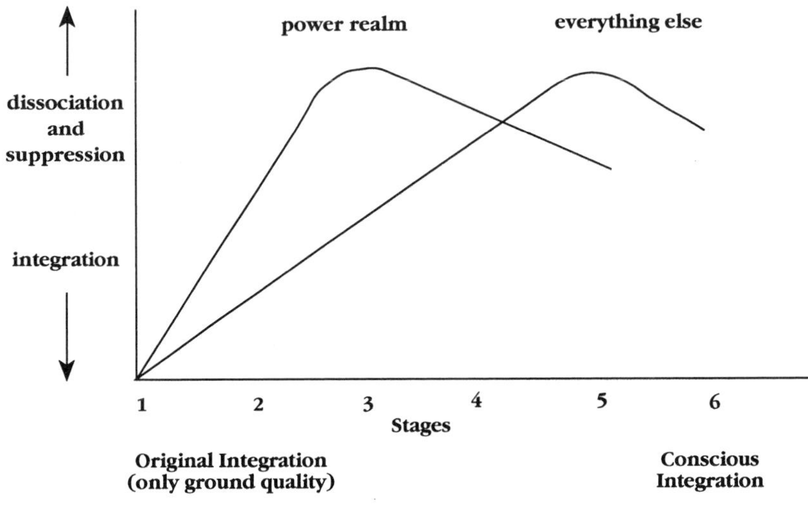

Figure 9.4

Democracy. Representative democratic governments were established with the explicit aim of giving power to the governed, first in France and the United States. This idea spread as the era progressed until it became the norm. Today representative democracy is widespread among the industrialized nations, and many other countries pretend to be democracies by using electoral forms. Even this is a positive development. The idea of democracy has become widespread and popular considerably beyond its actual implementation, but this popularity augers well for its future.

Of course, democracy as currently practiced is not fully successful in equalizing power. This is partly because it is representative democracy rather than participatory, and partly because of the large influence of wealth in the political process. What is more important, political democracy can never be enough because power is not exercised only through government. In the Modern era, power is wielded even more substantially through economic means.

Capitalism. Let's examine the power consequences of capitalism and the market economy in the Modern era. On the one hand, this new economic arrangement contributed to the breakup of entrenched feudal power structures, caused the rise of a large middle class, and provided the opportunity for people to move up the socioeconomic ladder. All these gains contributed to more equal distribution of power. On the other hand, it fostered the accumulation of large fortunes by some individuals and kept many others at the poverty level. It has also fostered a large imbalance in power between nations, with the industrialized nations exploiting the Third World economically. Overall, the market economy has been a mixed blessing in terms of power distribution.

The rise and fall of communism in the Modern era is connected to both the advantages and shortcomings of capitalism. Communism was an attempt to achieve power distribution by overcoming the tendency in capitalism toward economic exploitation and vastly unequal distribution of wealth. As an attempt in this direction, it was congruent with the overall thrust of the Modern era. However, it failed for two reasons. First, it had insufficient understanding of the problems of power distribution in the *political* arena and so fostered vast bureaucracies with their own power inequalities. Second, it failed as an economic system per se. Though it was somewhat successful in equalizing wealth, it failed to create a system of production and consumption that worked to provide the goods and services that people wanted and needed.

What we need in the future is an economic system that works fundamentally as well as capitalism but provides for better economic power distribution and less materialism. I will discuss this in a later chapter.

The Rise of the Middle Class. Capitalism and the general democratic trend of the era helped create a large, powerful, well-educated middle class. This had significant social consequences. For the first time since the Neolithic era, the majority of the population was able to participate in the wealth of the society. They had enough leisure to become educated and pursue their own personal development. Many of the privileges that in previous eras had been reserved for a very small minority (the nobility), were now available to most of the population.

Power Imbalance. In some important areas there was little or no improvement in power distribution. The oppression of women remained largely the same as it had been since the Archaic era. The only significant advances in this area have come so recently that they really belong to the transition into the next era. Racism and oppression of one ethnic group by another continued to be a serious source of pain and hardship. This often took the form of oppression by white Europeans (or European-Americans) of other races and cultures. There was also an important countertrend toward increasing tolerance of differences and appreciation of human rights, which I will discuss in the next chapter.

Those of you who are particularly concerned with the horrendous effects of poverty and oppression may wonder how I could assert that the Modern era represents any improvement in the power realm. I acknowledge that there are still very destructive imbalances in power, but these must be compared with those of previous eras. In the past, there were enormous discrepancies in power between the nobility and the peasants, and there were few attempts to alter this except for occasional rebellions of the oppressed. In the Modern era, though we still have a long way to go, we have taken important strides in the right direction.

All the major social developments of the Modern era—democracy, capitalism, and communism—have been attempts to engineer better power distribution. Capitalism had other motivations as well, and communism failed in its attempt, but the major thrust of the Modern era has been the attempt to improve power distribution.

Left versus Right. This struggle has produced the political distinction of left versus right, a Modern era concept where leftist politics represents the ground quality, power distribution, and the political right represents the status quo. These concepts don't completely correspond with the ground and emergent qualities, even if we limit ourselves to just the power realm. Consider the following: The political right doesn't always represent the emergent quality, social structure. There are forces on the right, especially the current libertarian position, that espouse a decrease in certain kinds of social structure.

The right can be most clearly characterized as always supporting either the current status quo or a return to the previous stage. Thus the right includes supporters of current corporate power (stage 5) and advocates of a return to fundamentalist religious and social values (stage 4). The left is always a champion for power distribution, or at least for the overthrow of the current structure of oppression. However, the left doesn't consistently promote power distribution in all areas. For example, the Communist Party promoted socialism as a form of economic power distribution without recognizing that a bureaucratic state apparatus decreases political power distribution.

Therefore, the concepts of left and right, though widely used today, are not very helpful in defining the real issues we face during this planetary crisis.

Integrating Structures. In my presentation of the model, the Modern era is the first place historically where there has been any integration of the ground quality with the emergent quality. Remember that the ground and emergent qualities *tend* to be opposed to each other but *can* be integrated. In order for them to be integrated, society must make a conscious effort to do so. A structure must be developed which promotes this integration. This structure needs to become legitimate and even preferred in the minds of the people, and the society needs to experiment with, adopt, and develop the structure. I call such a structure an *integrating structure*. Democracy, capitalism, and communism were all attempts at integrating structures, with democracy being the most successful. Now that humanity is in a transition to a new era, we will need new integrating structures in all realms.

Notice that creating an integrating structure is not the only way to try to solve a social problem. For example, oppressed people have struggled for at least five thousand years to free themselves from their oppressors and the hierarchical social systems they have lived under. There have been rebellions, slave uprisings, class wars, and wars of liberation since the Archaic era. Even though some of them succeeded, these struggles didn't change the fundamental nature of the oppressive system. They simply freed one oppressed group or enabled one social class to take the reigns of power from another.

An uprising is a more primitive way of addressing the problem of power imbalance. It can undo a particular injustice, but it can't provide a social evolutionary solution. Only a successful integrating structure can do that. Society wasn't mature enough to develop an integrating structure in the Archaic era. In the Ancient era, Rome and especially Greece provided the beginnings of integration, but we still weren't ready for a real evolutionary advance. Athenian democracy didn't last long enough and wasn't adopted by other societies in its era. It functioned primarily as a precursor to developments in the Modern era.

The central preoccupation in social thought and struggle during the Modern era has been the issue of power imbalance—oppression and exploitation. This was a new development in social evolution, that society actually made a conscious effort to try new social forms in order to solve a social problem. As an integrating structure is developed, it must have an *ideological framework* to explain what problem it addresses and why it is so important. That is why we have had such great ideological battles in this era.

I find this very encouraging for our current prospects. It is apparent from our history that it is possible to change the direction of social evolution, so to speak. We know that social evolution doesn't always move in a straight line, for example, toward ever increasing oppression. When humanity perceives a problem, we are capable of creating and actualizing a solution. When an emergent quality dominates in a destructive way, the ground quality can return and be integrated. This gives me hope for the resolution of today's crisis.

Precursors to Democracy. The democracy of Athens was not the only precursor to Modern democracy. The Iroquois confederacy developed a significant form of democracy, and there is even substantial evidence that the United States founding fathers had knowledge of it. Therefore there is a good chance that our own form of democracy was influenced by that of the Iroquois (Grinde 1991). How does this jibe with our model? The Iroquois were not even close to stage 5 in our model of social evolution. Materially they were at stage 2. How then, could they have developed a stage 5 social structure?

Remember that social evolutionary stages refer to the evolution of humanity as a whole, not to particular societies. Any given society may follow its own trajectory, different from the main sequence of stages, even to the point of being much more advanced socially than materially. In order for a development such as democracy to be considered a social evolutionary advance, it must be adopted by a significant number of societies in a certain era. If it is embraced by only one or two societies, I call this a *precursor* rather than a social evolutionary advance. When I say that we must be mature enough to develop an integrating structure, I'm referring to humanity as a whole. It is possible that the Iroquois had the required maturity, but other Native American tribes didn't. If the Iroquois system had spread to many other tribes, then it would have been considered an evolutionary advance.

This brings to mind Eisler's example of Crete, which seems to have had a peaceful, egalitarian society during the Archaic era. Not enough is known about their social structures to know if they also had a precursor to democracy, but it is possible. Precursor societies are ahead of their time; humanity as a whole was not ready for democracy until the Modern era.

Precursors are important in other realms as well. The Romantic movement in the Modern era was a precursor in consciousness which I will discuss shortly.

Table 9.1 The Evolution of Power

	Era	Qualities	Power
1	Upper Paleolithic		Egalitarian
2	Neolithic		Rank, stratified
3	Archaic		State
4	Ancient/Medieval		Republic, beginnings of law & market
5	Modern		Democracy, market economy

Summary. Table 9.1 summarizes evolution in the power realm. Looking at the ovals, notice that in stage 4, power distribution begins to grow again, now overlapping with social structure. Then in stage 5 it grows still larger with more overlap.

You may wonder why I list "republic" and the "beginnings of law and market" under stage 4. In the Ancient and Medieval eras, these were not the most prevalent power structures. Instead societies were primarily empires, city-states, and feudal domains. However, I'm not interested as much in the *predominant* social structure in each era, as the *leading edge* of social evolution in each stage. Thus empires and feudal structures were not new in stage 4; they had already been developed in stage 3. What was new in stage 4 was the notion of a republic and the beginnings of law and of market economies. These formed the leading edge of social evolution in the power realm during the Ancient/Medieval era. They were significant and influential even though they did not spread widely enough to become the predominant mode. Similarly, for most of the Modern era, democracy was the leading edge even though it wasn't the most prevalent power structure.

SCIENCE

Reflexive consciousness came to dominate over participatory consciousness in the Modern era. This, however, doesn't mean that participatory consciousness wasn't the primary mode for many people. It continued to be a widespread way of living. However, it was no longer respected, even by many of the people who relied on it. Intuition, emotion, and spirituality, for example, began to be denigrated or discounted. They were considered part of the inferior realm of women or the marginal realm of artists and clergy. In addition, participatory consciousness lost its influence in society. For example, in today's world, for a medical approach to have respect and power, it must be validated scientifically with experimental studies.

Where in stage 4 the primary vehicle for consciousness was religion and in stages 2 and 3 it was myth, in stage 5 it was science. For the first time the consciousness of an era was not dominated by something considered "spiritual." In some sense the "religion" of the Modern era was science. Today's Modern religions are not really full products of stage 5 consciousness; they are stage 4 religions that have adapted to stage 5.

Rationality. Stage 5 consciousness developed to its fullest the rationality that the Greeks had initiated. Rationality gives you the ability to step back from your experience and consider what would happen in the future under different possibilities. Through imagination and logical operations on these possibilities, you can get a clearer understanding of reality. In individual cognitive development, this corresponds to Piaget's formal operations stage (1977).

In the Modern era, everything was questioned, examined, and explored logically; answers were arrived at precisely, using mathematics wherever possible. This was a tremendous advance over the blind reliance on authority of the Medieval era. Researchers actually looked at reality and experimented with it in order to understand things. Whereas before advances in knowledge were stifled because everything had to fit into Church doctrine (in the West), now people were free to find out the truth, wherever it led, unhindered by tradition. Humanity emerged from embeddedness in faith on authority and took charge of its attempts to understand the world. This led to a tremendous growth of knowledge, especially knowledge about the physical world, and ushered in the industrial revolution.

Since it was recognized that participation could lead to bias and distort one's ability to know the truth, science attempted to wipe out all traces of participation in its methodology. This led eventually to a different kind of distortion.

Materialism. The dualism that began in stage 4 was taken to its extreme, with the philosophy of a separate body and mind, and separate material and spiritual worlds. Then as stage 5 progressed, since the mind and spirit couldn't be known scientifically and couldn't be studied without some participation, they began to be ignored. Eventually the spiritual realm was held to be nonexistent, and the mind was declared to be simply an epiphenomenon of the brain. The only thing that existed was the material world, the world that could be predicted and controlled with science and technology. This emphasis aided the Modern project of taking control of nature and allowed us to be amazingly successful at promoting comfort, power, and pleasure through technology. For the first time, humanity fully emerged from being at the mercy of natural phenomena and began to create the kind of environment it wanted.

Mechanism. Having reduced reality to the material world, Modern consciousness regarded it as a machine. Being enamored of the machines we created, we came to conceptualize reality as a machine. A machine model has the advantage that if you understand it, you can precisely predict and control what it will do. Thus insofar as reality is a machine, one can attempt to control it completely, and that was the project of Modern science and technology. Even human bodies and minds were conceptualized as machines, leading to advancements in medicine (as well as dehumanization).

Science proceeded to analyze its machine models into smaller and smaller pieces and learned how to predict and control the pieces, leading to successes in physics and chemistry. We hoped that when we got to the bottom we could explain and control everything. Lately we have been rudely awakened to the fallacy in this.

Along with conceptualizing reality as a machine, Modern consciousness began to actually make reality into a machine. Our mechanistic consciousness went hand in hand with constructing a machinelike physical environment through technology and urbanization, and fashioning a machinelike social environment through bureaucracy and other social structures.

As the influence of religion faded, the primary goals of human activity were pragmatic. "It's what works that counts." "Nothing succeeds like success." Results were what was important. The subjective side of life was seen as frivolous and dispensable. The participatory aspects of life—emotional, spiritual, and artistic pursuits, which give life meaning—were relegated to second place. This pragmatism was associated with the loss of participatory consciousness. When there is no participation, there is no meaning, and the only option is pragmatism.

In all these ways, reflexive consciousness triumphed over participation. Morris Berman describes this situation at the beginning of the Modern era:

> Finally, what is real for the seventeenth century is what is abstract [reflexive]. Atoms are real, but invisible; gravity is real, but, like momentum and inertial mass, can only be measured. In general, abstract quantification serves as explanation. It was this loss of the tangible and meaningful [participatory] that drove the more sensitive minds of the age . . . to the edge of despair. (Berman 1984, 40)

AUTONOMY IN CONSCIOUSNESS

Stage 5 witnessed an emergence from dependence on authority and tradition. There was a breaking away from the dogmatism of the Church. Greater numbers of people began to think for themselves. Knowledge was no longer viewed as something to be handed down from on high by the Church or the Bible or even the great classical authors. Instead it was to be learned directly from nature or from one's own experience. The Reformation was an assertion of the liberation of the individual from the Church and its hierarchy. The Protestants declared that the ultimate authority for relating to God and understanding the Bible rested with each person rather than with the priests. This was an important step toward autonomy.

In science, autonomy manifested as the philosophy of empiricism, where one learns about nature by studying it directly, not by speculating about it or consulting previous authorities. The scientific method was developed to guard against subjective bias so that the truth could be learned directly.

There was also a growing autonomy from tradition and culture. People came to realize that the story told by their religion and culture was not the only possible way to understand the world. They felt freer to choose from existing stories about reality or even to create their own. This development has important implications for our current capacity for change and will be discussed in a later chapter.

Humanism and Progress. The Renaissance ushered in the philosophy of humanism, in which for the first time people placed their faith in human beings rather than in religion or the supernatural. People began to trust in humanity's power to solve its problems.

Progress became a hallmark of the consciousness of the era. The cyclic time of stages 2 and 3 had given way to a historical time sense in stage 4, but in that era, history implied a sense of decay. Ancient peoples saw their own time as a diminished version of a golden age in the past, whose glory could never again be approached. In the Modern era, historical time began to be positive and forward-looking. This was nurtured by the millennial visions of Christianity, and especially by the humanistic faith in humanity's ability to solve its own problems and move ahead. As the era developed, the notion of progress nurtured the theory of evolution and the twentieth century belief in the technological wonderworld of the future.

Humanism and the belief in progress were steps toward the autonomy of humanity. As I have explained before, choice and autonomy are important outgrowths of reflexive consciousness. When you have emerged from embeddedness and can reflect and conceptualize, then you gain the ability to choose.

Modern Success. This belief in a positive future was fostered by the great success of reflexive consciousness. With materialistic science and pragmatic technology Modern society was able to work wonders. We gained unparalleled understanding of the physical world in mechanical terms and used this in manifold technical inventions that improved the quality of life. For the first time in history, we began to be in charge of our lives and our future. We gained some control over nature in the raw, and even began to understand ourselves a little. It began to look as if we would soon understand everything and be able to create exactly the material and social environment we wanted.

Of course, now in the middle of the transition to the next era, the problems with Modern consciousness are becoming apparent, but in its time it was a very exciting advance.

MORALITY

Looking at morality from the point of view of the model, as a subrealm of consciousness, the emergent quality is principled (reflexive) morals and the ground quality is relational (participatory) morals.

Figure 9.5 Morality

The Evolution of Morality. I mentioned in the discussion of Ancient Consciousness that stage 4 saw the emergence of the first systems of morals. This is not strictly true. Stage 1 peoples were generally quite moral. They had few inequalities in wealth and little in the way of destructive warfare. They were concerned about the welfare of the other members of their band and tribe. This, however, was not a reflexive ethics; it was not based on principles of good and bad, right and wrong. It was instead based on empathy and relationship, on community and tradition. I will call this *relational* morality. Hunter-gatherers cared about the members of their band because they were personally close and often related by blood. They also had a strong sense of connection to animals and the earth and consequently had a much more developed sense of ecological ethics than we do today.

In stages 2 and 3, as the size of societies grew and intersocietal contact increased, each person had more and more interaction with people outside their intimate community. Relational morality by itself tends to be *parochial*, that is, limited to those in one's group, so it gave little help in guiding intersocietal and intercultural contact. By stage 3 this lack of moral direction played into the violence and oppression of that time.

Stage 4 culture attempted to remedy this situation by instituting religious and philosophical concepts of good and bad, which included the belief in the value of each human being. Thus relational morals were supplemented by principled morals in the emergence of reflexive consciousness. This introduction of moral principles and laws was necessary in the large, complex empires of the time with mixes of many cultures, races, and religions.

However, even though stage 4 morals were an improvement from stage 3, they were not sufficiently evolved as principled morals. There were clearly formulated concepts of right and wrong promulgated by each religion, but many people followed them out of sense of tradition rather than any personal understanding. They lived by certain moral beliefs because it was the religious thing to do or because God had so decreed. Therefore it was easy for the morals to be perverted into something not moral at all. For example, women could be burned at the stake as witches based on certain moral conceptions of the church. I will call this *dogmatic* morality.

Stage 5 Morals. In stage 5, the sense of principled morals grew stronger and more autonomous. People emerged from embeddedness in moral traditions and began to examine their moral grounding and formulate their own beliefs using reflexive consciousness. Understanding the actual principles became important, rather than simply following specific religious or secular laws. Modern ethics, through its support for the intrinsic worth of each person, has led to the demise of slavery as an institution, an interest in human rights, and the legitimation of democracy. Our intercultural and intersocietal morality has improved.

However, with the suppression of the ground qualities of belonging and empathy, relational morality is greatly diminished in the Modern era. And because of the loss of community and the decline in the importance of tradition and religion, traditional morality has also diminished. Our new reflexive, personally chosen morality is not sufficient when dissociated from relational ethics, especially in dealing with our everyday personal lives. This has led to a kind of Modern amorality, which I will call *detached morality.* Our moral principles are so removed from our participation in life that they don't really guide us properly. Selfishness and competitiveness are lauded; we treat most people as objects to be manipulated or used. Only with close friends and family do we relate from a sense of caring. Our day to day economic interactions are based on getting the most for ourselves and "let the buyer beware." There is much competition and back-biting in corporate relationships.

Intercultural versus Interpersonal Morality. How can I account for the fact that intercultural morality seems to have improved in stage 5 while interpersonal morality seems to have declined? Let's look at the trajectory of the morality of intersocietal and intercultural relations over the span of social evolution. In the early stages of social evolution, there was little contact between different cultures and also little understanding. By stage 4, intercultural morality advanced with the introduction of principled morals, and this continued in stage 5. Thus there has been a steady improvement in morality dealing with our relations with those who are foreign and strange to us. This has been supported by the increasing contact and interconnection between different societies and cultures. The loss of relational morality has not hurt our intercultural ethics very much, because relational morality, by itself, tends toward parochialism.

On the interpersonal side, in our dealings with people who are part of our own society or subculture, there has been a steady decline in relational morality over time. This is because of the breakdown of community and the substitution of mediated, institutionalized relationships. However, the relational morality that has been suppressed in the overall culture today is still generally valued by women (Gilligan 1982). In this way an oppressed group is containing a ground quality that has been dissociated from the emergent quality in the dominant group. This is a frequent occurrence which I will discuss later in the book.

I am not claiming that people are less moral today in our interpersonal dealings than in our intercultural ones, but rather that the two have moved in opposite directions. Our interpersonal morality, which was fairly strong at the beginning of social evolution, has been weakening, while our intercultural morality, which started weak, has advanced over time.

INDIVIDUALITY

Medieval Lack of Individuality. Surprising as it may seem, life in Medieval times was lived entirely publicly and in groups, with little privacy for individual reflection or intimacy.

> On the village commons and in the palace courtyards, people were always in each other's presence. Rarely, if ever, did individuals stray from the pack or venture out on their own. . . . Withdrawal from group activity was frowned upon or openly chastised. (Rifkin 1991, 154)

Children were treated as incomplete adults, with no attention paid to their unique needs and development.

> From the age of seven, most children left their birth homes altogether [to be] apprentices. From the beginning of their apprenticeship, they were considered small adults and were expected to contribute to the commonweal, to the extent that their training and experience al-

> lowed. . . . Childhood was still an undifferentiated age, in which affiliation was first, and foremost, with the commune. (Rifkin 1991, 163)

Modern Developments. This changed in the Modern era, when people had space and time for privacy and solitude, and the special needs of children were considered important. In the West, privacy and childhood are Modern developments associated with the growth of individuality.

All the consciousness developments mentioned above also contributed to the Modern growth of individuality. With autonomy from religious and cultural authority and the breakdown of community, individuals came to depend on themselves for a sense of worth and dignity. With the loss of meaning from participation, the only thing that mattered was what a person could create for him or herself.

People began to define themselves primarily in terms of their personal qualities and achievements and only secondarily in terms of belonging to a community or ethnic or religious group. With this came a needed freedom and autonomy, allowing people to attempt to live their lives as they saw fit, rather than being forced to conform to external standards. Societies increasingly recognized the intrinsic worth of each person.

Individuality had its pluses and minuses. On the positive side, it encouraged the move toward personal development through educational, creative, and spiritual endeavors. The valuing of the individual had a positive influence on the development of democracy and the movement toward better power distribution. On the negative side, individuality contributed to the estrangement of people from each other as the Modern era advanced.

Individualism. Some observers of the Modern era have noted the degree of conformity that exists, even in advanced industrialized nations such as the United States. They make the point that we are dominated by *individualism,* in which each person struggles for personal gain and power. I agree with these criticisms. Individualism is not true individuality, which would be oriented toward the development of the person's capacities for genuine enjoyment, creativity, intimacy, and openness to nature and spirit, as well as achievement and competence. The individualism of the Modern era is a distorted version of individuality, warped by the Modern suppression of natural living and participatory consciousness.

THE ROMANTIC PROTEST

In each era there are movements that represent the ground quality as it develops in relation to the emergent quality. During the Modern era, the

Romantic movement was a strong and vital protest against the hegemony of reflexive consciousness. Emanating primarily from the arts and humanities, especially poetry, this movement celebrated participatory consciousness. The Romantics reminded us that there was another side to life, different from the mechanistic, dehumanized worldview that ruled the day. They wrote of love, spirituality, and passion; they told of the virtues of aliveness and feeling.

At first glance it might seem that the Romantic movement was an anachronism, since it attempted to bring back participation, but the Romantics didn't try to blindly return to the past. They created vital works in the present which were both Modern and participatory. They weren't influential enough to change the tenor of the Modern era, so the Romantic movement can't be regarded as a true evolutionary advance. Instead it was a precursor to the next era, to the current transition, when participation must be integrated with reflexive consciousness.

Therefore in Consciousness as in the other realms, the emergent quality has taken over and thoroughly suppressed the ground quality. Table 9.2 recounts the developments in the Modern era and summarizes the entire evolution of society to date.

Table 9.2 Stage 5

Realm	Description
Material	Industry, technology, scientific method, fossil fuels, mass production
Social	Democracy, capitalism, reign of economics, specialization
Consciousness	Rationalism, empiricism, science, pragmatism, humanism, progress, materialism, individuality, principled morals, autonomy

	Era	Qualities	Material	Social	Consciousness
1	Paleolithic		Hunting & gathering	Family, band	Magic, animism
2	Neolithic		Horticulture, herding	Village, chiefdom	Myth: Goddess
3	Archaic		Agriculture, bronze	City, early state	Myth: gods & heroes
4	Ancient/ Medieval	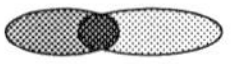	Gradual advance	Historic empire	Religion, philosophy
5	Modern		Industry	Democracy, capitalism	Science, autonomy

PART TWO

THE CURRENT CRISIS

The Modern era has run its course and is coming to an end. The innovations of this era, which were once exciting evolutionary advances, are now outmoded and threatening to destroy our ecological support systems. Consequently we are now in a planetary crisis that is part of the transition to the next era. Let's look at this in terms of emergence.

Emergence through mediation involves a separation from our biological ground, but it isn't complete separation. The human capacity for mediation is also part of our biology. Our faculty of reflexive thought, our ability to create technology and social structure—these are all biological, too. Emergence really means giving precedence to a certain part of our biological endowment. We use it to mediate between ourselves and the world. We use it to mediate between one part of ourselves and another. If we aren't careful, we develop a split between the mediating part of ourselves and the rest of ourselves. We end up living in a world of concepts rather than direct experience, a world of artifacts rather than nature. We become divided.

We can't really extract ourselves from our biology. No matter how much technology we use to protect us from nature and enhance our power and pleasure, we are still biological animals. We still need sunlight and flowers, bird song and oceans. We need quiet and space. We also can't extract ourselves from our ecological surround. We can't indiscriminately destroy our topsoil and ground water, our genetic diversity and our climate. If we proceed as if we could escape the laws of ecology, we will destroy ourselves.

Similarly, no matter how successful we are with social roles, we can't escape our deeper biological needs. No matter how much money, status, and power we have, we still need love, we still need to belong, we still need companionship and community. The mediated relationships are pale substitutes for our true needs. The famous mid-life crisis is proof of this.

No matter how much we live in a world of concepts, we still need to feel the wind on our faces, to touch friends, to experience grief and joy, to find creativity and spirituality, to directly experience our lives. Without direct contact with our biology, we feel alienated and confused or we frantically search for substitutes for what we have lost. Life loses meaning and we deaden ourselves. In the process, we destroy our environment, we wage war constantly, and we cause untold misery.

Even if there is a spiritual part of humanity that is independent of our biology, as some believe, our biological part is very real and must be given its due. We can emerge from biology but we can't escape. *The tragedy of today is that we tried to escape from biology. Now the truth is hitting us in the face; things are coming apart all around us. We must learn to integrate the vitality of our biological heritage with the positive forms of mediation that have emerged during social evolution. If we can manage to do this, we will not only surmount the planetary crisis, we will also return to our depth, our aliveness, and our connectedness. We will rediscover our roots and reawaken joy.*

In terms of the model, the pretense of escaping from biology is the suppression of the ground qualities. Without a conscious effort to integrate the ground and emergent qualities, they tend to oppose each other. A split develops between the qualities. As the emergent qualities become more prominent, they take over and the ground qualities are diminished. In the extreme (which is where we are today) the ground qualities are suppressed to the point where their loss causes serious problems for society, for individuals, and for the world. At this point, active forces for integration must become prominent.

The crisis of a historical transition always has two aspects. (1) The old way of living is breaking down and causing a host of societal problems. (2) The new way is beginning to take shape for evolution into the next era. This part of the book will focus on the first aspect—the dangers and problems of the current crisis. Part 3 will focus on solutions to the crisis which will enable us to evolve in a healthy way into the next era.

I will study this transition from the point of view of the model of social evolution I have been developing, which has two aspects—the driving forces and the evolving relationship between the complementary qualities. Chapter 10 deals with the ecological crisis and chapter 11 with the related population explosion. Chapter 12 deals with the social realm, especially the loss of community and the way that economics has come to dominate our lives. Chapter 13 deals with the contribution of the consciousness realm to today's crisis.

X

THE ECOLOGICAL CRISIS

Human society is facing a crisis in every realm, but the most dangerous by far is the ecological crisis in the material realm. Our current technology has been designed without regard for its impact on the environment. We have focused only on what we can get from our technology—power, ease, speed, pleasure. As a consequence, we have now arrived at the point of disrupting our environmental life-support systems (and those of other creatures). As has happened many times during social evolution, we are facing a population/environment crisis. As a consequence of our growing population, the magnitude of our technology, and our extensive consumption, we are outstripping the carrying capacity of our environment. As before, we must surmount the crisis or see our global society collapse.

Effects of the Crisis. The dangers and effects of this crisis are well-known—destruction of the ozone layer, global warming, loss of biodiversity, pollution of all kinds, depletion of topsoil and ground water, and so on. Less well known are its effects on human health. As an example, researchers have just recently become concerned about the long-term effects of widely used chemicals called organochlorides on human reproduction and the immune system (Hawken 1993, 40–44).

This illustrates perhaps the greatest danger in our ecological situation. There are so many things scientific researchers don't yet know and so many delayed effects they are just finding out about, that the problems we are currently worried about may just be the tip of the iceberg. In addition, many ecological problems interact with each other, producing much more damage in tandem than any one could by itself. As yet very little is known about such interactions. What problems may be developing insidiously without our knowledge?

UNIQUE DANGERS OF THE CRISIS

In today's ecological crisis there are two factors that make this crisis different from those of the past—the waste problem and the fact that the crisis is worldwide.

The Waste Problem. Until now, in discussing population/environment constraints, I have looked at the interaction between increasing population and a shrinking resource base. This is not the whole story. Human consumption not only depletes resources, it also produces wastes. And when the increasing population is using advanced technology, these wastes are significant. The wastes include not just garbage, but any byproduct that cannot be reused. Especially important are toxic and nuclear wastes, which are not broken down and absorbed by nature, and all forms of pollution, including those gases that are destroying the ozone layer and causing global warming.

In the past, our total impact on the environment was not nearly so great as it is today, and therefore wastes were not nearly so important a factor as resources. Though there might have been air pollution from the massive burning of wood in Europe in the fourteenth to sixteenth centuries, this was not as big a problem as the fact that the forests were being depleted. Today, this is reversed. For example, even though our world reserves of oil are limited and quickly being drained, we will probably not run short of oil. We will be forced to stop using it because of the damage from its waste byproducts. The carbon dioxide released from oil burning is changing the composition of the air we breathe and threatening us with the greenhouse effect and global warming.

This is just one example of a waste hazard. In the past the problem was that humans would eat ourselves out of house and home. Now a bigger problem is that we are poisoning our home, fouling our nest. This means that we can't simply solve this crisis with more technological advances involving new energy sources and agricultural techniques. We have hit the limits on the amount of waste the earth can absorb. In addition, we aren't just running short of energy and food, we are depleting many of our valuable ecological resources, all at the same time. We are quickly using up fresh water, topsoil, arable land, and even our precious genetic heritage. Even if someone invented a miraculous source of energy, these other problems would still be unsolved.

A World-Wide Crisis. When other population/environment crises have occurred, they were contained to certain areas. If the crisis couldn't be solved, people could always migrate to new locations that weren't so crowded and still had a good supply of natural resources. If one society collapsed because it failed to meet the crisis, others continued until someone found a new way to extract more food and energy.

Some people imagine that we can solve our environmental problems with a new migration, into outer space. However, simple calculations show that this is not viable. The amount of resources, especially energy, required to send a person into space is so great that we can't ecologically afford to send enough people away to make the slightest dent in our population problem.

In previous times, the total world population was also small enough that the environment could absorb new technologies and the larger populations they supported. There were population/environment crises in particular locations only. Today, for the first time in history the total world population has reached the point where it is straining the limits of the earth as a whole. The combination of our population size plus our level of consumption is producing not only local ecological problems but global ones such as the greenhouse effect and the loss of biological diversity.

Today's world population is not only huge but still growing rapidly in the preindustrialized world. The greatest proportion of the world's population is in those poor nations that don't enjoy our current level of technology. If today's Third World population were to use resources and produce waste at the level of the United States, it would break the planet many times over. And it is still growing rapidly!

It is hard to imagine any technological breakthrough that would allow today's entire world population to live at U.S. standards of living. It is even harder to imagine one that would allow the world population to continue climbing as it is. Society has reached our limit of growth. Regardless of what we can achieve with technology, we have to stabilize our population. Though this population/environment crisis is similar to those in the past, we can't solve it the way we have before.

Population. In the past societies resolved their population/environment crises by adopting new technology that allowed them to extract greater amounts of food and energy from the same amount of land, so they could support greater populations. Today we still need technological breakthroughs of this nature, but they will not be enough. In addition we must stabilize our population. To imagine that *any* technological advance can allow us to resolve this crisis without regulating population is simply wishful thinking.

This crisis will be solved by technology—the technology of birth control. At this transition point we have an advantage that no other society has had—reliable, effective birth control. This is what must bring us through this crisis. We must now make the political and cultural changes to bring this technology into widespread use so that we stabilize our population as quickly as possible.

Energy. Along with population, we will also have to change the way we use resources, especially energy. Historically, all of our technological innovations have provided ways of tapping into and using more energy. Now we will have to reverse this process. We must create technology that uses less energy because of being in harmony with the earth. This doesn't necessarily mean that we will get less from the technology; by using it intelligently, we may even get more. It is interesting to look at an analogous situation from ecology. Biologists have noted that the organisms that are most successful ecologically are those which are able to maximize the flow of energy they use. However, this isn't the whole picture.

> It is now acknowledged that maximizing [energy] flow-through is a common response in the early stage of an ecological system's development, when there is still an excess of available energy present. However, as various species begin to fill up a given ecological habitat, they are forced to adapt to the ultimate carrying capacity of the environment by using less energy flow-through more efficiently. The early stage of maximum flow-through is generally referred to as the colonizing phase, and the later stage of minimum flow-through as the climatic phase. . . . The transition from a colonizing to a climactic mode of existence is the most profound change our species will ever have to make. That crossroads is now before us. (Rifkin 1981, 54–55, 69)

Ecological Crises in the Animal World. Not only have ecological crises happened before in human history, they are not uncommon in the nonhuman world as well. Ecologists have studied many situations in which a species becomes dominant within its ecological niche, and then through its use of resources and production of wastes, it gradually changes the ecology of the niche so that eventually it can no longer survive there. It unknowingly destroys its own life-support system.

A good example of this is a niche where there is a predator and a prey species, such as fox and rabbit. If the niche is simple enough that there aren't multiple ecological pathways, the predator can become so successful that it wipes out most of the prey, and then suddenly its own population crashes because of lack of food supply. This is similar to the situation humanity is now facing in our world wide niche. We are consuming and fouling our environmental supports, and unless we change, we will suddenly discover that our population is crashing. Luckily, we have the intelligence that could allow us to foresee this outcome and do something about it. Let's hope we use it in time.

We are facing this crisis now because of our success in surmounting previous ones. We created the technology to allow us get the most from the earth while our numbers kept growing. This was a completely natural and understandable strategy until recently. We are now forced to change it because our success has altered the entire situation. We are in trouble because we now have the power to do the earth serious damage, and the driving forces have shaped our culture toward technology and consumption. It is more compassionate to understand our crisis in this way. Rather than blaming human nature or Modern society or the capitalist ruling classes for our disconnection from the earth, I prefer to see our predicament as a natural outgrowth of our evolution and our ignorance, which now must be corrected.

This is an important message of this book. We have a much better chance of working together to solve our problems if we refrain from anger and blame, if we understand our failings and destructiveness with compassion, if we see ourselves through the wider lens of our history as a species in process, struggling to survive and prosper.

Future Prospects. How serious is this environmental crisis? How much time do we have? If we don't change soon, how severe will the destruction be? No one can predict with certainty the answers to these questions. There are too many variables and too many environmental processes that we don't understand yet, but it is clear that it would be foolhardy to wait. We must make fundamental changes as soon as possible.

In a superb book (1992), Dana Meadows and her colleagues study the possibilities for creating a sustainable future and the consequences of continuing the status quo. They wrote the well-known book *The Limits to Growth* in the early 1970s, which was one of the first warnings about the ecological crisis. Their new book, *Beyond the Limits,* explores a wide range of possible scenarios for the future based on our current knowledge. They use computer modeling to envision what may happen under a variety of different circumstances. They study the global effects of instituting technology and policy for pollution control, enhancing agricultural yields, erosion protection, resource efficiency, limiting consumption, and most importantly population control.

Their conclusion is that humanity can avoid ecological collapse, but to do so we must institute these changes soon. If we wait twenty years it may be too late. The assumptions built into their simulations, while not unreasonable, are quite hopeful. It is not possible to accuse them of being doom sayers; they have done their best to be optimistic. We must take their conclusions with utmost seriousness. I will discuss the population aspects of their work in the next chapter.

THE SUPPRESSION OF NATURAL LIVING

In addition to the ecological crisis and related to it, there are other problems in the material realm at this time. Let's explore these through the model of social evolution. First we'll review the definitions of the ground and emergent qualities in the material realm:

Figure 10.1 Material Living

Natural living: Using material processes which work with the flows of nature. *Technological living*: Using both artifacts (especially machines) and specialized techniques in the material aspects of life.

Human Nature. It is important to realize that we human beings are part of the natural world, so when we speak of harmony with the natural world, we don't just mean air, water, and topsoil. There are a host of technologies we have developed which have important interactions with the human body and therefore can enhance or damage our health and well being. These include technologies for food production and distribution, medicine and healing, exercise, birth, and birth control. The technologies we have in these areas have been valuable for us in many ways, but as they have evolved into forms that are increasingly alien to our natural biological condition, they are creating as many problems as they solve.

The Problems. By today at the end of the Modern era, technological living has grown large at the expense of natural living, causing ever more critical problems:

1. Our health is being seriously threatened by chemicals in our food, clothes, and buildings, by toxic wastes, air and water pollution, etc. Diseases of the immune system are increasing ominously. There are the obvious ones such as AIDS, cancer, and arthritis, and the less obvious one such as chronic fatigue syndrome, environmental disease, allergies and a host of subtle undiagnosed maladies. Our bodies are being assault-

ed by our environment, and our immune systems were never designed to cope with this level of intrusion.

2. The state of being estranged from our roots in nature decreases the quality of our lives and our experience. Natural living has a feeling side, the internal experience of living in harmony with the earth. It means being in tune with the natural world, being alive to the sights, sounds, and smells—the touch of earth or sand on the feet, the call of a lark, the feeling in the air after a thunderstorm. It means living in the rhythm of the seasons, noticing the changes, letting them affect your life. It means interacting with nature—cultivating a garden, planting trees or shrubs, conversing with local deer or chipmunks.

We lose more than we realize when we are alienated from this. It affects us in subtle, insidious ways that we may rarely notice. Our creativity is stimulated by contact with the wonder and variety of the natural world, so we can become dull and mundane without it. Most people live lives of constant activity, high stress, overstimulation, overcrowding, even lack of adequate sleep. This is partly because our Modern, urban society often requires this, but I suspect much of it is due to our lack of connection to the natural world—the world we evolved in. People who have lived for long periods of time on farms or in the wilderness report that after a while their whole consciousness changes. They slow down, become more present. They become calmer, less aggressive, more centered, more at peace.

3. We have allowed the ecological crisis to become so dangerous because of our lack of an experiential connection with the natural world. Scientific studies are important, as well as data on environmental degradation, but ultimately we base important decisions on our intuition and emotions. If someone tells you that destruction of the rainforests is dangerous you may believe them, but the priority you will give it depends on your own personal relationship with nature. I love the rainforests I have visited in Hawaii and the magnificent redwood forests of California. When I hear that the rain forests are threatened, it goes to my heart. Someone who has lived only in cities and has no feeling for nature will not likely be moved by even the most alarming statistics; facts tend to touch us only when they coincide with our deeper values.

DISTRIBUTION OF THE MATERIAL QUALITIES

Ideally, each person and group would have an integrated balance of the two complementary qualities in each realm. However, when two qualities are opposed and one is much stronger, the qualities become split or dissociated from each other and the weaker quality is suppressed. The dissociation takes place both psychologically and socially. Psychologically the split happens within people, when they deny the existence of the weaker quality in themselves or denigrate the quality as being unimportant, shameful, or evil. I will discuss this in a later chapter.

The Social Split. Dissociation happens socially through uneven distribution of the qualities among the world's people, groups, and societies. Today this is happening in all realms. Here I will explore it in the material realm.

The industrialized nations are characterized by *artificial living*, and we unfortunately set the tone for the values the rest of the world aspires to. However, most of the world's people, those who live in the preindustrialized nations, probably belong in our *primitive living* category. Many of them have so little access to technology that they have inadequate food, shelter, or health care. There is tremendous imbalance in the world, with a small part of the world's population having access to most of the resources and technology.

However, despite the difficulties of primitive living, it is not primarily their lack of technology that makes the lives of preindustrialized people so wretched. It is their oppression, exploitation, and lack of power over their lives because this results in far more than just inadequate technology. I will discuss this more in the chapter on power. For now let's look at the ecological consequences of the material dissociation.

The Ecological Consequences. Poor people often are forced into unecological practices (such as chopping down the only trees for firewood) in order to simply survive. When your back is against the wall, you can't be worried about anything except how to get by. Only those of us who are relatively comfortable can afford to look at the longer term consequences of our actions.

We in the industrialized world have a built a lifestyle based on using a great deal of the earth's bounty. We have publicized it to such an extent that almost everyone in the world covets it. However, it isn't sustainable, even for us. If preindustrialized development proceeded as planned, and they began to use resources as we do, the world would quickly go to ecological hell. The only hope is that these tremendous imbalances be evened out and population stabilized. It won't be easy for us to give up some of our material benefits, and it also won't be easy for the poor people of the preindustrialized nations to realize that we were really wrong and they can't hope to live like us after all. However, the future of the planet depends on it.

XI

THE POPULATION EXPLOSION

Not only has population been a prime driving force in social evolution, it is one of the most important factors in our current crisis. Despite our overconsumption and environmental negligence, if the world's population wasn't so large, we wouldn't be threatening to destroy ourselves ecologically. If the preindustrialized population weren't so large and growing, it wouldn't be so difficult for them to achieve sustainable development.

These relationships can be analyzed using Paul Erhlich's formula I = PAT, which means Impact = Population × Affluence × Technology (1991, 58). The environmental Impact equals the size of the Population multiplied by the degree of Affluence (which means the amount of consumption) multiplied by the level of Technology. Thus all three of these factors are important. We need to stabilize our population, reduce our consumption, and develop ecological technology.

Let's look at this in terms of carrying capacity, which you'll remember is an ecological term meaning the maximum number of organisms that an area can sustain indefinitely:

> When is an area overpopulated? When its population can't be maintained without . . . degrading the capacity of the environment to support the population. If the long-term carrying capacity of an area is clearly being degraded by its current human occupants, that area is overpopulated. *By this standard, the entire planet and virtually every nation is already vastly overpopulated.* (Ehrlich and Ehrlich 1991, 39, italics in original)

Of course, the industrialized nations are over-populated now because of our current degree of technology and consumption. If we all lived as Third World peasants, we wouldn't be degrading our environment as much. Nevertheless, our population is crucial. The world currently has 5 1/2 billion people and our numbers are growing rapidly. About a quarter of these people are in the industrialized nations where our population growth is relatively slow. We need to stop our population growth soon, especially because of our high consumption. The preindustrialized nations contain the other three-quarters of the world's people, and their population is still increasing quickly. In the industrialized world the average family size is often close to two children per couple; this is called replacement fertility. In Third World countries it can often be four, five, or even six children per family.

Population Momentum. There is an even more ominous difficulty here. The age of the preindustrialized population is greatly skewed toward young people. There are many more people aged 0–20, for example, than aged 40–60. This is a natural consequence of the fact that the population has been growing rapidly. Since the younger age groups were born later, they are larger. But this means that even if the Third World miraculously reached replacement fertility starting tomorrow, their population would continue to grow for many years to come. This is because there are so many more people in the child-bearing years or younger, so even if each pair has only two children, this would amount to a greater percentage of the population.

We're not talking about a small difference here. In *Beyond the Limits*, they estimate that even if the world reached replacement fertility in 1995, the population would not stabilize until 2040 at 7 1/2 billion. An abrupt change to replacement fertility is, of course, not possible, so the best we can hope for is to stabilize at 9 or 10 billion, almost twice what we have today. This is the probable limit of what the earth can support, even with reduced consumption and sound ecological practices.

The industrialized nations have a population problem, too. Our population is also increasing, though at a slower rate, and any population growth on our part has a much greater impact on the earth because of our high consumption of resources. Furthermore, our population increase is not uniform. It is much higher among our poor than among our middle class. This is because poverty is one of the root causes of population growth today.

Tradeoffs. One of the most striking insights from the simulations in *Beyond the Limits* relates population and material standard of living. When the world's population is eventually stabilized, there will be a trade-off between its size and our overall standard of living. On a finite earth, the lower we can keep our final population, the better standard of living we all can have. It's obvious when you think about it, but it is quite powerful to have it stated so clearly. *The longer we wait to control our population, the less we will have materially.* Of course, the sensible thing to do in the long run is to gradually reduce population, but first we must stabilize it.

The question is not *whether* population will be controlled but *how*. If humanity doesn't control our population, the resulting ecological catastrophe and associated social breakdown will do it for us. "We shouldn't delude ourselves: the population explosion will come to an end before very long. The only remaining question is whether it will be halted through the humane method of birth control, or by nature wiping out the surplus" (Ehrlich and Ehrlich 1991).

And if we fail, the tragedy will not only be the suffering of those who die. The whole world will be embroiled in calamity in ways that can't be predicted.

THE REPERCUSSIONS OF POPULATION

The effects of our population size are all around us, but people rarely see them. We read that a certain preindustrialized country has doubled its GNP in the last twenty-five years but is poorer than ever. How can this be? Because it *more* than doubled its population in the same span of time. The only hope for the Third World to lift itself out of misery is to control its population. We read about the flooding in Bangladesh and the massive loss of life. These people were forced to live on lands that they knew were flooded periodically; there was nowhere else to go. Bangladesh has an enormously high population density.

We read about famine in Africa and how it is caused by droughts and civil war. How severe would this have been with a smaller population? We read of the horrors of ethnic cleansing and atrocious war between cultural groups. Again there are many causes, but how much of this would have happened if population were low enough that there was land for all?

We know about crime in the inner city, and the rampant poverty and racism, but how much of this is also caused by the incredible population density that people must live with? We see developments going up all over, and we bemoan the loss of our beautiful countryside and our peace and quiet. This is happening because our population is growing.

I live in a suburb of New York City, which is fairly crowded and noisy. However, when I go into Manhattan I am struck by the speed at which people drive and the way you are treated with surliness and contempt. I have a vacation home in the country, and when I go there I am struck by how slowly people drive and how friendly and at ease they are. My home in the suburbs is, of course, in between those two extremes. I ask myself what causes these striking differences. One of the main factors has to be population density.

The next time you read the paper or hear stories of societal problems, especially ecological ones, ask yourself how much population might play a part. It is rarely mentioned, but it is all too often a major factor. The Population Institute has a slogan, "Whatever your cause, it is a lost cause if we don't control overpopulation." And they are absolutely right!

NORTH VERSUS SOUTH

We in the industrialized world must be careful not to lay the major blame for the ecological crisis on the doorstep of the preindustrialized nations. We are currently causing the greatest amount of the ecological damage because of our high degree of consumption and use of technology. The resolution of the crisis must include both population stability (by the preindustrialized world) and moderation in use of resources (by the industrialized world).

These days at international meetings there are often arguments between the industrialized North and the preindustrialized South over who has the greater responsibility for doing their part. It is certainly appropriate for the South to remind us northerners that we must control our consumption as well as asking them to control population. However, it is a grave mistake to argue that only one part is necessary. In order for us to succeed, both parties must do everything they can.

Another specious North-South debate is about population growth and poverty. One side says that population growth produces poverty because poor nations continually have more hungry mouths to feed, and any increases in GNP are eaten up by greater increases in population. The other side says that poverty causes population growth because poor families have an economic incentive to have more children. However, both sides are right! This is another case of circular causality, where each factor increases the other and a vicious cycle is created. Society must try to stop such a cycle by working on both sides simultaneously.

It is especially upsetting to hear people on the side of the South claim that the preindustrialized world has no population problem, that it is all the fault of the North. It may indeed be all our fault, in the sense that we have contributed to the population explosion in the South, but we can't fix it alone. It is a tragedy to take any stand that doesn't encourage the preindustrialized nations to find a solution to their population crisis. If they don't succeed, they will suffer the most. The poorest people usually bear the brunt of problems, and global warming is likely to cause the most damage in the tropics.

There is even a stronger reason why it is in their best interest to stabilize their population. They naturally would like to climb out of poverty and take their share in the riches of the world. This is only possible if there aren't too many of them. Currently the North is causing most of the ecological damage, but that is because of our wealth and power. Even in an ecologically sane world of the future, wealth will still use resources, so if the south begins to take their fair share of the world's wealth with such large numbers of people, it will be an ecological nightmare. The only hope for them to gain their rightful place in the world is with smaller numbers.

Of course, we in the North have plenty to do at home. We must curb consumption and develop an ecologically sound economy. We must stop exploiting the South economically. We must provide them with as much aid and technical assistance as possible to help them not only stabilize their population, but also develop in ways that are democratic and ecologically sustainable. In the end, we all must work together to surmount this crisis.

XII

MARKETS NOT COMMUNITIES

In this chapter I discuss the current problems in the social realm and their effect on our lives and on the ecological crisis.

THE LOSS OF COMMUNITY

In the social realm, the complementary qualities are community and social structure.

Figure 12.1 Social Realm

In the current crisis, social structure has suppressed community. Let's look at the effects of this.

A Natural Need. The need for local community is an intrinsic human need. We all have a need to be interacting in our daily lives with people who know us and care about us, to be part of a local group with shared values and traditions. It is wonderful to say "Hello" to the corner storekeeper, to personally know your child's schoolteacher, to be part of a congenial church group or work team, to have a group of friends for recreation and mutual aid, to stop by at a neighbor's house for coffee or babysitting. Of course, the gossip and back-biting of small towns are also well known, but we all have a hunger for the positive aspects of community. Those needs are built into us as social animals, and we ignore them at our peril.

In today's world, we *are* largely ignoring them. We in the industrialized nations have lost our sense of local community, especially in urban and suburban areas. Each family tends to be an isolated unit, with minimal connections with nearby families and community groups. Even at work, where many people spend forty or more hours a week, there is sometimes little closeness or connection. The extended family is disappearing. Even the nuclear family is disintegrating into single-parent families, blended families, and isolated singles. Oppressed and ethnic groups tend to retain some sense of community as a defense against prejudice and poverty. However, mainstream middle-class people often lead lives of *alienation*, bereft of the warmth of community.

The little community that is available at regional or national levels is mainly through the media, so it doesn't provide much of the personal, human element that is so necessary, and it really can't make up for the experience of belonging has been lost at the local level.

Child Rearing. The loss of community, and especially of extended family, is a dangerous portent for our future. It is very difficult to do a good job of raising a child in a nuclear family, and it is even harder in a blended family or as a single parent. Children need a great deal of attention, patience, encouragement, and love in its many forms to grow up as healthy, confident, loving people. As a psychotherapist I know this all too well through exploring the childhood problems of my clients. It is very rough for one or two parents to handle this job properly without considerable help, especially today's busy parents, both of whom are often working full time.

In the past, child rearing was shared with live-in grandparents, aunts, uncles, older children, and others. The child had many places to turn, many resources. Today it's all on Mom and Dad, or maybe just Mom, and not surprisingly, we're doing poorly at raising our children. Our children are our future, and our lack of extended family is threatening it.

Crime. Our lack of community is perhaps the most important root cause of the increasing crime in our industrialized societies. When it is working, community provides an economic safety net for those who might be tempted to steal, a sense of belonging for people who would otherwise be isolated, and alternate sources of nurturing for neglected or abused children. Taken together, this covers most of the primary causes of lawlessness. Community also can provide a sense of togetherness in working to combat crime, and methods of justice based on restitution and reconciliation rather than punishment. The lack of these community functions predisposes our societies to a high crime rate. All this is explored in an excellent issue of *In Context* (van Gelder 1994).

POWER

Power is a subrealm of the social realm. The complementary qualities are power distribution and social structure.

Figure 12.2 Power

In this time of transition, humanity is struggling to achieve a better distribution of power. This means that everyone would have relatively equal access to goods and services, influence, and the ability to make their life what they want. This would certainly be a desirable state of affairs. From a moral point of view it seems only fair. It also benefits society by allowing everyone a chance to actualize their full potential. However, it seems to be very difficult to achieve in actuality, except in very small groups.

Difficulties in Achieving Power Distribution. Some would claim that this is because of the need for incentive; those people who work hard and take the initiative and risks and therefore contribute most to society must be rewarded in greater amounts than others. There is a fear that without this there will be no initiative and the system will bog down, as in Communist countries. However, in the United States today the ratio of the highest pay to the lowest within corporations is 135 to 1; this large a gap has little to do with rewarding initiative and risk. In addition, there are too many examples that contradict the incentive notion. Some of our poorest people are the hardest workers, and many people have to choose between jobs that pay well and those that make a contribution to society.

There is certainly some need to reward contribution, but to do this through large income disparities reflects a narrow individualistic, materialistic viewpoint, which is outmoded in today's world. I think it is possible to reward innovators and hard workers in meaningful ways without the need for great power imbalances. However, this will not be easy; it is one of the tough tasks to be faced in designing a just economic system.

It is natural to want power because power means being able to get what you want. So inevitably some people will want as much power as possible. (An exception to this is that people generally don't take power at the expense of those they are close to, so tribal peoples had fewer problems with power.) Therefore those people (or groups) with advantages often take more than their share of the power. Thus one might say that desire or greed is a factor that makes balancing power difficult.

There is a tendency among social justice advocates to emphasize this greed factor and to see the problem as one of the immorality of privileged groups and the lack of power of oppressed groups. While there is truth in this, I think that it misses the more important issue—that it is very difficult to arrange power distribution in a large complex society.

Group Size and Power. Let's explore the relationship between power distribution and the size and density of a social group. Only in small group settings it is relatively easy to have equal power distribution, and even then, there may be problems. Whenever an organization becomes much larger than that, the difficulties in functioning effectively require a greater amount of social structure, and this tends to concentrate power, unless a special effort is made to circumvent that.

When small progressive organizations bravely attempt a radically equal power distribution, for example using the consensus process, they frequently run into problems. Even when they succeed, it requires a great deal of energy and creativity. At the level of a nation with 250 million people, these difficulties are multiplied exponentially.

I'm not saying that the problem can't be solved. I'm saying that it involves far more than morality. To have power distribution in a large society, we need a social structure that encourages this. The sentiment is not enough. We need an *integrating structure* that is consciously designed to promote power distribution. As I have discussed, in the Modern era we have made strides in this direction with representative democracy. In the next era we need to go further.

The Value of Social Structure. The value of power distribution is obvious. The most important value of its complementary quality, social structure, is that it is necessary to make a society or organization function effectively. In all but the smallest groupings there must be structures that govern the production of food, the distribution of goods, the resolution of conflicts, the making of decisions, and so on. Without these, not much would get done, and everyone would lose. The lack of enough social structure for a society to function properly is called *anarchy*. Other than stage 1 bands, societies without much social structure do not survive long. The larger and more interconnected the group, the more social structure is necessary. At the level of a nation, the need is tremendous.

Another important reason for social structure is that it promotes the exercise of power by more humane means. It may not improve the distribution of power, but social structure sometimes ensures that power is exercised by law or by economic means or by vested authority rather than by force. (Of course, societies also use force to back up the other means.) While these other means aren't necessarily as humane as we would like, they are often better than the raw exercise of power by violence.

Intersocietal Power. This is most clear in examining the power situation at the world level, which is very different from the national level. *Within* most nations there is a high degree of social structure, so that, for example, conflicts are usually resolved by law rather than by violence. Thus the conflict over abortion in the United States takes place primarily through legislative and judicial struggle, with only sporadic violence. In a similar vein, you never hear of border skirmishes between New York and New Jersey or armed conflict between the Air Force and the Marines.

At the world level, the situation has been very different. Until recently there were no institutions that governed the exercise of power *between* nations. Even now the only political institution that might serve this function is the United Nations, and it has been kept weak. The nations of the world have been unwilling to give up much of their sovereignty, and so at the world level there is inadequate political social structure. Therefore the world is inundated with war and terrorism. If there is a conflict between two nations that isn't resolved through negotiation, there is no recourse to a higher power to decide it. Violence or the threat of violence is the only resort. At the world level *anarchy* reigns and therefore power is largely exercised by inhumane means—war. This is now beginning to change because of the development of a world economy, which tends to decrease the importance of war as a means to power.

Ideally social structure enables a society to function intelligently, to understand its situation and formulate its goals wisely, and to achieve its goals effectively. In this way, social structure has a valuable function to serve. It is rightly looked on with suspicion because it is so often used to uphold oppression. The healthy goal to strive for is an integration of social structure and power distribution.

Anarchy and Oppression. Since social structure so often accompanies societal size and density, and these so often produce social oppression, one might get the impression that smallness automatically produces equality. This is not necessarily the case. In the past, minimal size and social structure have sometimes encouraged equal power distribution, as in some hunting and gathering societies. However, minimal structure can allow power imbalances as well.

A lack of social structure can set the stage for the powerful dominating the less powerful. This is true at the world level today with the powerful nations dominating. In primitive societies it can mean that physical power predominates. In small groups today it can mean that those with charisma or controlling personalities take over. Even in the smallest of groups, a marriage, it is all too well known that one person can thoroughly oppress and abuse the other. In some of these situations, social structure can be used to improve the situation, to promote power distribution.

ECONOMICS

Let's consider for a moment the different ways that societal power can be exercised. Force or violence is the oldest and most basic. Power has also been exercised by vested authority, either religious or political, the king or the priest. Power has been distributed according to class, race, ethnic group, gender, and religion. Most recently power depends on wealth and economic clout. At a personal level there is also charisma, intelligence, moral influence, and so forth.

The Reign of Economics. The most striking thing about societal power today is that it is increasingly exercised through economic means. Vested authority has largely fallen by the wayside with the Modern move toward autonomy. Force operates mainly in a situation of anarchy. The more social structure, the less importance it tends to have. Political power is still quite strong, but the political process is heavily influenced by wealth. Furthermore, with the rise of the multinational corporation, our national governments have less and less control over our business institutions.

The success of capitalism and the market has put economics into first place in the exercise of power. This is not necessarily bad in itself, but it presents us with a serious problem. We as a world are aware of the dangers of *political* oppression, that is, oppression based on force, class, and vested authority. We know about kings, tyrants, slavery, and so on. We have struggled with it for five thousand years and are actively working on ways to eliminate it. The rise of democracy in the Modern era and its current popularity in the world are testimony to this.

We are not so aware of the danger of *economic* oppression or exploitation, that is, oppression based on wealth, finance, and ownership. This has only been a serious problem for a few hundred years, and its most visible opponent, communism, has failed. Therefore we don't tend to worry about the fact that there is little democracy within the corporation, that businesses can destroy communities and nature, that corporate lobbyists have undue influence politically, that multi-national corporations exploit Third World people. We naively think that if we have "free enterprise" and "free trade," everyone has a fair chance. As a world we have not yet fully awakened to the peril of economic oppression and figured out how to combat it.

We tend to think the market itself constrains corporations to work in society's best interests. It is true that the market, as long as it is competitive, does force corporations to maintain efficiency and control prices, but society needs more than this. The market doesn't compel corporations to be democratic or ecological. In fact, under an uncontrolled market economy, corporations are virtually forced to pursue profits only. Even those corporate leaders who might have ethical concerns for exploited peoples and the earth, don't have much room to act on them. If their concerns conflict too much with their company's bottom line, the concerned business leaders can lose their jobs or bankrupt their firms.

Just at the historical point where humanity has finally developed an integrating structure for the political side of the power realm (representative democracy), the power game is getting switched on us. Now economics has the reins of power, and we don't yet have an integrating structure for the economic side. Thus even though we have made important strides toward integrating power distribution, there is still massive oppression and exploitation, especially economic.

People still tend to think about power in national terms—which nation is the most powerful, most competitive economically. However, one of the most important trends in today's world is the growing influence of the multinational corporations. Some of them have GNP's approaching those of medium sized nations. Soon they may be the dominant players on the world stage, more powerful than nation-states. We have yet to take this seriously in our thinking about power. David Korten's book *When Corporations Rule the World* (1995) discusses this issue in depth.

Economic Colonialism. The place where power is most unbalanced in today's world is in international economic relations. There is an enormous split between the power and wealth of the industrialized nations and the rest of the world. There is a small but growing number of countries that fall in between the rich North and the poor South, but there are not yet enough of them to promote a reasonable balance.

Much of this imbalance is the result of earlier colonial policies, when the European powers divided up much of the preindustrialized world. They would conquer a preindustrialized land, govern it politically, and convert its economy from subsistence farming to export crops. They took away the land that was owned and worked by the peasant farmers and converted it to large agribusinesses devoted to growing single luxury crops, such as coffee or sugar, for export to the motherland.

Even when the colonies gained their political freedom, they frequently were unable to undo these changes. An upper class developed which was devoted to maintaining its power and wealth through continuing the economic practices of the colonial masters. When colonial governments left, multinational corporations based in the industrial powers moved in, with the cooperation of the local upper class. The people continued to work for minimal wages on large corporate farms. Then as population grew and agriculture became more efficient, many were forced to leave the land altogether and move to the cities to menial jobs and lives of poverty. Thus the oppression of the local people continues, now largely through economic means. Of course, this is just one scenario for economic colonialism. There are many variations, but the resulting poverty and misery are much the same.

The United States is torn about what to do. Some people in our government, clearly concerned about the pain and suffering of Third World people, attempt to improve things by offering aid and pushing for democratic reforms. However, this is often not in the best interests of the powerful multinational corporations, which benefit from continued oppression, so much of our policy ends up supporting the status quo. In addition, even when the powers would allow it, it is often difficult to set up democratic government in the Third World, because the people have been oppressed so long that they often lack the information, communication skills, and sense of empowerment that are necessary for democracy to work.

As I explained in the last chapter, this international power imbalance is also contributing to the ecological crisis, by encouraging profligate use of resources by the north and forcing desperate measures on the people of the south.

Intersocietal Power in the Model. The subrealm of power was presented as one in which the evolution of the emergent quality moved quickly resulting in full-blown oppression in the Archaic era, followed by some integration of power distribution in the Modern era. This is only true for power *within* societies. Let's take a look at the subrealm of intersocietal power. Figure 12.3 illustrates the power issues at this level.

Figure 12.3 Intersocietal Power

Here the ground quality is *societal autonomy,* which of course, was fully realized in stage 1 and has gradually eroded as societies have become more interconnected. The increase in interactions between societies and people from different societies has resulted in greater intersocietal *structure,* including *intersocietal oppression,* either by conquest and subjugation or by economic colonialism. Thus oppression *among* societies has been gradually increasing over time. The Modern improvements of democracy and market economies haven't yet encouraged power distribution in the international arena, so intersocietal oppression has become increasingly worse because of the greater interconnection of societies.

In terms of the model, intersocietal power follows much the same trajectory as the rest of the social realm (and the other realms), not the faster trajectory of power within societies. This means maximal suppression of the ground quality in the Modern era. Our job in moving into the next era is to begin integration.

Economics and the Selection for Power. The reign of economics is especially important in the international arena. Here power has historically been exercised almost exclusively through war. Now for the first time, there is a significant degree of social structure at the international level, so that war is becoming less important in determining global power. The global social structure I am referring to is primarily economic, because we now have a truly worldwide economy. This power is exercised by the multinational corporations, the World Bank, the International Monetary Fund, and the group of seven industrialized nations. Of course, the United Nations is a growing political organization at the planetary level, but it has much less power than our global economic institutions.

War is, unfortunately, not yet obsolete. It still has a part to play in global power contests. It is still widespread in the preindustrialized world, and military power is still used by the industrialized nations to maintain Third World regimes that are friendly to their economic interests. However, economics has taken over. It makes less and less sense to try to take power militarily in the world today, especially among industrialized nations. Your enemy is likely to be a major trading partner. And the final test of a society's power is its economic competitiveness. Military might is used primarily as a support for economic power.

The clearest evidence of the reign of economics comes from Japan and Germany. They are two of the most powerful nations on earth, despite the fact that Japan's military has been limited in size and action and Germany's has until recently been under the control of the West. They have become global powerhouses based on their economic success alone.

This shows that the parable of the tribes is changing. Throughout history the selection for power has been entirely based on military power. Now it is coming to be based primarily on economic clout. The demise of the Soviet Union is a clear indication of that. It matched the United States and NATO stride for stride militarily, yet it collapsed because it couldn't compete economically. The selection for power is now favoring economic competitiveness rather than military strength.

In one sense this is good. Economic competition is far preferable to war, and a society shaped for economic competitiveness is likely to be better off than one honed for war. We are moving in the right direction, but we have far to go. The powerful nations of the earth are shaped for economic power; they thrive on high consumption, growth in technology, wasteful practices, and a constantly expanding economy. All these processes are destroying our environment. The market system as it now stands shapes our industrialized societies toward ecological destruction (Schmookler 1993).

There are two other social aspects of the current crisis that need to be mentioned—the dangers of cultural homogenization and overspecialization. These will be covered in chapters 16 and 20.

XIII

LOSS OF MEANING AND VITALITY

Most of the effects of the consciousness realm on society are indirect, though no less important or powerful. Figure 13.1 shows complementary qualities in this realm.

Figure 13.1 Consciousness

IMPAIRMENT OF EMPATHY AND MEANING

Meaning. Currently in our industrialized societies, reflexive consciousness is dissociated from participation and participation is suppressed. This puts us in a situation of *detachment* where the only kind of understanding that counts is based on empirical data and logic. Neither of these, by itself, can tell us much about meaning and purpose in our lives. The understanding of life purpose is grounded in the emotional, the intuitive, and the spiritual. We have devalued these participatory modes so much that we have lost our sense of what life is all about.

A sense of life purpose comes from feeling part of something larger than ourselves, something that gives our lives meaning through its own intrinsic value. People of earlier eras were much more connected with such a larger sense of meaning. In the Modern era, since many of us in the industrialized world have the power to get nearly anything we want in the way of material things, we often choose this to the exclusion of participation. Therefore we feel separate from nature, isolated from community, out of touch with the emotional and creative, and disconnected from the artistic and spiritual. In this vacuum, struggling to build a happy life as an individual or a family, without higher goals, we feel bereft of purpose and meaning. We dedicate our lives to money, security, power, and appearances. In our detachment we are forced to rely on that which can be objectively counted, and this leaves our lives barren and sterile.

The impact of this detachment goes beyond the individual level. Modern societies are also bereft of meaning, and the directions we pursue reflect this. We blindly chase economic growth and technological innovation thinking they will make our lives happier. We covet power and control in order to feel safe. We apply quick fixes and band aids to the great problems of our time such as drug abuse and homelessness. There is no larger vision of where we are going.

The United States seems to have no other goals than maintaining our material standard of living and our status as number one world power. Even our noble goal of bringing democracy to the world has become lost in concerns about national security and power. For decades we have supported any dictator who provided us with markets and military bases.

Empathy. Along with the loss of meaning, detached consciousness brings about an impairment of empathy. When we don't participate in the feelings and meanings of our own lives, we also can't participate in others'. We tend to see everything in objective and machinelike terms, treating other people, other nations, and the natural world as objects to be controlled and used. Thus we can talk about millions of "acceptable" deaths in a supposedly limited nuclear war. We can torture and enslave animals by the millions for dubious ends and allow wholesale destruction of species and habitats because we have lost empathy with the natural world. Lacking a sense of compassion, we permit widespread oppression and exploitation.

We have even lost empathy for ourselves. We tend to treat our own bodies and psyches as objects to be manipulated, and therefore our physicians overuse drugs and surgery on us. People look for behavioral quick fixes for psychological problems rather than the deeper personal growth that is required. We ignore ecological threats to our health and well-being.

In stage 1 our hunter-gatherer ancestors had deep empathy with the natural world and with the people of their tribe. As participatory consciousness has gradually been suppressed during social evolution, humanity has lost that resonance, resulting in our modern detachment. On the other hand, our early ancestors had very little understanding of people from different cultures, and this has actually grown over time with the increase in reflexive consciousness. However, it still falls short of what we need for a resolution of our international conflicts. In the next era we need to develop a kind of systemic empathy that includes both our own people and those who are different.

This loss of empathy has been encouraged by our Modern form of social structure. Our ancestors who lived in local community had intimate personal connections with most of the people they interacted with. They knew the local storekeeper, the schoolteacher, the town or village leaders, and most of the people they passed on the street or in the forest. Today we have personal contact with only a small number of people in our lives, and most of our interactions are impersonal ones in which each party is treating the other as an object. This erodes our sense of empathy and compassion for others.

Most of the imbalances of the material and social realms are supported by impairment of empathy and meaning in the consciousness realm. Of course, all this is beginning to change, but this is because society is moving *away* from detached consciousness as we transition into the next era. Participation, empathy, and meaning are returning, as they must if we are to survive.

VITALITY COMPENSATION

In all three realms, the ground quality embodies a vitality that we Moderns need. In the current crisis, these vital qualities of life have been suppressed, and we unconsciously attempt to substitute for the vitality we have lost. I call this process *vitality compensation.* Even though it happens in all three realms, I have included it here under consciousness because it is a psychological process.

In the material realm, our current artificial environment not only decreases our quality of life, but this decrease can in turn stimulate our need for more artificial living in an attempt to make up for what we have lost. Human beings naturally get a great deal of pleasure and satisfaction from our connection with nature—the soothing sound of the ocean, the excitement of river rafting, the beauty of desert vistas, the everyday richness of bird song, and so on. We come alive in these ways. When we are deprived of this natural vitality, we often seek substitutes. In the United States, our homes are filled with stereos, TVs, VCRs, partly to compensate for the natural sights and sounds we have lost. We buy expensive, flashy clothes, throw lavish parties, take drugs, covet racy cars. In this way we attempt to substitute technological living for the vitality we have lost through the suppression of natural living.

In the social realm people need the closeness and security that comes from true community. We need to feel loved and loving with our families and close friends. In the consciousness realm we need to be in tune with our creative and artistic nature, to be open to our emotional depth and our intuition. We want to be spontaneous and playful. We long to be connected spiritually, to have a sense of meaning in our lives.

When we are cut of from these experiences, our craving for vitality doesn't vanish, it becomes distorted. We seek vitality wherever we can, even in substitutes that don't fully satisfy. In Modern society we seek it in status, appearance, power, and wealth (social realm). We seek it in addictions and manufactured excitement (consciousness realm). Much of our interest in vitality compensation is encouraged by the market economy, through advertising.

A Vicious Cycle. This is another example of circular causality. In the Modern era, the increasing availability of technological and material goods and pleasures has contributed to the suppression of the aliveness of the ground qualities. This causes a need for vitality compensation. This compensation contributes further to the suppression of real vitality (the ground quality), and disempowers the person who seeks it. In addition, the substitutes do not really satisfy, because they don't really touch us at the core where our natural needs are. Therefore we constantly need more of them. Thus we are caught in a vicious cycle, depicted in figure 13.2. The more we seek these artificial pleasures, the more we contribute to an economy and a society that is excessively technological, power-oriented, and inauthentic. This society alienates us from our sources of natural vitality and makes us need compensation even more.

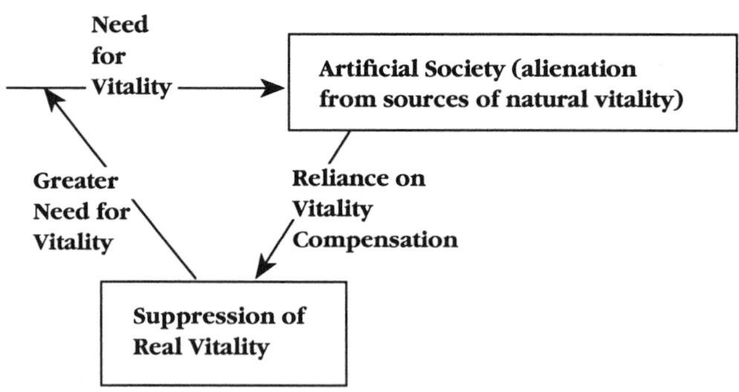

Figure 13.2

A vicious cycle is hard to change because it continually feeds on itself, but when enough of a change is made, then the cycle begins to work in the other direction. As we regain our natural vitality, we recognize that it is more satisfying than the artificial, and we seek it out more. As this happens with more people, society will begin to change to offer these natural pleasures, and the snowball may soon roll in the other direction.

EVOLUTION AND ADDICTION

This process I am describing may sound surprising similar to addiction. It is. Modern society is profoundly addictive (Schaef 1987), but this is only partly due to the suppression of the ground qualities. It is also comes from the success of the emergent qualities and how we handle that.

In the Modern era we live in a largely artificial environment. Even when this environment is not ecologically destructive or unhealthy for us, it is still artificial. It is not the environment humans evolved in. We are not biologically adapted to it. Here I want to discuss how this is related to addiction in modern life—addiction in the broadest meaning of the term.

Let's use our penchant for sweets as an example. The human race evolved to have a sweet tooth, to crave the sweet taste. Evolutionists speculate that this had the evolutionary advantage of encouraging people to eat the ripest fruits, with the most food value. At that time, there was no possible problem with this because our environment didn't contain an overabundance of sweet things. There was no chance that our early ancestors would have substituted chocolate cream pies for healthful vegetables. However, now we live in a situation where this is possible. We have created an environment that is more to our liking than the original, but we now have the possibility of overdosing on what we like.

This of course applies to all the obvious addictions—food, alcohol, drugs, cigarettes, coffee. We now have the means of altering our consciousness through artificial means, and nothing to control it except our own choices. Although there is some responsible use of drugs for personal growth, most drug use is quite destructive, while altering consciousness through more natural means is almost universally healthy and growthful for the person. However, these other means—meditation, chanting, fasting—require discipline, patience, and the right attitude, thus historically ensuring against overuse or abuse. Now we can alter our consciousness at the pop of a pill, and we are not evolved to handle this easily.

The Range of Addictions. Modern addictions go far beyond these obvious ones. We have the possibility of unlimited stimulation in a passive state—from TV, video games, movies, recorded music, and so on.

We can simulate just about any human activity without contact with other people or the natural world and without taking any initiative or risk. We can have sex from a porn video without the interpersonal risk. We can enjoy fine food at a restaurant without the skill to prepare it. We can wear interesting clothes and jewelry without the creativity and patience to design and make them. We can live an entirely pretend life through TV and movies. Virtual reality is the ultimate in living a simulated life. All these activities are destructive in a subtle way, sapping our initiative, our creativity, our sheer engagement with life.

Passivity can show up in other ways. We can go anywhere or talk to anyone without exercising our bodies. Through video games we can even play sports without much physical engagement. This has led to the medical dangers of a sedentary lifestyle. Of course, I'm not saying that we shouldn't enjoy a good restaurant or movie. I'm exploring the larger implications of the sheer amount of artificial and passive pursuits that are available to us.

The more engaged, real activity is always more intrinsically satisfying, but the artificial activity is very seductive. Humanity didn't evolve in an environment where it was possible to overindulge in these activities, so we don't have built-in biological mechanisms for dealing with this. Since we are now surrounded by addictive possibilities, our challenge as a species is to develop the psychological and cultural means to control these addictions where our biology can't help us. We must make choices that will foster our long-term development as individuals and societies, rather than our short-term gratification.

In addition, the addictions are so tempting because our natural ground qualities have been suppressed. We must not only learn to control our addictions, we must also regain and integrate the ground qualities so we will have access to healthier alternatives.

The larger point here is that our tendency toward addiction is not simply due to moral shortcomings or some intrinsic fault in our culture. It is the byproduct of the suppression of the ground qualities and of our success with technology, which has placed us in a situation we are not biologically prepared for. It is helpful to approach this problem with compassion for ourselves, not contempt.

Summary. Even though the most dangerous crisis the world faces comes from the material realm, this crisis is sustained and exacerbated by the problems in the other realms. In the social realm, it is supported by the loss of community and the international power imbalance. In the consciousness realm, it is enabled by vitality compensation and the impairment of empathy and meaning. In all three realms, the emergent quality has become dominant; it has dissociated from and suppressed the ground quality. In addition, each realm affects the others. It is actually more accurate to say that these realms are only different facets of one larger reality.

Table 13.1 summarizes the characteristics of the current crisis in each realm and adds an extra line to the era chart, representing the current crisis.

Table 13.1 Current Crisis

Realm	Description
Material	Ecological crisis, population explosion, waste problem, limits of the earth, health problems
Social	Economic colonialism, world economy, loss of community, selection for economic power
Consciousness	Vitality compensation, impairment of empathy and meaning, addiction

Era	Qualities	Material	Social	Consciousness
1 Paleolithic		Hunting & gathering	Family, band	Magic, animism
2 Neolithic		Horticulture, herding	Village, chiefdom	Myth: Goddess
3 Archaic		Agriculture, bronze	City, early state	Myth: gods & heroes
4 Ancient/ Medieval		Gradual advance	Historic empire	Religion, philosophy
5 Modern		Industry	Democracy, capitalism	Science, autonomy
Current Crisis		Population/ environmental crisis	Economic colonism	Loss of vitality, empathy, meaning

Part Three

SOLUTIONS

I have traced the evolution of society from our origins as hunter-gatherers to the current planetary crisis. Now I explore how to resolve this crisis and build a healthy global society. Chapter 14 takes an overall view of the model of social evolution as it relates to integrating the ground and emergent qualities. In chapters 15–20 I look at integrative societal solutions in the various realms. Chapter 15 deals with political and economic power and chapter 16 with gender and culture. Chapter 17 deals with the material realm and population. Chapters 18 and 19 deal with consciousness. In chapter 20 I have included those aspects of the social realm not already covered before.

I don't pretend to have all the answers to what is needed to surmount the planetary crisis. I point out the general directions society must take based on the model I have been developing. Some of the specifics have been elucidated by other social theorists, some still have to be explored, and all must be worked out through social interaction and trial and error. Those approaches that have been explored by others I mention briefly with references to the original authors. I go into detail where there are important solutions that haven't been sufficiently explored or where the issue is particularly helpful in understanding how to apply the model. I don't deal with the very important question of how *to bring about the changes that are needed, how to get from today's world to a healthy stage 6 social arrangement. That is an enormous topic in itself and outside the scope of this book.*

In chapter 21, I explore how the complementary qualities are distributed among the population and how to understand the position of various groups and movements with respect to the planetary crisis. Chapter 22 applies the model to understanding how a person's life choices can contribute to resolving the crisis.

XIV

OVERVIEW OF THE MODEL

The model of social evolution is built around ground and emergent qualities in each realm. These qualities are complementary in the sense that they represent aspects of human and societal nature that tend to be opposed unless a conscious effort is made to integrate them. There is a dynamic, dialectical relationship between the complementary qualities, which is driven by the selection for power and population/environmental constraints.

Steps in the Model. This relationship evolves through certain steps—original unity, emergence, dissociation and suppression, and integration.

1. First there is an original unity which consists of the ground quality alone. The emergent quality has yet to assert itself.
2. The emergent quality gradually arises from the ground quality and becomes increasingly prominent.
3. After a long while, the two qualities become dissociated from each other and the emergent quality becomes dominant. The ground quality is suppressed and often devalued.
4. Finally society chooses to redevelop the ground quality in integration with the emergent quality. This allows both qualities to continue developing, now integrated with each other. From this point a new cycle can begin.

Table 14.1 shows how these four steps correspond to the stages and eras we have been studying.

As I suggested earlier, this is not the only possible sequence of stages for social evolution; it is the one that the leading edge societies have taken. Other societies may have taken alternative trajectories in the past, and current societies not yet in stage 5 may take a different trajectory in the future. I'm especially interested in the circumstances under which a society can stay relatively integrated during emergence and therefore avoid dissociation and suppression.

Table 14.1 Steps in Social Evolution

Stage	Era	Step	Qualities
0	Lower Paleolithic	Original Unity	
1	Upper Paleolithic		
2	Neolithic	Emergence	
3	Archaic		
4	Ancient/Medieval		
5	Modern	Dissociation & Suppression	
6	Next	Integration	

Note: I have represented the "Next Era" graphically as a complete integration of the ground and emerging qualities. This is only to show the ideal situation. We cannot know what form will actually arise as the ground qualities are integrated.

One possibility is that a society may stay integrated if it doesn't pass through the oppressive empires of stage 3. It may be that oppression in the social realm sets up a split within the society that leads to dissociation in other realms as well. Those societies that appear to have avoided an oppressive phase, such as Crete and some Native American tribes, may have retained a relatively integrated culture until they were conquered later.

Another possibility is that a society can remain integrated during emergence if there are already existing models for integrating structures which can be used by that society. These models can come from more advanced societies. For example, as the industrialized nations create models of ecological technology and industry, those societies currently in stage 4 or earlier might adapt some of these models for their own development. This way they could avoid going through the material dissociation of stage 5.

These models can also come from other levels of social structure. For example, there has been some success at developing democracy at the national level. Now we need to create a government at the world level, and we probably won't have to endure the level of oppression at that level that we did at the national level, because an integrating structure for democracy is already known. It just has to be applied at the more inclusive global level. As we move into stage 6, we also have the task of developing corporate democracy. I hope we will use some of what we know about national political democracy in that task.

DIALECTICAL VIEWS

A number of other scholars have also perceived our history in dialectical terms. A dialectical view of process sees trends as moving in a certain direction until they run into a contradiction, which then nurtures the emergence of a counter-trend that attempts to correct the problem. This second trend then proceeds in another direction until it too encounters problems, and there is the necessity of a synthesis of the two which resolves the conflict at a higher level. There is a long history of thinkers who have seen consciousness or history in these terms, the most famous being Hegel and Marx.

Charles Johnston's Creative Model (1984), on which my model is based, uses a dialectical approach that views today's transition as a turning point. In this model, something is being brought into form during the first phase, which then reaches a transition point, where it becomes dissociated from the ground of its creation. Then there is a phase where it integrates with its ground. When applying his model to social evolution, Johnston sees today's crisis as the transition to the integration phase.

Richard Tarnas reaches a similar conclusion in his highly acclaimed summary of Western philosophy, *The Passion of the Western Mind* (1991). In this book, he traces the entire history of Western thought, from the ancient Greeks to the present. Arrived at independently of mine, his view is consistent with my understanding of the evolution of the consciousness realm. He frames the polarity between reflexive and participatory consciousness in terms of the masculine/feminine polarity.

> The evolution of the Western mind has been driven by a heroic impulse to forge an autonomous rational human self by separating it from the primordial unity with nature. . . . But to do this . . . the Western mind has been founded on the repression of the feminine—on the repression of undifferentiated unitary consciousness, of the participation mystique with nature . . . of the community of being . . . of mystery and ambiguity . . . of imagination, emotion, instinct, body. (Tarnas 1991, 441–42)

This is a clear description of the suppression of participatory consciousness by reflexive consciousness and individuality. He then goes on to suggest that our evolution until now has been the first step in a larger dialectical process whose next step is the integration of the ground/feminine:

> But this separation necessarily calls forth a longing for a reunion with that which has been lost—especially after the masculine heroic

> quest has been pressed to its utmost one-sided extreme in the consciousness of the late modern mind. . . . Then man faces the existential crisis of . . . living in a world . . . that matches his world view—i.e., in a man-made environment that is increasingly mechanistic, atomized, soulless, and self-destructive. *The crisis of modern man is essentially a masculine crisis,* and I believe that its resolution is already now occurring in the tremendous emergence of the feminine in our culture. . . .
>
> An epochal shift is taking place . . . a reconciliation between . . . the long-dominant but now alienated masculine and the long-suppressed but now ascending feminine. . . . I believe that this has all along been the underlying goal of Western intellectual and spiritual evolution. *For the deepest passion of the Western mind has been to reunite with the ground of its being* . . . to differentiate itself from but then rediscover and reunite with the feminine, with the mystery of life, of nature, of soul. And that reunion can now occur on a new and profoundly different level . . . for the long evolution of human consciousness has prepared it to be capable at last of embracing the ground and matrix of its own being freely and consciously. (Tarnas 1991, 442–43, emphasis in original)

Thus Tarnas senses and foresees the dialectical integration of participation (feminine) with reflexive consciousness and individuality (masculine). He focuses, of course, on consciousness, but his work lays the philosophical ground work for the integration of the ground qualities, not just in consciousness, but in all realms.

Ken Wilber's model (Wilber 1995) is also dialectical, but in a different sense than mine. I discuss his work in detail in chapter 18.

SOCIAL EVOLUTION AND THE NATURE OF REALITY

At this point I would like to introduce another perspective on the model of social evolution, which involves the degree of alignment between society and the underlying nature of reality. This will help us to understand the character of the integrative solutions needed now.

In the early stages of social evolution, society was organized according to principles that fit the nature of things because society was largely embedded in the natural world. We had not yet emerged. Let's look at this underlying nature.

The Nature of Reality. Looking at reality as a whole, including human, social, and material reality, I believe that it has certain intrinsic properties. *Reality is an integrated organic, systemic whole that is participatory, vital, and meaningful.* These assumptions about the nature of reality are at such a deep philosophical level that they probably can't be proved or disproved. They must be taken as fundamental assumptions. However, this view of reality is consistent with that of many scholars today.

Reality is an *integrated whole* because its parts are related and connected to each other and it contains subwholes (and they contain subwholes, etc.) that are also integrated. The physical world has been shown to be integrated by subatomic physics, by ecology, and now by general systems theory and the science of complexity. The social world has always been integrated at the level of community and is now becoming more and more integrated through social structure at the world level.

The world of life is *organic* in that it is organized according to the principles of biology. Ecosystems, organisms, and human communities all have a natural, alive, flowing kind of order to them that is different from that of a machine or bureaucracy. Even the nonliving world and the sub-worlds of chemistry and physics have a *systemic* interrelatedness that transcends machine models.

Reality is *participatory* in that all parts participate in the whole; no one can be a completely separate observer. When observing the nonhuman world, we can achieve a certain amount of objectivity, but even this has been shown to be limited by atomic physics. When it comes to the human and social world, a pretense of complete objectivity can lead to serious misunderstandings.

Reality has an intrinsic *vitality* and aliveness, and it is *meaningful* in a spiritual and emotional sense, rather than simply being a mechanism. I believe that meaning is not just something that we humans attribute to reality but an intrinsic quality of it. Moreover, the meanings we give reality arise from it in a natural way, since we are part of reality, not separate observers.

All these properties I have attributed to reality are also ground qualities in this model. They are the qualities of society in its early stages when it is completely embedded in biology. Thus society is naturally and unconsciously aligned with reality because it has yet to emerge from embeddedness.

Emergent Control. During human social evolution, to better control reality for our well-being and security, we emerged from being embedded in it and made relatively objective observations and analyses of it. We differentiated it and organized it through mediation. We did this in two ways, by conceptually dividing reality into various pieces and analyzing the relationships among them, and by actually carving up reality so that it became more differentiated materially and socially.

We emerged from nature and studied it. We divided it into parts and analyzed the parts and their interactions with each other. We built tools and machines to change the world to our liking. We created an entire artificial environment to live in, and we organized this world according to mechanical principles.

We emerged from our original communities and created large societies. We differentiated social reality into sectors and fields and professions and occupations, into finer and finer pieces as each person became a specialist or a cog in the social machine. In order to allow such fragmented societies to function, we organized these pieces according to the principles of bureaucracy and monetary exchange.

Unsophisticated Emergent Quality. We have emerged from organic embeddedness and naturally aligned societies, and created societies with our minds and our technology. However, our understanding and our methods of creation were, and still mostly are, unsophisticated. Modern society analyzes reality in mechanistic, fragmented ways that ignore the connected organic nature of things. Our technology and our social structure are also largely immature. We aren't yet sophisticated enough to recognize the actual nature of reality, which is the basis for the ground qualities of natural living, community, and participatory consciousness. Therefore we not only fail to understand these qualities in the design of our societies, we also undermine them through the changes we make in reality, and so our world seems to lack them.

However, we can't fully destroy them, because these ground qualities are built into our nature and the nature of reality. We made the mistake of imagining that our unsophisticated view of reality captured the truth. We had the hubris to think that we could really control things completely. As our power to control reality has grown in scope and depth, we have tried to organize more and more of reality for our own ends with our unsophisticated methods. We have taken over more of the earth and more of genetic and subatomic reality. Now the true nature of reality is being revealed to us because we are incurring massive and unprecedented side effects, consequences that we didn't intend but are happening because of the interconnected, organic nature of things.

Nature *is* organic and integrated, so when we treat it as a machine, we generate ecological breakdown. Human beings need community, so when we treat our institutions and societies as machines, we foster social breakdown. We also need vitality, creativity, and intimacy, so when we perceive ourselves as isolated, passive thinking and pleasure machines we engender psychological breakdown.

The emergent qualities aren't intrinsically at odds with the underlying nature of reality. It is our current unsophisticated, dissociated versions of the emergent qualities that misconstrue reality and treat it in fragmented ways. Earlier in our history, when our methods were even less sophisticated, we weren't able to control as much of reality, so we couldn't cause as much damage. In the future as our methods become more sophisticated and tuned to the real nature of things, we won't cause as much damage because we will be more congruent with reality. In the meantime, to modify an old saying, "A medium amount of knowledge is a dangerous thing."

Integration. To evolve further, we need to integrate the emergent qualities with the ground qualities, or to say it another way, the emergent qualities need to evolve further, to improve their effectiveness. Our emergent methods need to become more sophisticated in their recognition of the nature of reality.

We must recognize that we are participants in a larger whole, not completely separate observers, so in studying reality we must become participant-observers. We need to understand the organic connected nature of reality, and differentiate and organize it in a way that respects this. We should structure our societies in a way that respects the human need for community and equality. We need to design our technology in a way that respects the organic quality of nature. Our concepts should reflect the organic relational nature of reality.

We must exercise power that is governed by an understanding of the deeper meaning of life. When we exercise power over nature and society and over our own bodies and minds, we need to do it with goals that are informed and motivated by the vital and meaningful nature of human life and the earth. For too long we have exercised power for selfish ends without any thought to the larger consequences to society and the earth. We have striven for economic growth for its own sake, technology for profit, and political power for the sake of status and personal advantage. Now we must exercise power for the sake of the well-being of humanity and all of the biosphere, informed by our deepest love and wisdom.

However, this is not just a moral issue. It is a matter of understanding the true nature of reality. It's not only something we should do as good people; it is also the only approach that makes sense. It is exciting to me that as our emergent qualities become more sophisticated and accurate, they will naturally be turning toward the ground and integration. Table 14.2 summarizes these notions.

Table 14.2 Ground and Emergent Qualities' View of Reality

Ground Qualities	Emergent Qualities	Unsophisticated & Dissociated Emergent Qualities
Vital, meaningful	Instrumental	Control hubris
Participatory	Emergent	Separate observer, objective
Organic, systemic	Organized, mediated	Mechanistic, bureaucratic
Integrated	Differentiated	Fragmented

INTEGRATION OF GROUND

In order for integration of the ground quality to occur, the following steps are necessary:

1. Recognition of problems. The society recognizes that there are serious problems because of the dissociation and suppression of the ground quality.
2. The society makes a conscious decision to integrate the ground quality as a way of solving these problems.
3. *Integrating structures* and supporting ideologies are developed and put into action.

As discussed previously, an integrating structure is a social structure that integrates the ground and emergent qualities, and a supporting ideology is an explicit rationale for the integrating structure that explains why it is advantageous for society. For example, in the power realm, for centuries there was a widespread recognition of the problem of oppression. In the 1700s this resulted in the adoption of the integrating structure of representative democracy in France and the United States. Since then, this structure has spread to many of the industrialized nations, and its ideology has been accepted almost worldwide.

For these steps to happen, a reasonable degree of reflexive consciousness is necessary. It is rare for the complementary qualities to integrate automatically. Without conscious effort they tend to oppose each other. These steps require a societywide ability to analyze and make conscious decisions. This is one of the reasons why the integration of the qualities doesn't usually happen as the emergent quality is evolving and instead it takes a fairly advanced society.

It may seem paradoxical that an integrating structure is a social structure, and yet "social structure" is the emergent quality in the social realm. However, at our current stage of social evolution, our population is large enough that we can't function adequately without social structure. Therefore, any integration must be a social structure, even if the purpose of that structure is to promote community, equality, or other ground qualities.

Throughout part 3, I will be exploring examples of integrating structures for stage 6 in the various realms.

Integration versus Equal Strength. Integration of the ground and emergent qualities doesn't necessarily mean that their strengths are equal. For example, in writing this book, I have been strongly oriented toward reflexive consciousness, developing a highly abstract theory. I have brought in participatory consciousness by giving it an equal place in the theory and by relying extensively on my own emotional/intuitive/spiritual side in developing my ideas. Therefore the work is integrated in that the two qualities work together, but the form of the book emphasizes reflexive consciousness.

On the other hand, it is possible for the qualities to be balanced in strength without being integrated. For example, an organization might have two warring factions, nearly equal in strength, one advocating an intellectual approach to some problem and the other advocating an intuitive approach. As long as they were at odds rather than working together, this would not be an example of integration.

The ground and emergent qualities need to work together, and there needs to be a minimum amount of each, so that neither is suppressed or ignored. However, it is not necessary for a person or group or institution to embody equal amounts of the qualities.

Ways to Integrate. There are a variety of ways to integrate the ground and emergent qualities. Each of these possibilities illustrates a way for those of us who want to foster societal health to design an integrating structure:

1. *Ground as Goal.* The emergent quality can promote the ground quality. For example, democracy is a form of social structure (emergent) that promotes power distribution (ground).
2. *Ground as Nature of Reality.* The emergent quality can recognize that the ground quality is the nature of things and

take this into account in pursuing its own ends. For example, ecological technology may still have the emergent goals of power, ease, and pleasure, but it recognizes that the best way to achieve this is to work with the flow of nature (ground).

3. *Being in Ground, Using Emergent*. Since the ground quality brings vitality, we may want to live in the ground quality as much as possible, and use the emergent quality only when we need it to accomplish something. For example, for economic well-being a community should be as economically self-sufficient as possible (ground), but it will need to trade for certain items that it can't produce (emergent).
4. *Choosing According to Situation*. We may want to choose between the qualities according to which one is more appropriate to the needs of the situation. For example, in corporate life, community promotes not only the well-being of the employees but also better productivity. Therefore a work group will want to spend some of its time in activities that promote personal connection and cohesiveness (ground) and, of course, other time in activities that directly produce revenue (emergent). It will probably choose to spend time on community when there are problems with morale or personal frictions, and it will need to focus its time on production when there are important deadlines.
5. *Dynamic Balancing*. A society or organization may aim to recognize when one quality has become dominant and the other suppressed. Then it can purposely focus on the suppressed quality to bring it back to appropriate strength. For example, an organization might monitor its degree of structure versus spontaneity and if either quality diminished too much, endeavor to restore it.
6. *Simple Ground*. In some cases, only the ground quality is needed in a simple society or organization. For example, in a very small society or group, not much social structure is necessary. Everything can be done informally, and only the ground quality, community, is required for healthy functioning. Therefore this situation can be considered integrated.
7. *Advancing Emergent Requires Ground*. In some cases, it is only possible for the emergent quality to advance, to become more effective, if it integrates the ground. For example, often organizations can only become more effective in their

own terms (productivity, efficiency, profitability) if they incorporate community and equality.

Development of the Ground Qualities. Let me emphasize that the ground qualities as they appear today are not the same as the ground qualities in the early stages of social evolution. Modern participatory consciousness is vastly different from the participation of tribal society. The ground qualities go through their own development in each stage of social evolution. They naturally absorb some of the emergent quality even when there is dissociation. For example, a Modern person who embodied the ground quality of participant consciousness would nevertheless be much more capable of rational thought than a member of a hunter-gatherer tribe. In addition, the ground qualities also change because of having to deal with their suppression by the emergent qualities. For example, Modern people who are born with a natural inclination toward, let's say, emotion and intuition, will end up either feeling bad about themselves because of this, or they will learn to be proud of their ground quality inclinations in the face of societal denigration.

Most importantly, the ground qualities change even more as a result of being integrated with the emergent qualities (as do the emergent qualities). For example, as mythical thinking is integrated with rational thinking, we take myths as stories of psychological depth to learn from, whereas people who lived in stage 3 took their myths literally.

This should make it very clear that my call for the integration of the ground qualities is not an attempt to return to the past. It is an invitation to reclaim those aspects of ourselves that have been suppressed in the forward movement of social evolution, but this involves reclaiming in a new form, which comes from the integration of the past and the present.

With integration, the ground quality is not only reclaimed and integrated, but also has a chance to develop further. The emergent quality can in some cases actually enhance the ground quality if it is designed to do so. For example, in the material realm, through travel and education people can develop a deeper appreciation of the variety of nature. In the social realm, through consciously integrating individuality and diversity into community we can deepen our connections with each other. In the consciousness realm, through the conscious use of specific psychotherapeutic and spiritual practices that involve reflexive consciousness, we can participate more deeply in the exploration of our psyches.

Development of the Emergent Qualities. As integration happens, the emergent quality also continues to grow. Remember that the emergent quality develops in two ways—by becoming more pervasive and by becoming more effective. As it integrates the ground quality it becomes more effective because it recognizes and therefore deals with the true nature of reality. Ultimately the emergent quality needs the ground quality to attain its most advanced form. For example, social structure (emergent) currently suppresses community and equality (ground). However, it is becoming increasingly clear today that for a society to be *most* effective it needs to include a high degree of community and equality. This produces cooperation rather than divisiveness, and it allows the best talents, perceptions, and understandings of all people to be utilized. Therefore for social structure to attain its most advanced form, it needs the ground qualities of community and equality.

In addition to integration, there are ways that the emergent qualities are continuing to develop on their own, to become more effective in their intrinsic goals. For example, in the material realm, technology is advancing to an information/computer society. This is an advance in the emergent quality, which is independent of whether it is integrated with the ground. Some of these advances in emergent qualities are valuable for our evolution into the next stage, especially if they don't involve dissociation from the ground. Therefore I will also discuss these in the chapters that follow.

STRATEGIES FOR CHANGE

When thinking about solutions, an important question arises about strategy in working for healthy change. Does one realm underlie the others? Traditional Marxists see the economic realm as underlying and determining all the others. Some feminists see gender this way. Many spiritual writers see consciousness as the central realm. If it were possible to identify a realm that truly determined or shaped what happened in the other realms, then it would be wise to focus our energies primarily in this area.

I don't believe that there is one realm that underlies or is more important than the others. The realms interact very strongly, each affecting the others, but I don't think that any one can be singled out as having the primary determining effect. Our consciousness certainly influences our social structures; for example, the Protestant work ethic supported the growth of capitalism. However, our social structures also affect our consciousness; for example, our competitive economic system affects how easy it is to develop caring, cooperative approaches to problems. Therefore in working to promote social transformation, I believe that we must work toward change in all realms simultaneously. We can't expect to first improve everyone's consciousness and then work on our social systems, or vice versa.

It will probably work as follows: By affecting a little change in, say, consciousness, this will allow us to make small institutional changes. These then will facilitate further changes in consciousness, which will enable greater institutional change, and so on.

XV

COOPERATION AND DEMOCRATIC ECONOMICS

I will begin our discussion of solutions to the planetary crisis with the power realm because this realm is involved with the process of social change itself and therefore affects changes in the other realms. The complementary qualities are represented in figure 15.1.

Figure 15.1 Power

For the purposes of our analysis I have further differentiated the power realm into the subrealms shown in figure 15.2.

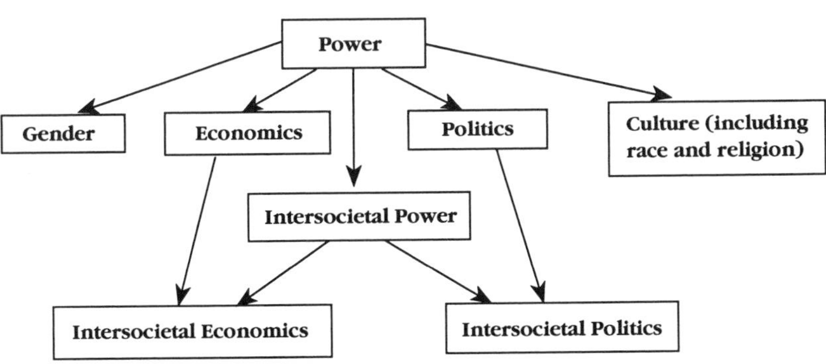

Figure 15.2

I will deal with gender and culture in the next chapter; the others are covered here.

POLITICAL POWER IN THE MODEL

Figure 15.3 Politics

Under political power, the ground quality is *political participation* (not to be confused with participation in the consciousness realm), meaning the participation of the people in the process of governance. This was certainly present in tribal societies and was largely lost by the Archaic. As *political structure* grew in order to coordinate the larger societies, participation was suppressed and vested power was kept in the hands of small groups, promoting *oppression*. I have discussed how the Modern era saw the beginnings of an integrating structure, representative *democracy*, which has given us some integration of political participation with political structure.

Since this is a realm in which there is already some integration, the next step will be an advancement of this integration, to incorporate more participation and power distribution and also to enhance the effectiveness of the social structure. This needs to happen through the improvement of our democratic process and the development of *cooperation*.

IMPROVING DEMOCRACY

The Influence of Wealth. The biggest problem with the prevailing form of government in the industrialized world, and particularly in the United States, is the extent to which wealth is used to influence the political process. Corporations have enormous power through campaign contributions and the accompanying lobbying. This radically distorts the political process and prevents it from either representing the will of the people or being in the best interests of society. There have been attempts to change this through various kinds of electoral reform, but it is very difficult because those in power are products of the current system and beholden to its wealth brokers. Fundamental change in this area can only happen when enough people recognize its importance.

We need a principle of the separation of politics from the influence of wealth, similar to our principle of the separation of church and state and our conflict of interest rules for politicians. Since there is so much more power inequity in the economic realm our only hope is to separate politics from this influence. Such a principle would outlaw any undue corporate influence and any kind of arrangement that gives more power to those with more money.

Participatory Democracy. Our American form of democracy could be much more participatory. We need political structures and cultural values that promote more active participation of all the people in the political process. (For further discussion, see Bradova 1993; Lappé and DuBois 1994.)

Decentralization. Democracy is also enhanced when political power is exercised at the lowest level possible. In other words, national governments shouldn't have power to control things that can be handled adequately at the state or local level. The only powers that should be national in scope are those that address problems that are national in scope. This follows the principle of federalism, which I discuss later at the global level.

The bioregional movement (Sale 1991) promotes a form of decentralization that follows ecological contours. It proposes that people learn to emotionally inhabit the bioregion in which they live, and that political divisions follow these natural geographic and ecological regions. This movement involves both the material and social realms. It promotes democracy, community, and ecological sensibility.

However, decentralization by itself is one-sided. Taken to an extreme, it would limit our mobility and therefore decrease international understanding and the appreciation of diversity. People must be both members of their bioregional communities and citizens of the world.

COOPERATION

Electoral Politics. A key component of stage 6 is the process of cooperative politics. One of the biggest drawbacks to our current form of government is its adversarial nature. For example, our elections are oriented toward winning and losing rather than toward picking the best leaders. This is evident from the emphasis in the media on a candidate's campaign strategy rather than on substantive issues. Even our legislative and judicial proceedings are seen primarily as battles with clear winners and losers. Often it seems that it is more important that the president win (or lose) his latest contest in Congress than that the most useful legislation be passed.

Most of the participants in the political process (both representatives and citizens) are primarily concerned with their own special interests rather than the good of the whole nation (let alone the whole earth). Even environmental organizations that often have the good of the whole in mind are seen as just another special interest. Disadvantaged groups fight for their fair share of the pie. Groups that currently enjoy advantages strive to keep them. Consequently our legislation is often reduced to the lowest common denominator through special deals and exceptions, through bargaining and lobbying, and it is very difficult to enact legislation with any vision or heart.

This is so deeply ingrained in our system that it is hard to imagine any other way. Envision what it would be like if our representatives really got together with the intent of coming up with the best program for improving things in this country rather than fighting for their constituencies and lobbying groups. Suppose they approached their political work with an open mind and a willingness to really listen to and learn from each other. Suppose that, when a bill was being debated in Congress, our representatives truly put their minds together in order to come up with the best legislation. Imagine that the citizens of the country were actively involved in the political process, both nationally and locally, and they also acted in this cooperative way. What a different way of doing politics! How much more effective this kind of governance would be. The resulting legislation would be better than any one party could do on their own. This difference is depicted graphically in figure 15.4.

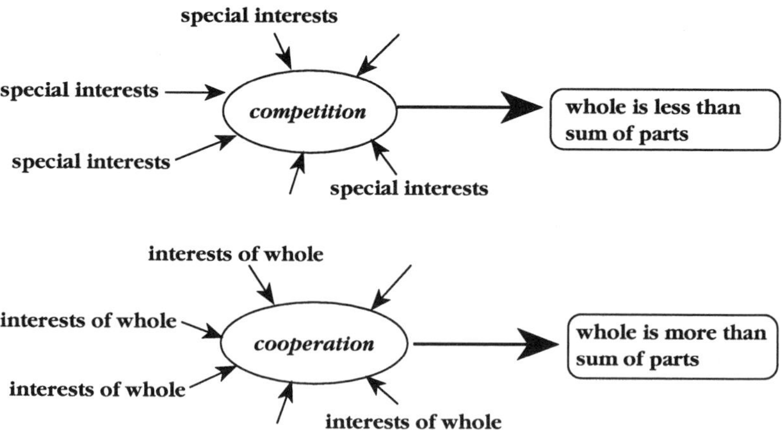

Figure 15.4

Law is another crucial area for the introduction of cooperation. Our current legal system is thoroughly adversarial, and this frequently results in excessive litigation, unnecessary anger (especially in divorce proceedings), exorbitant legal fees, and a general waste of energy which could be used more constructively. There is currently a movement within the profession to use mediation between contesting parties rather than litigation whenever possible. This is a promising sign for the future.

Social Change Politics. The principle of cooperation applies, not just to electoral politics, but to all types of political activity and social change work. In the past, activist groups have tended to do battle with corporations or government agencies in the courts or in the streets. It was always structured as a win/lose situation. "They" were the bad guys and "we" were the good guys. We were in a struggle to win. In progressive and leftist politics, this was so much the case that the word "struggle" was uniformly used to denote any political activity. If someone believed as "we" did, they were OK and should be enlisted in the fight. If someone didn't, either they were evil and should be defeated, or they were misguided and should be shown the light. This is a very easy and seductive way to approach social change, and I am sometimes unwittingly guilty of it myself. Social change agents must move beyond simplistic good/bad, left-right approaches to politics.

In standard social change work, for example, if an environmental group wanted to change the fact that corporations produce enormous waste, they would attack the corporation, through the media, through demonstrations, or through lawsuits. Until recently, they never thought to approach the corporation and suggest a joint venture where both sides might benefit. A few years ago, the Environmental Defense Fund did just that with MacDonalds, and persuaded them to institute a comprehensive waste reduction scheme which was quite successful. Now EDF has built on that by initiating a major program of testing and use of recycled paper by a group of major corporations, which has the potential to produce widespread corporate use of recycled products.

Too often social change work has been limited to protesting and fighting the worst abuses rather than having the vision and initiative to create healthy alternatives. Taking a combative stance has two striking disadvantages: (1) It pits people and organizations against us who could be working on our side, who might be open to doing things our way if approached intelligently and compassionately. (2) The best we can hope for is to stop something bad rather than create something good. This doesn't lead to basic change.

Fundamental change comes from a proactive stance—first trying out alternative ways of doing things, and then forging alliances to bring them to the mainstream. Let's keep in mind that most people (maybe all people) stand to benefit from the kind of changes that need to happen as society moves into the next era. This step in social evolution is not just for certain classes or groups. We can approach people with the aim of helping them to realize that fundamental change is in their best interest. If this effort fails and the world suffers ecological breakdown, everyone will suffer (though not equally). Many people in power do not realize this and may even attempt to profit from ecological problems, but if they can be helped to see that they and their children will suffer from the disaster that is coming, they may be amenable to change. We're all in it together, and a cooperative approach uses this fact.

Of course, there are situations where protest and struggle are appropriate. Sometimes the powers-that-be will not cooperate or even listen unless they are forced to by adversarial actions. In such cases, cooperation can easily turn into co-optation, accomplishing nothing. Cooperation is usually only possible between peers who are relatively equal in power. Sometimes confrontation and cooperation can be used together on the same issue, perhaps by different groups. The confrontation often needs to come first, and then when it has rallied the public or in other ways created a situation of power equity, cooperation can be most effective. Cooperation is not the only useful approach. There is a time to fight and a time to cooperate, and we must have the wisdom to know the difference.

The Model. Let's look at this from the point of view of our model. From the Archaic through the Medieval eras and into the Modern era, power distribution was suppressed, with resulting oppression. In this situation, cooperation would probably not have been the best strategy for social change. The establishment had all the power and therefore no interest in cooperating. Consequently the history of social change has largely been a history of rebellion and competition—competition to gain a relatively equal share of the power.

As I mentioned before, even revolt has not been enough in itself to produce an evolutionary advance in power distribution. Humanity needed an integrating structure (representative democracy) to code power distribution into social structure. Of course, we also needed the rebellion to force the oppressors to accept democracy. What we know about equalizing power comes out of these struggles, so naturally our first try at an integrating structure would reflect this. Therefore representative democracy is primarily an adversarial system. We now fight more often with votes than with guns, but we still fight. And this is natural and understandable given our history. It is the first step toward an integration of power distribution and social structure. Table 15.1 shows these steps in the evolution of political power.

Table 15.1 The Evolution of Political Power

Stage	Era	Political Power
1, 2	Paleolithic, Neolithic	Natural power distribution
3, 4	Archaic, Ancient, Medieval	Oppression
5	Modern	Adversarial democracy
6	Next	Cooperation

The Advantages of Cooperation. Now however, humanity is ready for the next step. Power in the industrialized countries is sufficiently equalized that in many cases cooperation will be effective. Furthermore, when it *is* effective, cooperation is much *more* effective than competition. A cooperative agreement spreads to other parties more easily because they see the possible advantages for themselves. It is more likely to be incorporated into mainstream institutions because the average person is less threatened. It is liable to have long-term beneficial effects because it grew out of proactive proposals rather than simply preventing something destructive. A cooperative arrangement is less likely to create enemies and engender a backlash.

The most advanced kind of cooperative politics recognizes that "we" don't have all the answers, that we can perhaps learn something from people who disagree with us. Using this approach, social change agents would attempt to find an answer through dialogue with others, rather than assuming that we had the right answer and must convince the others. This makes us much more effective at reaching people because we aren't condescending to them. Even more important, it recognizes reality. No one person or group or ideology has all the answers. We will do best if we all learn from each other. It takes a great deal of humility and confidence to follow this approach—humility to let go of the assumption that we're right and confidence to articulate our viewpoint anyway. For an excellent discussion of this topic, see the article "Transformational Politics" (Atlee 1991) and the entire *Thinkpeace* journal.

This approach is powerful for building coalitions because it naturally recognizes our commonalties with others. It also avoids the splintering that happens in groups and movements that believe they have the entire truth. Fran Peavey describes her experience with a cooperative approach in her book *Heart Politics* (1986).

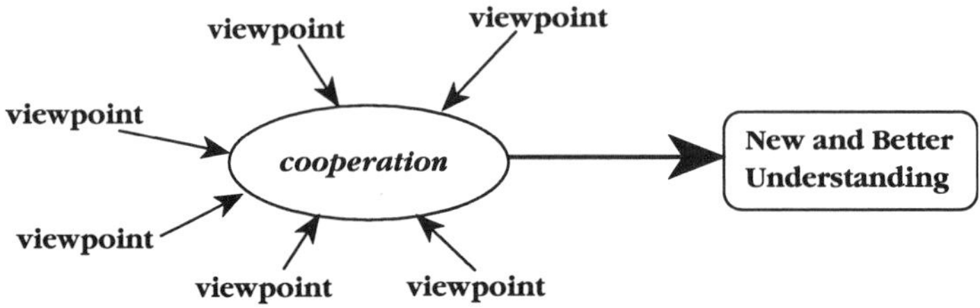

Figure 15.5

This cooperative approach is gaining ground today. It is the next step in the evolution of power. Remember that the emergent quality evolves by becoming more effective (as well as more pervasive). Cooperation represents the next step in two ways: (1) It enhances the ground quality, power distribution, and integrates it with social structure. (2) It makes the emergent quality, social structure, more effective. Thus cooperation is a higher level integration of the ground and emergent qualities, which can be called *synergy*. In general, a synergistic integration not only represents a way for the ground and emergent qualities to work together but to enhance each other. Cooperation not only improves power distribution, it also enhances the effectiveness of social structure.

Tom Atlee in "Collective Intelligence as an Approach to Transformative Social Change" sees the next step beyond equalizing power as *societal intelligence*. This means using a cooperative approach to decision making that involves all parties in a creative process to maximize the overall intelligence of the actions of the society, for the benefit of its citizens, the environment, and the world as a whole.

This book is specifically intended to foster cooperative politics. The model is based on the integration of emergent and ground qualities, showing that the ground quality (which is usually championed by social change agents) is not the only valuable quality. Looking at our predicament through the lens of history, it is apparent that those emergent qualities that are now causing trouble were once new and exciting evolutionary advances and are still a necessary part of any solution. I hope that this encourages a compassionate understanding and appreciation of all points of view.

A DEMOCRATIC ECONOMY

Economics is the next subrealm in our breakdown of the power realm:

Figure 15.6 Economics

Here the ground quality is a *caring economy.* Remember that the overall ground quality in the social realm is community, and part of the definition of a community is that it cares about the well-being of its members. A caring economy was enacted in the *simple societies* of stages 1 and 2 using reciprocity and redistribution. Today with such large, complex societies, these methods are not effective except in family and neighborhood settings. Without social and economic structure, the result is *anarchy,* a situation where there is not enough economic organization to coordinate the necessary economic functions for the society.

The emergent quality is *social structure,* as it is for the entire social realm. In stages 3 and 4, the emergence of states, empires, and feudalism moved the economic realm into a high degree of oppression. In stage 5, the Modern era, the growth of market economies promoted the growth of a substantial middle class which had a decent amount of economic power. This was the beginning of an integration of ground, and it also increased the effectiveness of the emergent quality, but it still left room for substantial *economic exploitation,* as we will see below. Table 15.2 depicts the evolution of these economic structures.

Table 15.2 The Evolution of Economic Power

Stage	Era	Economic Power
1	Paleolithic	Reciprocity
2	Neolithic	Redistribution
3, 4	Archaic, Ancient, Medieval	Feudalism
5	Modern	Market economy
6	Next	Democratic economy

The Market. The market is a very efficient and effective way of economic functioning for large social units. The failure of communist command economies leaves the market economy with no serious competitors. And rightfully so. The market economy has the important advantage that it functions through distributed decision making, where most important economic decisions are made through the accumulated actions of millions of actors, without there needing to be too much in the way of a centralized control structure. Society needs more social structures with this property.

However, despite being a step in the right direction, the market has serious drawbacks. Left to itself, the market tends toward economic exploitation, resulting in enormous imbalances in wealth. In addition, our form of capitalism allows corporations to function with little or no internal democracy. This leaves workers with only one option for dealing with exploitation—quitting the job—and with high unemployment this is not a viable option for many. Therefore the market system needs to be augmented with other structures that cultivate caring for the well being of all the people of the society. I am calling such a social structure a *democratic economy.* By this I mean a system where economic power is wielded by the people, distributed more equally, and used for the benefit of all the people.

Need for an Integrating Structure. Political democracy, even participatory and cooperative, can't go far enough to achieve power distribution, especially today when economic power has such influence in the world. We need a new integrating structure, which I am calling a democratic economy, which will be for the next era what representative political democracy was for the Modern era. This would allow us to integrate power distribution with social structure in the economic realm.

Some social critics see the situation primarily in moral terms—the greed and power hunger of corporate executives, or the evil machinations of the ruling class. While there is truth in these views, I think the primary problem is that the economic system itself is flawed as it now stands. Other critics feel that the market is so intrinsically oppressive that an altogether new economic structure must be found. I don't believe this. I think that the market only needs to be augmented to serve our purposes. As efficient as the market is in making certain economic decisions, it is not a structure that naturally leads to power distribution.

To foster positive social change, we need more than moral exhortation or rebellion. We need to devise a social structure that will truly promote economic democracy, and we need an ideological framework for it that makes sense to the average person. In my earlier discussion, I mentioned that an integrating structure needs a strong ideological explanation in order for it to be adopted. Communism not only didn't work as an integrating structure, it also didn't work in the United States as an ideology because it didn't properly address the issue of economic freedom. As society move into the next era, we need an integrating structure for economic democracy that preserves adequate economic freedom, and an ideology that explains its worth without violating important existing social values.

I don't pretend to have such a structure worked out. That is beyond the scope of this book. The European experiment with social democracy, especially in Sweden, has been an attempt to promote a democratic economy and therefore has important lessons to teach us (Milner 1989). There are currently a number of alternative thinkers who are exploring new economic structures (Cobb 1990; Daly and Cobb 1989; Hawken 1993). James Robertson (1990) has sketched an excellent comprehensive proposal for a new economic system, which emphasizes empowering people and communities and includes ground-breaking new ways of thinking about money. I believe that a critical endeavor for the near future would be a highly visible proposal for a democratic and ecological economy that could ignite people's excitement.

Workplace Democracy. Some management consultants are beginning to understand the importance of allowing workers flexibility, variety, responsibility, initiative, and creativity in their jobs. There is a current trend toward self-managed work teams and a realization that large, hierarchical organizations are not flexible and innovative enough to prosper in today's economy. A more fundamentally important idea is *cooperative ownership*, where the employees of a corporation own and control it, thus truly promoting workplace democracy (Morrison 1991). This could be encouraged within our current market structure by providing credit for starting cooperative businesses and training people in the skills necessary to run them successfully.

Political Guardianship of the Economy. Any economy that is truly democratic must be under democratic political guardianship. This doesn't mean that it should be a bureaucratic command economy such as that of the communist countries. It means that the rules of the market should be under political control. The market is like a game with certain rules, where each player strives to maximize the number of points so as to win. If everyone strives to win, then the market performs certain economic functions efficiently.

The government shouldn't try to take over this function. However, the government must set the rules of the game so that it not only maximizes efficiency but also power distribution, ecological health, and perhaps other criteria that citizens value. The government can constrain the game so that the players (corporations, consumers), in maximizing their bottom lines, naturally make decisions that also engender equality, cooperation, etc. This is illustrated in figure 15.7. For example, governmental support for cooperatively owned businesses would naturally tend to lead toward more equality of income and power. (See "An Ecological Economy" in chapter 17 for further examples.)

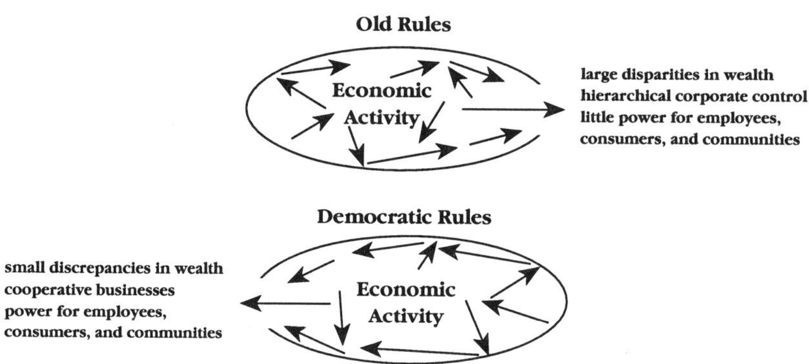

Figure 15.7

Individual corporations can only go so far in this direction on their own without being disadvantaged in the competition for profits. That's why guardianship is necessary. This only works, of course, if the government is truly democratic and reasonably decentralized. Otherwise, instead of being constrained for the benefit of society as a whole, the game becomes tilted to the advantage of certain players.

Though it's not well understood these days, we citizens have the right to do this. Paul Hawken explains: "Corporations are chartered by, and exist at the behest of, citizens. Incorporation is not a right but a privilege granted by the state that includes certain considerations such as limited liability. Corporations are supposed to be under our ultimate authority, not the other way around" (Hawken 1993).

Of course, steps toward guardianship have been taken in the past with legislation supporting labor unions, worker safety rules, social security, and so on. However, too much of this was done in a top-down bureaucratic way and was therefore expensive and somewhat ineffective.

In experimenting with a democratic economy, we need to find methods that don't rely so heavily on coercion from the top.

The Myth of the Free Market. The idea of the wonderful operation of the perfectly free market is a myth. Market economies depend on certain restrictions and conventions of trust and reliability to work at all. For example, without any control, a market economy tends toward monopoly and price gouging, at which point it is no longer free. In addition, the successful operation of the market depends on certain moral qualities such as honesty, freedom, initiative, and lack of corruption, which must either come from the community or be enforced by the government (Daly and Cobb 1989, 49–51). For example, our Wall Street financial system could not work without clearly enforced restrictions on stock trading based on inside information.

Our markets have always been constrained politically in order for them to work at all. They need to be guided even more to foster economic democracy and ecological health. The government needs to be the rule maker and referee of the game, not the coach or quarterback. These roles rightly belong to the corporations. The referee sets and enforces the rules, but within those rules, the market should remain free.

A danger is that the teams try to bribe the referees to set the rules in their favor. This happens far too often through campaign contributions and lobbying from corporations. Society must reduce or eliminate this through the principle of separating the political from the influence of wealth.

An even greater danger is that the largest corporations have become multinational. Their influence in the international arena has advanced rapidly and political control has not kept up. The multinationals, through their size and ability to relocate from one country to another, have kept themselves too free from political restraint. I will continue this discussion under the topic of global governance below.

Internal Markets. One of the hottest new ideas in management is that of handling much of the decision making internal to a corporation through market mechanisms (Halal, Geranmayeh et al. 1993). Managers are realizing that for companies to be flexible and innovative enough to compete in today's fast-paced global marketplace, they must replace the usual top-down, bureaucratic control with different mechanisms that encourage more initiative, creativity, and efficiency.

> While Russia privatizes its great state enterprises so as to recapture the dynamism of the marketplace, U.S. enterprises are abandoning their own central-planning apparatus in favor of internal markets. In

> fact, one of the most striking trends of the past decade is the appearance of internal entrepreneurs . . . internal customers, and other internal equivalents of the external marketplace.
>
> The ideal situation is to treat each unit as a small, separate company, free to manage its own affairs, while integrated into the parent corporation. All units need the freedom to conduct business transactions both inside and outside the firm. Without that freedom, managers are subject to the monopoly and bureaucracy of their organization, roughly the same forces that led the Soviets to over-control their economy. (Halal 1994)

Of course, the internal units must be held accountable to the overall goals of the corporation and controlled in various other ways to make this work.

This new approach has the potential to make businesses more internally democratic as well as effective.

> Internal markets will greatly change the role of workers. It makes sense, in hierarchical systems, to treat people as employees with only limited freedom of action and rigidly defined responsibilities. But an internal market system requires workers to [be] . . . given an opportunity to use their talents, with all the freedom, self-control, risks, and rewards associated with being an entrepreneur. (Halal 1994)

This approach can also be applied to government, education and other organizations, perhaps making them much more democratic, responsive, and cost-efficient than currently. However, what is most exciting to me is the parallel between internal and external markets. Just as internal markets are effective only if controlled from above by corporate leaders, external markets are only truly effective if controlled from above by a democratic government, as I discussed previously. Instead of autocratic corporations operating in an uncontrolled marketplace, the world needs levels of market behavior and levels of control, internal and external to companies, internal and external to nations. This combined with cooperative, participatory democracy could perhaps truly provide us with a governance system appropriate to the complexities of the planet in the twenty-first century.

GLOBAL GOVERNANCE

I will go into some detail in my discussion of global governance and the global economy, partly because the subrealm of intersocietal power is important in its own right, and partly because it provides a good illustration of how to use the model to understand current questions. Let's look at the intersocietal area.

Figure 15.8 Intersocietal Power

One aspect of the social evolutionary trend towards greater social structure has been the movement toward greater *intersocietal structure*—necessitated by increasing trade, travel, war, and political conquest or merger. In recent times this has meant a trend toward *global* structure. In this area, as mentioned, economics has moved faster than politics, and the world already has a global economy before we are ready for a global system of governance.

The ground quality is *societal autonomy*, which was almost absolute in stage 1 since societies (bands and tribes) had little contact with each other. As societies have become more connected, societal autonomy has lost ground, through conquest, leading to *intersocietal oppression*. However, the struggle for autonomy is not dead, as evidenced by liberation and secession movements around the world.

The Need for Global Governance. Stage 6 needs to continue and complete the trend toward global structure and governance, especially politically. The emergent quality of intersocietal structure needs to advance further. This has two crucial advantages. The first is that a true system of global governance will end war. Once there is a global governing institution that is empowered to decide disputes between nations and has the military power to back up its decisions, war won't be possible. Not only would this be a wonderful humanitarian advance, it would also end the selection for military power. No longer would societies need to be warlike or militarily strong to survive. It could allow societies of a different nature to grow and develop.

The second advantage is that it would give us a better chance to guide the world economy and the multinational corporations. As I mentioned, political guardianship of the economic system is essential for a democratic economy, and right now the only global institutions with significant economic power are the World Bank, the International Monetary Fund, and similar institutions that are not democratically elected. These institutions are completely controlled by the industrialized nations and their multinational corporations. A democratic world governing body would have a better chance of guiding the world economy in a way that would be in the interests of the people of the world as a whole.

Global Federalism. Society needs an integrating structure for world governance, which would integrate societal autonomy and global structure, providing the global coordination we need while respecting as much as possible the autonomy of specific societies. Such a system of world governance would need to be *federal* in nature, meaning that the individual nations would only delegate those powers to the global government that need to be exercised at a global level. These should eventually include military might, decisions that affect the global commons and impact the environment in a global way, and setting the rules of the global market economy. The rest of the power that currently resides with national governments could probably remain with them. It is especially important that nations have the power to retain their own cultures and traditions, as long as they aren't unduly oppressive. Moreover, since some nations are made up of a number of different cultures, perhaps these powers should even devolve to a lower level. The principle of federalism states that political power should reside at the lowest level where it still can be effective.

At the moment Europe is groping with difficulty toward such a federal structure. At the global level, the United Nations still has relatively little power, but it is now becoming apparent that it needs more, especially in dealing with increasingly widespread violence and genocide. Nations are very reluctant to give up any of their sovereignty, but global governance is the direction of social evolution, even if it takes another hundred years.

This is not an all or nothing situation. Each time the United Nations is strengthened in some way or made more democratic, it is a step in the right direction. Society will have to move toward a world government in stages. It may even be good for this to happen gradually, because it would be wise to make sure that any world government is truly democratic. We don't want to take a chance on political oppression at the global level. However, we must strive for political unification of this nature because the much greater danger is economic oppression at the world level. This is already happening to some extent, as I discussed in chapter 12.

THE GLOBAL ECONOMY

Let's now take a look at what will be required to achieve a democratic economy at the global level. Figure 15.9 shows the complementary qualities in this subrealm.

Figure 15.9 Intersocietal Economics

The Disadvantages of Free Trade. Right now most economic power is national or international in scope. Some economic control is still retained locally, but that is changing. Local and even national economics are losing ground in the push for *intersocietal trade* with few restrictions, called "free trade." More and more economic power is now exercised internationally. Let's consider what might be best here. The current wisdom is that virtually all political power should stay with the nations, while most economic transactions should be globalized. This is a potential recipe for disaster.

Through *economic colonialism,* many preindustrialized nations were forced away from subsistence agriculture and into export crops. This was a move away from local toward global economics. It removed their power to sustain themselves in their own way and made them dependent on the global market, where they have no credit, expertise, high technology, or modern business savvy. They were forced into a game they were bound to lose.

Then they were encouraged to take the path of "economic development," to become like the industrialized countries. However, this hasn't been working for most of them, and environmental limits make it impossible for very many of them to become industrialized. Global economics, known as "free trade," though theoretically free and fair, is far from it. Those who have the current power can use this system to become more powerful, and those who don't are left in the dust, worse off than before. Furthermore, free trade isn't really free for all parties, because capital and resources can move to find their best advantage, but labor can't, so workers can easily be exploited.

Free trade is touted in the name of economic efficiency. There would be no tariffs or trade barriers. Businesses would move to those locations that are most advantageous to them. Every locale would specialize in producing a specific item for global trade because it would be able to do that most efficiently. In many ways free trade is a good idea. The world doesn't need massive protectionism for the sole purpose of propping up inefficient local industries, and we don't want trade barriers to get in the way of international communication and understanding.

It is probably also true that free trade would increase efficiency and beef up the global economy, but let's ask what the cost would be. Unless it is guided politically, free trade works against economic democracy. Corporations can relocate to those nations or cities that offer the cheapest labor, the least taxes, and the most lax environmental controls and worker safety standards. Corporations can get nations or cities to bid against each other to offer the best climate to attract business. This is a guarantee that corporations will not be controlled by the people of any nation.

The Fallacy of Economic Growth. Since free trade is promoted primarily as a way of achieving economic growth, it is important to look carefully at this issue. The accepted point of view in the U.S. government, among leaders of both parties, is that we must have continued economic growth to have a healthy economy, especially to avoid excessive unemployment.

However, this thinking is based on a fundamental fallacy. The reason we have needed constant economic growth for the last few decades is that we have been losing large numbers of jobs to automation, and millions of women have been entering the job market for the first time. This means that the United States has had fewer and fewer jobs for more and more workers. The only way we have kept up with this situation is through high levels of economic growth. By now the majority of women have already entered the workforce, so this part of the problem is abating, but automation will continue to decrease the number of available jobs for the foreseeable future. This problem is dealt with in Jeremy Rifkin's *The End of Work* (1994).

If we can find a way to handle this difficulty, we may not need continued economic growth. One suggestion for handling the unemployment problem is to adjust the work week downward to fit the amount of available work as automation progresses. This would reduce or eliminate unemployment and provide the economy with an additional boost from the extra workers who would have income to spend.

An even bigger fallacy is the idea that our world economy can grow indefinitely on a finite planet. Economic growth consumes resources and produces waste. We have reached the limits of what the biosphere can handle. For ecological reasons we *must* have a steady-state economy that can be healthy without growing (Daly 1988).

> A condition of nongrowth can come about in two ways: as the failure of a growth economy, or as the success of a steady-state economy. . . . It is precisely to avoid the suffering of a failed growth economy (we know growth cannot continue) that we advocate a steady state-economy. (Daly 1977, 126)

I'm not suggesting that creating a steady-state economy will be easy, just necessary. Innovative thinking is needed about how to structure the economy to achieve this.

Thus the primary goals for our economy can't be efficiency and growth. We can't tolerate much more growth, and though efficiency is important, our current economic system handles it adequately. What it doesn't handle adequately are power distribution and sustainability. This is where society must put its efforts. We need an economic system that places economic power in the hands of the greatest number of people and which controls the tendency of an economic system to destroy the natural environment.

Self-Reliance. *Self-reliance* is crucial to an economic system that is democratic. This means that each locale or region or nation would conduct a reasonable amount of its economic business within itself. Food would be grown locally as much as the climate and growing conditions permit. People would patronize locally owned businesses, except when they needed something which couldn't be reasonably found at home. For example, there is no reason why consumer electronics should be assembled in Taiwan and shipped to the United States. Trade outside a region should be used mainly for those items that cannot be properly produced or extracted within it. The current system and a self-reliant one are contrasted in figure 15.10.

This helps to ensure that the region (or city or nation) is strong economically and not unduly dependent on the swings and vagaries of foreign markets. To understand this, let's look at the opposite extreme. Suppose a region decided to specialize in producing just one thing—bananas or consumer electronics—because they could do it most efficiently and therefore would do well in the global economy. Then suppose someone else manages to produce it more cheaply. The whole region would be thrown into economic jeopardy, just because of a development on the other side of the world. If, instead, a region is largely self-sufficient, then it can be economically strong and in charge of its own fate.

Self-reliance also means that energy will not be squandered on unnecessary transportation costs. It means that a region cannot be exploited economically by foreign powers. Exploitation can happen only when a region is dependent on the world economy, and a self-reliant region participates in the world economy only as much as it chooses. Therefore the people of the region retain their economic power.

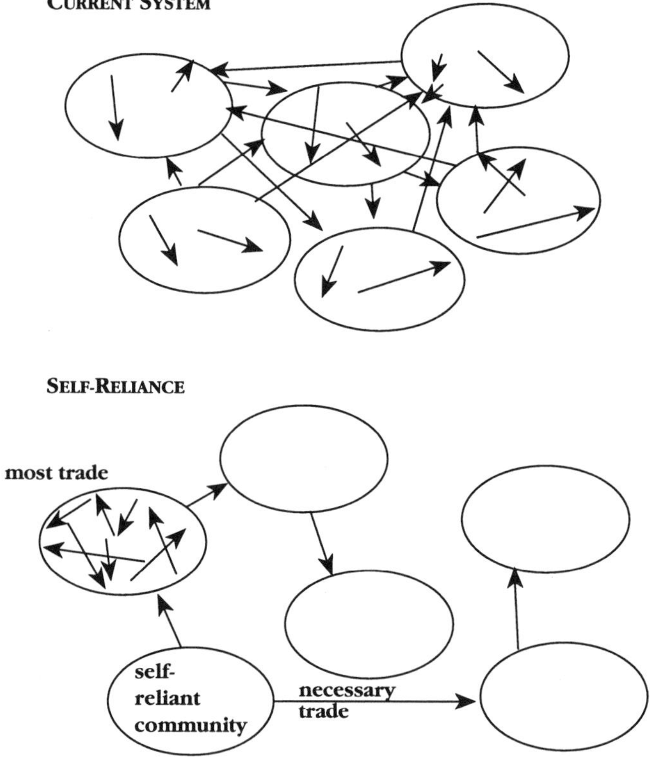

Figure 15.10

Self-reliance goes hand in hand with community. It depends on the organic wholeness of each community and bioregion, which is lost if there is too much intersocietal trade. The more local economic interaction the more it helps to build community within the region (town, city, nation). The more there is a sense of caring and shared tradition in an area, the easier it is to promote local economic transactions. For an excellent discussion of free trade and its relationship to community I recommend *For the Common Good* (Daly and Cobb 1989). This book describes an economics that is truly oriented toward community and ecological health.

Subsidiarity. There is an important principle that helps to integrate self-reliance with intersocietal trade: *Subsidiarity* means that economic decisions are made as locally as possible and otherwise at the largest scope necessary for them to work. (Korten 1993; Morris 1993) For example, global warming and the depletion of the ozone layer are clearly global issues. If these are dealt with through such measures as a carbon tax or a ban on CFCs, this should be done at the global level.

If the scope of acid rain damage is a single continent, such as North America, then solutions should be implemented at that level. It would be unduly oppressive for laws designed to protect against acid rain to be made at the global level. It is not the business of Europe how North America solves its acid rain problem. However, this problem can't be solved at the national level if acid rain from American factories is destroying lakes and forests in Canada. It must be done at the level of the North American continent. Water pollution, in most cases, can be handled at a regional or local level, so there may be no need for national solutions to this problem.

No Limits on Guardianship. A second aspect of subsidiarity is that decisions by larger political entities should be allowed to *specify* economic guardianship, not *limit* it. For example, if a world decision is made to set certain standards (for levels of contaminants in food or worker safety precautions or carbon dioxide emissions), these should be minimal standards that each nation must comply with. However, each nation should have the right to set tighter standards if it chooses, because their situation seems to warrant it. The world governing body should not have the right to set a maximal standard that no country may exceed. In other words the world shouldn't have the right to *limit* the guardianship that any country is allowed to exercise on its own economy. The world should have the right to exercise political restraint over those things that are world issues, but it shouldn't limit any additional restraint that nations desire.

Unfortunately the latest GATT free trade agreement does exactly that. A committee of GATT can overthrow laws of their constituent countries if they consider them to be in violation of free trade. So if a country wants to protect itself through tight environmental laws and levy tariffs on imports that don't meet its standards, GATT could overthrow such laws in the name of free trade, thereby undermining a democratic and ecological economy and violating the principle of subsidiarity.

The Need for Integration. For social evolution to advance, society needs an integration of the ground and emergent qualities, and therefore an integrating structure to accomplish this. This applies to all the realms, but I examine it in detail for the subrealm of intersocietal economics because it offers a good illustration of the principle.

Self-reliance is the ground quality. It was our starting point for social evolution. *Intersocietal trade*, or free trade, is the emergent quality. In the current debate, there is a well-founded fear that free trade agreements are taking us further away from a democratic economy. As social change agents, what shall we do? If we fight against free trade and take the principle of local self-reliance to an extreme, this is a form of reverse splitting, where we simple-mindedly denigrate the emergent quality. This would mean a step backwards economically, a return to *protectionism*.

It could also mean serious economic inefficiency. If local industry is protected from having enough competition to ensure that it does its job well, it can end up being lazy, uncaring, and wasteful. Consider the condition of the American auto makers before Japanese cars came on the scene. Self-reliance shouldn't be taken to the point where it eliminates necessary competition. In addition, the trend in social evolution is toward greater world interconnection. We would be foolish to simply fight it. Clearly we need some protection of local businesses to promote self-reliance, but we also need some intersocietal trade.

Fair Trade. One solution would be to strive to have trade agreements written so that the degree of environmental, community, and worker protection that we have in the United States is required for our trading partners. Not only would this prevent the worst abuses of free trade, it might even serve to spread ecological and democratic practices to other nations. This type of principle has been used in the past within the United States federal structure. For example, federal civil rights laws have been used to encourage racial equality in those states that would not have chosen it on their own.

With an integrated approach, local self-reliance would still be important, the principle of subsidiarity would be maintained, and free trade, properly done, could also be embraced. This combination is being called *fair trade*. This gives us a healthy integration of the ground and emergent qualities and a good shot at a truly democratic economy.

This is an example of what is needed in all realms—a conscious choice on society's part to create an integrating structure that is in its best interests. The economic changes proposed here would make the economy not only more democratic, but also more ecologically sound. In a later chapter, I will suggest other economic changes that are needed for ecological sustainability.

A VISION

Vision and Life Purpose. One of my strongest motivations for working on social change is my vision of a healthy society. Though I am interested in the specifics, even more important is my hope that it is possible for us to live together in ways that connect us with each other and the earth, and give each person a chance to find joy and fulfillment. I hold this in my heart as a vision for our future that imbues my life with a sense of deeper purpose.

In each "Solutions" chapter, I share some of my vision of a healthy society. As you read, think about your visions and hopes for the future of our world. Let yourself imagine what it would be like to live in a healthy society. Open your heart to this possibility.

A Vision for the Power Realm. What would it be like to live in a truly democratic world? I see a political system that is more participatory, more cooperative, and removed from the influence of wealth. There is greater involvement of citizens' groups, nongovernmental organizations, small study circles, and activists. These groups don't just protest against wrongs, but actually provide some of the governance of society. The government puts constraints on the market in such a way as to foster self-reliance, cooperative ownership, and other democratic practices.

I see economies that are largely built around cooperatively owned businesses, so that everyone has an opportunity to work in an egalitarian atmosphere with initiative and responsibility. I see a reduced work week creating increased job opportunities and greater power for workers (not to mention greater leisure), allowing almost everyone to have a chance to work and enjoy their share of the wealth.

I see a federal structure where groups of self-reliant communities inhabit bioregions, where bioregions are grouped together into nations, and where there is a global governing body. In this structure political and economic power resides at the smallest level possible, and everyone also has a global outlook and cares about the interests of the whole world.

I see economic self-reliance developing in the nations and communities of what is now called the Third World. I see those peoples regaining the right to grow their own food and care for themselves, and learning how to do this with technology that is appropriate to their needs.

Global trade agreements are forged which spread the best of our democratic and ecological economic practices throughout the world. Table 15.3 summarizes these recommendations. For each realm, I have divided the solutions into those that involve an integration of the ground and emergent qualities, and those that involve advancing the emergent quality or the integration.

Table 15.3 Political and Economic Solutions

Realm	**Integration**	**Advancing Emergent or Integrated**
Politics	Democracy	Cooperation
Economics	Democratic economy	
Intersocietal Politics	Federalism	World governance
Intersocietal Economics	Fair trade, subsidiarity, guardianship of economy	World economy

Note: There is no entry under "Advancing Emergent or Integrated" in the economics realm because the only recommendations I made in economics were for integration.

XVI

CULTURE AND GENDER

CULTURAL OPPRESSION AND LIBERATION

Oppression has frequently been based on differences in culture—in ethnic group, race, and/or religion—with a dominant cultural group oppressing one or more other groups. When each cultural group is also a different society, this amounts to intersocietal oppression, which has been covered in an earlier chapter. Here I want to analyze cultural oppression within a society. This means looking at the power issues confronting a society that is made up of more than one culture. This can be viewed as a subrealm of power. In the United States today, this is particularly apparent in difficulties in race relations.

Figure 16.1 Culture

The ground quality is *liberation*, which means that a each cultural group in a society is able to maintain their cultural integrity and power. The organic wholeness of their community is maintained. They can stay intact as a group and continue to practice and value their culture. In addition, they are able to be powerful as a group and as individuals. The larger society doesn't deny them their share of influence because of membership in their cultural group. Early in social evolution, liberation was widespread because there were virtually no societies containing more than one culture. Each tribe consisted of a single culture and there was little contact between different tribes.

The emergent quality is *cultural integration*, which means the degree to which the various cultures in a given society share values and ways of living. This means that a society consisting of many cultures nevertheless contains an underlying set of cultural values common to all its people. This is important for its people to work together and get along. During the span of social evolution, through immigration and conquest, societies have grown to consist of more and more widely differing cultural groups, increasingly in contact with each other. Therefore they have been forced to find some minimum underlying basis of cultural agreement, partly through cross-assimilation, but more frequently by one culture coming to dominate the society. Either way, this has resulted in increasing cultural integration

As cultural integration has grown, liberation has often been suppressed, and the result has been cultural oppression or homogenization. With *cultural oppression*, the members of one cultural group are oppressed by the members of the dominant cultural group within the society, as with blacks being oppressed by whites in the United States. This can be institutionalized, as with slavery or segregation, or it can happen more subtly despite official efforts by the state to eradicate it, as with current day prejudice against blacks. With *cultural homogenization*, members of a cultural group are assimilated into the larger society in such a way that they gradually lose their original culture and adopt the ways of the group in power. In this situation they may not be oppressed as individuals, but the richness of their culture is lost. This can be fostered by cultural oppression, where people often want to assimilate in order to escape prejudice and disadvantage, and it can also happen because of people's natural tendency to try to fit in to a country they have immigrated to.

In the opposite situation, liberation without cultural integration results in *parochialism*, where each culture considers itself superior to all others. This was the original situation in stage 1, when each tribe thought that it knew the only way to live and to understand reality. Today parochialism often promotes cultural conflict and violence. Parochialism can take the form of reverse racism or other kinds of reverse splitting, where the oppressed group promotes the idea that they are actually superior to the oppressing group. This is often a necessary temporary step toward liberation, but ultimately it must be transcended in a larger understanding of pluralism. Liberation without cultural integration can sometimes take the form of *separatism*, where an oppressed group strives to protect itself by separating completely from the group in power, sometimes even forming its own society.

Integration. In the political and economic realms I discussed *social* integrating structures—economic systems, methods of governance, principles to guide societal institutions. In this subrealm society needs a *cultural* integrating structure consisting of cultural values and ways of living. Ideally this would foster a society that would consist of many cultural groups, each of which is not only tolerated but valued by the others. This is called *cultural pluralism.* In this situation, not only are homogenization and oppression eliminated, but the society gains from the richness and interplay of the various ways of living and seeing reality.

Cultural pluralism will be more likely if the society maintains some cultural integration—a minimal underlying set of values that almost everyone subscribes to (Kidder 1994). A society can afford to tolerate diversity if it is held together by some shared values that transcend the diversity. Without this shared cultural base, pluralism would tend to fragment a society and therefore could not be tolerated.

Advance. In addition to the integration of pluralism, there is an importance emergent advance that is happening as we move into stage 6. This is the development of *cultural freedom,* where people are free to choose or create their own traditions. This is an advance brought on by the emergent qualities of social structure and individuality. People can remain with their heritage, or choose to adopt a different culture, or create their own unique life style and values by combining and synthesizing elements of existing traditions. Sometimes a group of people even create a new culture gradually through this process.

Not all cultures are equally good for their members or society. For example, some are more oppressive, constricting, and narrow, and others are more egalitarian, free, and expansive. In a pluralistic society, I would hope that the underlying shared values would be healthy enough to weigh against the influence of any destructive subcultures. In a society with cultural freedom, people will tend over time to gravitate toward more positive cultures, and therefore will incorporate those values into the shared set.

Historical Trajectory. This subrealm has followed much the same historical trajectory as the power realm in general. It reached a height of dissociation during stages 3 and 4, when there was widespread oppression based on cultural differences. During stage 5 the ground quality, liberation, has regained some of its strength with the elimination of slavery, an increased concern for human rights, the gradual extension of the vote to various oppressed groups, and worldwide condemnation of such things as genocide and apartheid. Of course, cultural oppression is still widespread, but society has made some steps in the right direction.

This process has been aided by the growth and popularity of democracy and by the ascendance of reflexive consciousness. I discussed previously how reflexive consciousness means emergence from being embedded in family, nature, tradition, and so on. As people have been increasingly exposed to the viewpoints of other cultural groups and reflexive consciousness has grown, we have emerged from being embedded in our cultures of birth. We can now see that our heritage was just one option among many, rather than the truth. Since no culture, race, or religion can legitimately claim superiority, the growth of clearer vision through reflexive consciousness has promoted cultural pluralism.

Constructivism. Even the average person has begun to understand the ideas of culture and world view, and to realize that there are many stories about life and reality and many ways of living. We see that reality is something we construct with our consciousness rather than a given. This is called *constructivism* (Anderson 1990), and it has greatly improved our chances for advancing to a world of cultural pluralism and freedom in stage 6.

Our current transitional time has seen a wide variety of liberation movements in the United States, starting with blacks and then encompassing women and spreading to gays and other groups. These are part of the larger historical movement in which the ground quality (liberation) is returning and being integrated with the emergent quality (cultural integration).

Global Homogenization. Intersocietal connection is still increasing; international travel, trade, communication and coordination are all on the rise. There is a tendency for the dominant culture of any society to take over and for other traditions to be assimilated so thoroughly that their uniqueness and special qualities are lost. Today there is a tendency for the dominant global culture, which is that of the Western industrialized democracies, to take over the world at the expense of other ways of living. This tendency toward homogenization is a greater tragedy than one might at first think. Not only does it mean a loss of cultural diversity and vitality, but also it frequently means a loss of those values and customs that might be most helpful in advancing into stage 6. Oppressed cultures often hold the suppressed ground qualities that must now be integrated. They must be preserved so that their people can aid the world in the current transition. I discuss this further in a later chapter.

It seems that because of constructivism and the strength of the liberation movements, the increase in global interconnection in some cases may actually encourage pluralism as well as cultural integration. The more contact people of different cultures have with each other on relatively equal footing, the better is the chance of their appreciating the validity of each other's cultures. In addition, the most socially advanced members of the industrialized nations are realizing the limitations and potential destructiveness of an exclusive reliance on their own culture, and therefore some of them have reached out to study other traditions to enrich themselves and their societies. Thus there are tendencies toward both pluralism and homogenization.

Valuing People and Cultures. A crucial factor in these developments is how much a given heritage is valued, both by its own people and by people of other traditions, especially the dominant culture. The historical tendency has been for the dominant tradition to be valued above all others, not only by its members but by members of oppressed cultures as well. This helps to support the oppression. There are exceptions to this, of course. For example, the Jewish people have survived so long as an oppressed group because they have valued their own culture highly. When a culture is moving toward liberation, it is very helpful for its members to value it. Gay pride and "Black is beautiful" are just two examples of this valuing process. Once an oppressed culture is openly valued by its own members, it is more likely to be valued by the society at large.

Notice that there is a difference between valuing the people of a culture and valuing the culture. Both are important aspects of a healthy society, but they have different impacts. Stage 4 began the process of valuing everyone regardless of culture; the universal religions preached this and were open to all people. This helped to diminish cultural oppression. This ethic has continued growing during stage 5 and is now being extended to a valuing of animals and all the natural world. This is a consequence of the growth of reflexive consciousness and particularly principled morals; it is sorely needed to help us resolve the ecological crisis.

However, if this is not accompanied by a valuing of each culture, it still leaves open the possibility of cultural homogenization. It allows the possibility that the stance of the group in power might be, "All people are OK, as long as they adopt my religion (lifestyle, ideology, etc.)." A healthy society must value not only all its people but also each of its cultures; this leads to true pluralism.

This is a difficult proposition, because not all cultures are equally healthy. In our concern for societal health, we need to be able to criticize those aspects of a culture that are not beneficial for its people and the world while recognizing its good points as well. This is tricky, because we may be biased in making this evaluation. Nevertheless we can't retreat from this task. We must strive to be aware of our prejudices while retaining the right to criticize.

I have not mentioned oppression based on class in this chapter. Class oppression is a stratification in a society based on factors other than race, religion, ethnic group, and so on. A power split develops within a single culture. Once this becomes entrenched, then the upper and lower classes may develop different cultures, but the power imbalance is not based on culture. Class oppression therefore falls under the general realm of power rather than under this subrealm.

GENDER

Oppression based on gender is similar to that for culture, with one prominent difference. The genders were never separate historically as cultures were, and therefore the emergent quality isn't cultural interconnection or its gender equivalent. Instead it is *social structure*, the general emergent quality for the power realm.

Figure 16.2 Gender

The ground quality, *liberation*, refers to liberation of women. This was fairly strong in some stage 1 and 2 societies and women generally were not greatly oppressed in the early stages of social evolution, though gender liberation was not as widespread as other ground qualities. The liberation of women was suppressed with the growth of *social structure*, especially in the Archaic era, resulting in *sexism*, the oppression of women. In the Modern era, with the rise of feminism, liberation is returning. Women have begun to value themselves as women and to demand equal power in society, both crucial components of liberation.

Reverse Sexism. However, as frequently happens, the ground quality is returning in a way that is not always integrated with the emergent quality. So some women's groups are promoting the view that women are better than men, a form of reverse splitting known as *reverse sexism*. They see the destructiveness that is happening in the world today, mostly caused by men and by masculine values. They understand that a macho attitude often underlies destructive wars. Our industrialized societies are plagued with hyperrationality and objectification, lack of relatedness to others and the earth, and many women associate these with masculinity. They realize that most violence is perpetrated by men, and that men are primarily responsible for steering the world toward disaster. Therefore they believe that there is something wrong with masculinity and that femininity is superior.

This is an understandable conclusion, but it is based on a fallacy. The problems in the world today are caused by a distortion of masculinity, not a true masculinity. This distortion is a result of the suppression of femininity and other ground qualities, not by intrinsic problems with masculinity. True masculinity can be powerful but not destructive, forceful but not intrusive. It can be rational but not detached, organized but not alienated. Just as the emergent qualities are not destructive in themselves, only when they are dissociated from the ground qualities, masculinity is not bad in itself, only when it is dissociated from femininity. What the world needs is a true masculinity integrated with a true femininity.

In saying this I am not claiming to know exactly what true masculinity (or true femininity) is, but I have hints of it, from my own inner work and from the men's movement. For example, Robert Bly (1990) has popularized the concept of the "deep masculine," which refers to the archetypal masculine energy deep in the male psyche.

Integration. The obvious stage 6 cultural integrating structure is as follows: Women must gain equal power with men in all aspects of life, resulting in *gender equality.* This means both institutional and legal equality of opportunity, but also equality in terms of cultural values and psychology. Both men and women would value women as highly as men and grant them the same freedom that men have in terms of power over their lives. However, this doesn't mean that women would become like men or that gender differences would disappear. Each gender must be valued for its own unique qualities.

Advance. In addition, as the emergent quality is advancing, women and men are becoming liberated from gender role stereotypes. This will result in *gender role freedom,* the freedom for each person to define for themselves what it means to be a man or a woman, not constrained by social norms and stereotypes. While there are no doubt significant differences between men and women, and some of them are probably innate, it is hard to tell exactly what the intrinsic qualities of each gender are. However, even where we can pinpoint the differences between the genders, these are usually statistical averages, with many men and women being more endowed with the qualities associated with the opposite sex.

With gender role freedom, each person has the liberty to define what their gender means to them personally. Women who identify with traditional women's interests and talents such as child rearing, intuition, caregiving, and so on, can celebrate these aspects of their femininity. And women who lean toward intellectual pursuits or sports or achievement in business can also claim their right to pursue these (or anything else). And of course, the same with men. People need to be able to appreciate the strong points of their gender, define these strong points in their own way, and pursue other interests if they so choose.

Power of the Women's Movement. Of all the liberation movements, the women's movement is the most exciting to me, not only for what it is doing for women, but even more importantly how it can help society overall. Women have so much to offer us in this time of transition because they often hold the ground qualities that society needs to advance. And the women's movement seems to be unstoppable. Other oppressed groups can be marginalized and put in ghettoes. They are often kept separate enough that they can be ignored by the group in power. However, women cannot be ignored. They are an integral part of the dominant culture. They are an intimate part of the lives of men. Now that they have realized their oppression and begun to find their voice and their power, they can't be stopped. Already in mainstream America, middle-class girls now growing up take for granted a degree of liberation far beyond what was known by their baby-boomer mothers. This holds exciting promise our advancement into stage 6.

Gender in the Model. Let's examine the question of using gender as an overall metaphor for the complementary qualities. Notice that the emergent qualities in each realm—technological living, social structure, reflexive consciousness—tend to be masculine qualities. Men are more often oriented toward technology, social power, and intellectuality. The ground qualities in each realm—natural living, community, and participation—tend to be feminine qualities. Women are more likely to be feeling, intuitive, and oriented toward personal relationships. It's not so clear that women are more oriented toward nature than men, but overall the correspondences hold. This makes it tempting to base the whole model on a gender metaphor, with masculinity and femininity the emergent and ground qualities and androgyny the goal for integration.

In fact, many writers have used this metaphor. The quote from Richard Tarnas at the beginning of part 3 illustrates how he does this. Even though it is true that men tend to favor the emergent qualities and women the ground, I prefer not to use gender theoretically or metaphorically in this way. First, it only points to averages. Some champions of natural living or power distribution have been men. Some great scientists have been women. The exceptions are endless.

What is more important, to use gender in this way seems to perpetuate gender stereotypes in a subtle way. Though there are intrinsic differences between men and women, it is hard to know exactly what they are. Our socially induced stereotypes and gender roles are so powerful in their influence on us. Even though there are innate differences between the genders, there are also vast individual variations, so it is constricting to define femininity or masculinity. What about women who love technology or the intellect? What about men who love intuition or relatedness? I prefer to use more neutral terms for the complementary qualities in the model.

As the ground qualities have become suppressed during social evolution, women have tended to represent and contain these qualities, and therefore they have a special contribution to make in bringing these characteristics back. Women often embody the qualities that society needs to reown at this time in history. Other oppressed groups also embody certain of the ground qualities that society needs and therefore can help us to integrate and move into stage 6. I will explore this in detail in later chapters.

A VISION

My hope for the future is a world in which power and value are not distributed according to race, religion, culture, gender, sexual preference, or anything else. In this world, everyone has an equal chance to have a share in the wealth and in the power to make decisions affecting their life, to be respected, and to be fulfilled. All cultures and religions are valued for their unique worldview and way of living. Everyone is able to understand and value people of the opposite gender. Furthermore, people are not constrained by their gender or by their heritage. They are free to create or choose their own way of living based on who they really are without having to fit into a stereotype. Table 16.1 summarizes these developments.

Table 16.1 Culture and Gender Solutions

Realm	**Integration**	**Advancing Emergent or Integrated**
Culture	Cultural pluralism	Cultural freedom
Gender	Gender equality	Gender role freedom

XVII

ECOLOGICAL ECONOMICS AND POPULATION

In the material realm, to resolve the planetary crisis, there must be an integration of the ground quality, natural living, with the emergent quality, technological living. It won't work for natural living to replace technological living or even to achieve some sort of balance or compromise. Knowing the dangers of our current use of technology, it is easy to engage in a subtle form of reverse splitting by thinking that society needs less technology, that we should forego our current preoccupation with machines to live more in harmony with the earth.

Some radical environmentalists propose that in a healthy society humans intervene as little as possible in the workings of nature (Goldsmith 1993). However, the idea of unspoiled wilderness is somewhat of a myth. What people think of as wilderness has often been modified by the actions of early humans, animals, and even by the natural succession of ecosystems. Ecosystems don't necessarily stay intact forever, even climax ecosystems.

At this stage of history the job of Modern society is to take charge of biological evolution. In fact, as Walt Anderson points out (1987), we already have. We're just not doing a very good job of it so far. We need to improve our understanding and caring for the natural world, so that our governance of evolution preserves, restores, and enriches the earth. Social change agents shouldn't advocate leaving the natural world alone. First, that won't happen; humans are intrinsically inquisitive, meddlesome animals. Second, we have already caused so much damage that active restoration is often necessary. Most important, we humans are part of the natural world, so as Thomas Berry points out (1990), if we govern evolution wisely, from our sense of connection to the earth, then it is really the planet governing itself.

Therefore we need an integrating structure for the material realm, including ecological and appropriate technology, permaculture, and ecological industry.

ECOLOGICAL TECHNOLOGY

People tend to think of nature and technology as inevitably in conflict. This is understandable because that has been the case so far. However, what the industrialized world needs in the future is not "less" technology in any sense, but rather technology that works in harmony with the natural world. Robert L. Olson, in a provocative article in the *Futurist* (1991), suggests that this is exactly what truly advanced technology will be. Our future technology won't be as large or centralized or environmentally destructive as today's, but it will not be any less advanced or any less "technological." It will be as complex, more sophisticated, and more "intelligent" than today's.

Science and technology have never developed independently of society's perceived needs. They have always been directed by corporate, government, and military funding and other social choices. So far this has steered our technology toward military use and corporate profit, with no thought to the long term social or environmental consequences. We need to bring our technological choices under more democratic public guardianship. There should be studies about the consequences of a given proposed technology and then public debate about whether to pursue it. As our values change and we realize the danger of our ways, this will lead toward the adoption of technology that works in harmony with nature, including human nature.

Olson suggests six characteristics of what he calls "environmentally advanced technology." It would be (1) sustainable, (2) based on a safe and inexhaustible supply of energy, (3) efficient in the use of energy and other resources, (4) efficient in recycling and the use of byproducts, (5) intelligent, and (6) alive. "Intelligent" refers to the incorporation of information processing (computer) abilities directly into our tools and materials. "Alive" refers to the concept of living machines pioneered by John and Nancy Jack Todd (1993).

> Living machines composed of many types of organisms and advanced structural materials can be designed to perform many of the most vital functions in society, including food and fuel production, waste treatment, and water purification. Living machines emulate the design principles used by nature itself and display characteristics of living systems, such as self-repair and self-design to adapt to changing environmental conditions. (Olson 1991)

Appropriate Technology. In addition to this high-tech approach, we need to recognize the value of small-scale technology such as bicycles.

As promoted by advocates of appropriate technology, these "old-fashioned" machines can, in certain circumstances, be of more value than the latest technological wonder. For examples, a poor peasant in the Third World with a small plot of land would gain a great deal from having an ox and a plow, but would have no use for a tractor. Similarly, the judicious use of bicycles in industrialized nations can improve health and decrease pollution and energy waste.

Why pursue Olson's kind of advanced ecological technology rather than simply advocating small-scale technology? One reason is that we need some truly advanced technology to cope with today's vast, complex world. Another is that technology has much to offer in terms of improving our health and well-being. There is no reason to limit its development if it is guided toward ecological health.

A third reason is strategic. If, as social critics, we advocate an anti-technology perspective, this puts us unnecessarily in conflict with a large segment of the population and some of our brightest minds. If instead, we pursue ecological technology from an integrated perspective that recognizes the value of technology as well as the necessity of harmony with nature, we are in a win-win situation. Everyone can understand and believe in our goals. The environmentalist and the technologist can work together. This is another example of the value of a cooperative approach.

"Appropriate technology" has come to mean small-scale technology. However, this whole discussion is really about using appropriate technology in the broader meaning of the term. We should always aim to use technology that is appropriate—appropriate to the natural world, to its social context, to its impact on humans and the community in which it is used, and to the human goals for which it is designed. Until now our technology has not been designed with appropriateness in mind. We are now forced to change that.

Permaculture. An excellent example of the integration of natural and technological living is permaculture, a design system for creating sustainable human environments created by Bill Mollison, an Australian scientist (1990). Permaculture was originally oriented toward agriculture, but is now being expanded to deal with all aspects of society.

> The key to permaculture is respectful design. By respecting the inherent qualities of people, plants, landscapes, and structures, permaculture says we can free them to help us. Instead of focusing on changing and controlling them, it concentrates on placing them in relationship to each other so that they benefit each other and the whole system they are part of. Permaculture is a way of observing

> and working *with* nature rather than pushing it around. Ultimately it requires less human effort and energy resources because it designs systems to work by themselves. (Atlee 1992)

One of the key concepts in permaculture is that every problem can be used as a resource if it is looked at in the right way. Thus waste products from one process can be used as inputs to another. A boulder on a building site can be incorporated into the house design, for beauty and heat storage. A disagreement can stimulate greater creativity.

ECOLOGICAL INDUSTRY

The industrialized nations need to redesign our industrial processes to work in harmony with nature. Hardin Tibbs (1992) presents a blueprint for doing this which he calls "industrial ecology."

> Environmental debate so far has been focused on making a case for environmentalism, or arguing against it, and has not provided industry with a clear agenda for positive environmental response.
>
> The aim of industrial ecology is to interpret and adapt an understanding of the natural system and apply it to the design of the manmade system, in order to achieve a pattern of industrialization that is not only more efficient, but that is intrinsically adjusted to the tolerances and characteristics of the natural system. . . . An industrial system of this type will have built-in insurance against environmental surprises, because their underlying causes will have been eliminated at the design stage.

His suggestions include the creation of "industrial ecosystems," in which the byproducts of one process would become inputs to another, in the same or a different company or industry, creating a complex, interconnected web of "metabolic pathways" which would greatly reduce waste.

AN ECOLOGICAL ECONOMY

Through ecological technology and industry it is possible to achieve an integration of the ground and emergent qualities in the material realm. But how can our society make this happen? We can't just coerce companies to do this. How do we arrange our economic system so that this integration happens naturally? This leads to the social realm.

In a previous chapter I suggested that we needed a new economic system to achieve a democratic economy. Now I am expanding that idea. We need a democratic *and* ecological economy—one that encourages both power distribution and ecological harmony. We need an integrating structure that encompasses the social and material realms. Paul Hawken's book *The Ecology of Commerce* (1993) includes a number of innovative proposals for the design of an ecological economy.

An economy can be viewed in two ways: (1) as a set of institutions and material transactions, and (2) as an information system that determines what institutions and material transactions will happen. It is relatively easy to specify what institutions and material transactions would make up an ecological economy. It is harder to design an information system that promotes this. This needs to be done by setting the rules of the market game in such a way that corporations naturally act in ecological ways in the course of pursuing their ultimate goal—profits.

In other words, our society can't rely on companies to become ecological solely because of moral and spiritual considerations. A few may manage to do this, but in a capitalist economy, corporations must make a profit to stay viable, so under our current economic information system most businesses can't afford to be ecological if their competitors aren't. We need an economic system that is designed so that the most ecological way to do things is also the cheapest and most efficient. Then corporations will find a way to do it, and everyone will benefit (Hawken 1993).

Full Cost Pricing. When a corporation manufactures and sells an item, such as a refrigerator, there are certain costs that the company must incur—salaries of employees, cost of materials, overhead, etc. Since these are born by the company, they are called *internal* costs by economists. The company does its best to minimize them, because any success in this area is reflected in increased profits. These costs are reflected in the retail price of the refrigerator, which is also influenced by the market.

There are other costs that are not born by the company—for example, the cost of cleaning up toxic wastes, the health toll in the nearby community because of pollution, building highways and fiber optic networks which the company uses, handling the wastes when the products are eventually thrown away, the effect of eroded topsoil or diminished water tables incurred in extracting the natural resources to make the products. These costs are born by others—the government, the local community, certain individuals, or society as a whole. These are called *external* costs because they are not born by the company that produced the item.

The solution is to arrange things so that the company bears all the costs. The issue here is not fairness, it's economic incentive. If some of the costs are born by others, the company has no incentive to try to minimize them. It has no incentive to reduce packaging or to design products so they can be reused or recycled. It has no incentive to reduce pollution or to find better ways to extract natural resources. To the contrary, it has an incentive to ignore these issues. If a company spends extra time and money trying to minimize external costs and its competitors don't, the company could lose in the market competition.

The solution is to find ways to ensure that the company that makes the product bears the full brunt of the cost of the product. Some of this will, of course, be passed on to the consumer, but this is also appropriate. If the price of an item is higher because it includes external costs, then consumers will choose whether to buy, based on a price that reflects the true cost of the product to society. So with full-cost pricing, the market pressures both manufacturers and consumers to make their economic decisions based on the actual cost to society and the environment, and therefore to minimize the destruction of the environment. In this way, the market really works for the environment.

Implementing full cost pricing is not easy. Some of it can be achieved by levying taxes or fees that reflect the external costs. Communities already tax companies to pay for their use of the infrastructure of highways and railroads. Our society needs to add "green taxes" such as pollution taxes and taxes on the extraction of natural resources. These taxes should not be seen as ways to raise revenue, but rather ways to provide the economy with accurate information in the form of incentives so that it can function in a healthy way. Hawken suggests that income and sales taxes should be reduced proportionately to the amount of revenue from green taxes.

He also suggests a number of innovative proposals for internalizing external costs without using taxes. One is that manufacturers would be responsible for disposing of any cars or large appliances they make. This would encourage them to design the products to be long-lasting and modular, with reusable parts. Another is that toxic waste dumps would be "parking lots" in which companies that produced the wastes would have to rent and maintain the space in which their wastes were kept. Again this would encourage them to use toxic wastes as little as possible and to develop ways to handle and reuse the wastes or possibly convert them to harmless substances.

Full-cost pricing will encourage manufacturers to deal with ecological problems at the original design level, where the greatest advantage can be gained. In this way, it will promote ecological technology and industry. Especially valuable would be methods of achieving full cost pricing that minimize the use of detailed monitoring and the intrusion of government. This is an area where there is a great opportunity for creativity in the design of a new economic system.

Overall Limits. Internalizing external costs goes a long way, but it is not enough. Some external costs are so pervasive that it is impossible to assign them a specific number. They may affect the global environment in ways that cannot be priced. We can't put a price tag on the greenhouse effect or on the destruction of the ozone layer. We can't measure the cost of the loss of biological diversity. Some of these large-scale problems can be dealt with by agreeing on specific restrictions, such as with ozone depletion. Others can't be dealt with so easily because they are simply due to the sheer amount of material activity in our economy, because of our population size and level of technology.

Humanity is overrunning the ecological limits of the earth. To have an economy that is sustainable, it must not only be harmonious with natural process, it must be circumscribed in size, well within the limits of the biosphere. This means setting constraints on our population and our material activity. I have already discussed the need for a steady-state economy, and I'll explore solutions to the population problem in the next section.

In order for an economy to be truly ecological, it must have mechanisms for limiting the sheer amount of activity that uses energy and resources and produces wastes. Interesting proposals are beginning to emerge. Herman Daly (1989) suggests that there be an overall global limit at the source—a limit on the amount of energy and resources that can be extracted in a given time period. A limited number of permits could be issued which would be required to extract resources. These would be sold by the government to the highest bidder and could be exchanged on the open market.

Hawken (1993) suggests an expansion of the role of utility companies. Currently energy utilities are set up in such a way that they can make money not only by selling energy, but also by conserving it. Amory Lovins has encouraged many utilities to realize that they can actually be more profitable by encouraging energy efficiency than by the usual method of increasing sales by stimulating demand through advertising. Hawken suggests that all extraction of resources be done by utilities so that conservation and efficiency would be encouraged.

These are just two of many possible approaches to solving this problem. I mention them as examples of innovative thinking in this area.

It is indeed possible to design an ecological economy, and right now creative proposals are starting to surface. We are beginning the task of designing an economy that is democratic and ecological.

Cultural Values and the Economy. In addition to limiting material activity through economic measures, our Modern society needs cultural values that recognize that happiness is gained primarily through means other than consumption, that true satisfaction doesn't really come from material wealth. Beyond a certain level of material well-being, our well-being is not increased much by additional purchases or better consumer technology. Instead it comes from love, community, creativity, spirituality, and other things that don't involve much material activity. Our current economy actually destroys many of these vital qualities, by encouraging overwork, alienation, and disconnection from nature.

Our society is involved in a vicious cycle of causality, where our economic system encourages us to value wealth and status, and our materialistic value system supports a destructive economy. I find it tragic to read in the paper today that the economy is doing better because people spent a great deal of money on Christmas presents in the last weeks of December. Under our current economic information system, in order to prosper it seems we must destroy the earth. We have to find ways to break this cycle from both sides—designing a healthier economy and changing our cultural values. I deal with this in more detail in chapter 19.

A Global Ecological Economy. As the U.S. national economy becomes more sustainable, we also need to encourage others to do the same. One possibility is promote trade agreements that require participating nations to have a certain minimum standard of environmental guardianship. Another mentioned by Hawken is that we grant favored trading status only to nations who meet our environmental standards.

As mentioned before, by following the principles of self-reliance and subsidiarity, trade should be kept as local as possible, and this will cut down considerably on energy for transportation.

Cross-Realm Solutions. Notice that the idea of an ecological economy is an integration involving both the material and social realms. Solutions involving more than one realm will often be necessary. So far I have stayed within a single realm simply for convenience of exposition. In fact, the realms are somewhat arbitrary divisions of reality, so cross-realm solutions are to be expected.

Ecological Ethics. For example, society needs a fundamental change in moral values with respect to waste. This involves the intersection of the consciousness and material realms. We need to have a waste-prohibiting ethic that is thoroughly ingrained in our cultural values, so that everyone will automatically use reduced packaging, recycle, buy recycled materials, minimize use of energy, and so on. This needs to become just as deep a part of our morals as cleanliness is. Remember that during the Middle Ages, people didn't know that dirt and vermin spread disease, so during the Black Plague, when over half of Europe died, people did nothing to stop the infestation of rats because they had no idea that the rats were related to the plague.

Today, no self-respecting person would have a dirty kitchen, or eat food off the floor, or allow rats or insects to infest the house. However, we don't adhere to this standard of cleanliness to prevent disease; it is simply part of our value system. We will soon have to develop a similar ethic about waste and other personal ecological practices, so that no self-respecting person would waste energy or materials, not because they were constantly worrying about the environment, but simply because it had become an ingrained part of our way of living.

POPULATION

World population is skyrocketing, and to avoid disaster it must be stabilized quickly. Let's first explore why this is happening. There seem to be two main reasons, both having to do with the effects of industrialization—oppression and improved health.

Oppression. Stable communities in the early stages of social evolution tend to have mild rates of population growth. They do tend to grow, but not nearly as quickly as is currently happening in the Third World. When these societies are invaded and their people oppressed, birth rates and population tend to rise much more rapidly. This is perhaps because their stable cultural patterns have been disrupted, and the conquerors and their local agents have little incentive to hold down the population. The conquered people are often used for the power of their labor in the agricultural projects of the rulers, so they may even have an incentive to increase the indigenous population.

Health. Looking at the recent history of the West, it is evident that with the rise of industrialization, there was an improvement in sanitation and diet which produced a general enhancement of health and longevity. This meant that there was a decrease in the "death rate." Population growth is measured by birth rate minus death rate. If you decrease the death rate while holding the birth rate constant, population growth increases. This is what happened in the early days of industrialization.

Children as Economic Assets or Liabilities. Then as industrialization advanced, it led to a large prosperous middle class, which became educated and politically powerful. At the same time, Western societies developed full-blown market economies and lost a sense of community. These events had an interesting effect on population. In traditional peasant and farming societies, children are a clear economic asset for parents. They are a source of labor on the farm from relatively early ages, and they can be counted on to take over the farm and provide for their parents in old age. Thus the more children a family has, the more prosperous and secure the parents will be. As a consequence, traditions developed that encouraged large families. Women were valued for their fertility and mothering ability. Men were valued for their capacity to produce and support many offspring.

In advanced industrial societies, this situation is reversed. Children are an economic disadvantage. The working parent brings in a certain amount of income, and the more children there are, the more mouths to feed and the poorer the family. If the family is to get ahead, the children must be educated, and this costs more money. Furthermore, with the breakdown of community and family ties, children are not even expected to be the major providers for their parents in old age. This is handled by the state through social security or the individual through savings. All this reverses the advantage of having large families. Therefore in industrialized countries, values have developed favoring small families in which each child is groomed carefully for education and occupational advancement. Parents are valued for the success of their children, not the number.

The Demographic Transition. As a result of this, industrialized nations have made a transition from high birth rates to low, and their populations have begun to stabilize. This is known as the "demographic transition," as depicted in figure 17.1.

It has been a consistent enough phenomenon in industrialized countries that experts hoped population in the Third World would stabilize as it became industrialized. However, in most cases this hasn't happened. The problem is that the demographic transition requires much more than just a rise in industrialization and GNP. It requires that the nation truly develop a prosperous and numerous middle class, which benefits from the market economy. It requires the minimization of poverty and powerlessness. Most importantly, it requires the education and emancipation of women.

In countries that have industrialized without achieving these other developments, the demographic transition has not occurred. In countries that are still split between a small upper class and a large poor class,

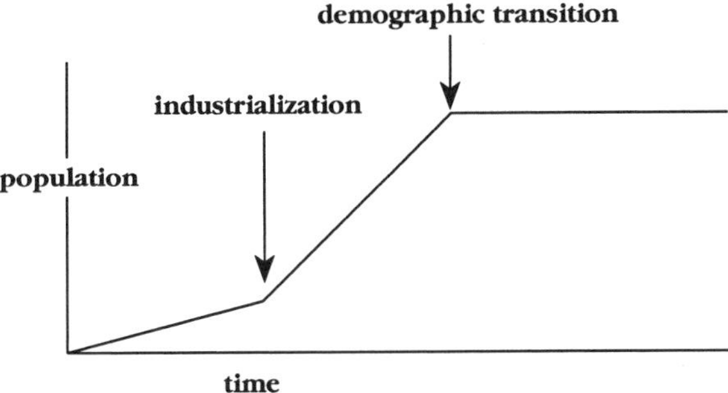

Figure 17.1

people continue to have large families and population continues to grow. Even in the advanced industrialized nations which have a much smaller underclass, those people who are poor continue to have high fertility rates.

Solutions. What must be done to stabilize population in the preindustrialized nations and among the poor within the industrialized nations? The first and easiest answer is to provide birth control to everyone who desires it, free of charge. We must go out of our way to make sure that even those in the poorest, most rural areas have easy access to birth control. However, we must be careful not to focus primarily on birth control. In some cases this has led to oppressive methods of population control, where people were duped or coerced into being sterilized or where laws were passed limiting family size. These methods are not only morally objectionable but they also don't really work in the long run without the people's support. The second answer is to try to change cultural values. We need to encourage people to change from valuing large families to valuing the quality of family life and the fulfillment of children.

The third and pivotal answer is the reduction of poverty and the oppression of women. People who have carefully studied the effects of various political and cultural changes on population have concluded that the single most important factor is the status of women. Societies in which women gain education and power have the best records in making the demographic transition and stabilizing population. The most important thing we can do to help the preindustrialized world stabilize their population is to end our economic exploitation of them. We must dismantle economic colonialism and promote power distribution and the emancipation of women. This has now been recognized at an international level through the Cairo conference on population.

Community. Ironically, the same forces of social structure that have destroyed family and community in the rich countries have also helped to stabilize population. This presents us with a difficult task. We must integrate community with social structure in ways that do not encourage people to begin having more children. One possibility is to return to the extended family that has been our form throughout most of history. Now it should include the option of choosing one's family, where people who are not related by blood can create familylike relationships. This provides opportunities for parenting without actually having children. We must also try to encourage the demographic transition in developing countries in ways that do not destroy their existing sense of community.

Long Term Goals. Our immediate concern must be stabilizing population quickly to avoid an environmental disaster. In the long run, the world needs to reduce population. Remember, we live on a finite planet whose limits have been surpassed. Our material standard of living in the future will be inversely proportional to our population. The more people there are, the less material well-being for all. Of course, we would be better off with less emphasis on materialism in the future, but nonetheless, it is still preferable to have as high a standard of living as possible without compromising the environment or our own spiritual values. This depends on reducing our population considerably.

FUTURE PROSPECTS

The material realm is where our greatest peril lies, so let's examine our prospects for evolving to stage 6 in time to avert an environmental disaster.

Driving Forces. All the industrialized nations have been shaped over the long haul for military power by the parable of the tribes and for extractive technology by population/environment constraints.

However, the situation is now changed. In today's world the societies that will be most successful in the long run are those that respond to our current population/environment constraints differently. In past crises, the successful societies responded by developing new technology that allowed them to extract more food and energy and therefore to increase their populations. Now that is not possible. Today the nations that prosper will be those that stabilize their populations, limit their consumption, and harmonize their technology with the earth. Now for the first time, the driving force of population/environment constraints is pushing us in a different direction—toward sustainable societies.

Currently the selection for power is shaping us more toward economic power than military power. Nations are striving to achieve high extraction, high consumption, growth economies. It appears as if an economy like that will be most successful in the future global market. However, this isn't really true. In the successful economies of today, such as the United States, Japan, and Germany, the side effects are beginning to overwhelm us, as discussed in chapter 10. Because these societies have ignored the realities of population/environmental constraints, the hidden health, social, and ecological costs are burgeoning. These ecological factors are not only destroying the earth, they are beginning to undermine our economies. Health costs are skyrocketing, partly because of environmentally related disease; waste disposal and cleanup is a serious problem; and all our other environmental problems are producing costs that drag the economy down. It isn't obvious yet that this is affecting our economy, but it will become increasingly clear as time goes on.

Conscious Evolution. The driving forces work over the long haul in social evolution, but now there is little time to work with. The world can't wait for the materialistic societies to convert to ecological sanity or collapse. The world is too interconnected. If they collapse they will take the planet with them. Therefore what is crucial now is not the *actual* driving forces but the *perceived* driving forces. As long as most people think that a high consumption growth economy is the way to success, our society will pursue it. Those of us who understand the consequences must find a way to help our people and our leaders see that such an economy will not work, that the most successful economies in the future will be steady-state ecological economies.

Our societies must move beyond the driving forces and rely on conscious choice to build healthy, sustainable nations and economies. We now have the knowledge to do this, and we *must* do it, because if we wait for the nonviable high-consumption societies to collapse, there will be vast worldwide ecological damage, and untold upheaval and suffering. We must take conscious charge of social evolution and move in the healthy direction of stage 6.

The Future. I believe that the world is headed that way, that the trends are clearly in the direction of the integration of the ground qualities. There are currently many promising ground quality movements, and we must work to insure their success. Part of this work is to be alert to the ways that such movements can fail—repression, co-optation, assimilation, or turning to evil (Berman 1990).

The world has little time. I don't know if we will change fast enough and smoothly enough to avert serious destruction. That is our great task at this time in human history. Robert Gilman (1993) presents an exciting and provocative scenario for how our entire economy could be turned around by 2003.

However, even if society doesn't adapt fast enough to the social and spiritual needs of our crisis, and the world goes through a time of ecological destruction and social decay, it can still recover and move into stage 6 at a later time. Even in the midst of a deteriorating world, those of us who see what is happening can work to make sure that our important psychological, social, and ecological understandings are deepened and spread, not lost. Then at some point, chastened by our failure, the world's people will be ready to work together to build a healthy society. We must do what we can now to avoid this fate, but if we can't avoid it, we must sow the seeds of a future recovery.

A Vision. I see in the future a world where technology and industry are designed from the start to work with the natural flows of the earth and the human body, and where the economy is organized so that corporations find it most profitable to follow these principles. In this world, people value those things that truly bring fulfillment and are less interested in material possessions. The economy runs almost exclusively on renewable resources and energy, and material processes are organized so that we conserve resources and minimize waste products that the environment cannot absorb. We have stopped destroying the habitats of existing animal and plant species, and so our planet retains what is left of its richness of life forms.

Birth rates have reached replacement level and some countries are choosing to temporarily lower them even further in order to stabilize their populations. Globally, long term plans are being formulated to gradually reduce population, so that everyone can enjoy a higher material standard of living and a greener, less crowded earth.

XVIII

THE EVOLUTION OF CONSCIOUSNESS

Before discussing solutions in the consciousness realm, I will discuss and critique existing models of the evolution of consciousness and society.

KAHLER

One of the earliest studies of the evolution of consciousness was done in the 1940s by historian Erich Kahler, before the word *consciousness* was commonly used. He sees social evolution as a process of humanity transcending the limits of its own being, and describes this in a way that leaves no doubt that he is talking about emergence through mediation: "This psychic procedure consists of two acts: the establishing of these limits by detaching and discerning a non-self from self [emergence] and the establishing of a new, conscious relationship between one's own existence and the clearly conceived non-self [mediation]" (Kahler 1956, 42–43).

My main point of disagreement with this excellent book is the timing of these two acts. Kahler sees them as happening sequentially in history, with stages 1 through 4 being devoted to the emergence of human individuality and stages 5 and 6 being concerned with efforts toward consciously organized human association. While it is true that there has been a gradual emergence of individuality and a concomitant increase in social structure, I see these as happening together throughout social evolution, rather than one after the other. Even more importantly, emergence through mediation is a process that encompasses all aspects of social evolution, and the mediation process involves much more than organized human association.

ELGIN'S MODEL

Duane Elgin (1993) presents a fascinating model of social evolution based on the evolution of consciousness. His model of consciousness evolution is congruent in many ways with mine and with Ken Wilber's (to be described next). Elgin conceives of a linear progression of stages, each one characterized by an increasing degree of perspective and detachment from the experience of the previous stage.

In his model, each stage of social evolution is characterized by a move to a higher dimension of "sacred geometry." For example, in moving from stage 1 through 3, the flat two-dimensional world of the hunter-gatherers opens up into the three-dimensional world of agriculture and the beginnings of civilization. The extra dimension is not a literal dimension of space, but rather one of consciousness, where people are able to step back and see themselves and the world from a wider perspective.

This is similar to the consciousness version of my concept of emergence, but his model doesn't include any deep recognition of the dialectical nature of our evolution. He does mention that humanity is now at a point of "'evolutionary inflection' where an arduous process of withdrawing from nature makes a decisive shift toward an equally demanding journey of returning to live in harmony with nature" (Elgin 1993, 256). However, his model doesn't contain any theoretical constructs such as my ground and emergent qualities which explain this dialectic.

He explores advanced spiritual stages of development and correlates them with projected future stages of social evolution. Let's briefly look at his view of our possible future: The next stage of consciousness (in his model stage 5) is the witness self where we are able to step back and view ourselves dispassionately. The corresponding stage of social evolution is that of mass communication and global reconciliation, where we learn to work together on solving the massive problems we are facing. I agree that global reconciliation is an important part of the next stage of social evolution, and this is reflected in my sections on cooperation, democracy, culture, and gender. His understanding of the witness self as the next stage of consciousness evolution corresponds in my model to a further development of reflexive consciousness. I believe that an equally important aspect of consciousness development for the next stage is the regaining and integration of participatory consciousness, which Elgin doesn't cover.

Elgin's stage 6 involves "oceanic consciousness," where we experience the underlying unity of creation. The corresponding social aspect of this stage is global bonding and community, where we are able to cooperate on building a sustainable world. In my view, this is really the next stage in social evolution and Elgin's stage 5 is really a transition to this stage, rather than a separate stage in itself.

Having completed this task, stage 7 involves "flow consciousness" and a societal time of experimentation in new creative endeavors. Stage 8 is characterized by our maturation as a planetary civilization, but this is too far removed and speculative to mean much to me.

Overall, Elgin's clear elucidation of the possible next two stages is exciting. Whether or not these stages actually occur as he projects, it is inspiring to consider our future prospects in such a hopeful light. He does this without ignoring in any way the dangers we face today.

WILBER

The spectrum model of consciousness was developed by Ken Wilber (1977, 1986), one of the premier theorists in transpersonal psychology. Wilber's scheme is based on the "Great Chain of Being," a view of reality as a spectrum of levels starting with the material world at the bottom, and progressing up through the body, emotions, intellect, and then various degrees of spiritual reality. Each higher level includes the levels below it, until one reaches the ultimate level, which is a form of pure spirit or consciousness that is the origin of all of reality. He uses this model to explain both the social evolution of consciousness and the development of consciousness during an individual's life.

Historically, Wilber sees consciousness as evolving up this ladder of being (1983), with hunter-gatherers functioning primarily at the body level, agriculturists at the emotional/imaginal level, and medieval and modern people at the mental or ego level, about halfway up. This corresponds to our stage 5 reflexive consciousness. He predicts that in the future humanity will evolve through a number of higher spiritual levels, which have already been explored by some enlightened individuals and by the great mystics and prophets, but now most of humanity is at the ego level. Wilber's work overall has been a major contribution to psychology by integrating in a single model the understandings of traditional psychology and psychotherapy with those of the world's spiritual traditions.

In his newest work (1995), Wilber connects his model to general and evolutionary systems theory in creative new ways, and relates it to the planetary crisis, especially gender and ecological issues. This book contains major new insights that prompted me to revise portions of this book, even though my manuscript was finished before Wilber's book came out. He is very lucid about the advancement of consciousness through emergence (which he calls transcendence), and he recognizes that the primary problem with Modern society is dissociation.

Critique. The following is a critique of those aspects of Wilber's thought that deal with social transformation. I have chosen to give such a detailed critique of his work not because it is especially deserving of criticism, but just the opposite, because I respect his ideas so much and because they are similar to my own. Thus in fleshing out our differences, I believe I can more fully explicate my own ideas and contribute to the advancement of our overall understanding of the evolution of society and consciousness.

One limitation of Wilber's model is that his view of ultimate reality seems to be completely derived from stage 4 consciousness. He applies stage 5 rational thinking to understanding stage 4 consciousness, but he assumes that the great spiritual figures of the Ancient and Medieval eras were able to understand the ultimate nature of spiritual reality and that by synthesizing their insights it is possible to comprehend this. (Of course, he recommends a lifetime of spiritual discipline in order to experientially participate in this understanding.) I personally think that reality is much more subtle and complex than that. I don't think that even the greatest minds and hearts of stage 4 were capable of providing us with final answers to these ultimate questions. I doubt that even stage 6 will do that.

In his scheme, the future development of consciousness is already laid out and has been explored by the world's great spiritual teachers by advancing up the Great Chain of Being. I believe that humanity's future development is only emerging as we evolve, and that we are likely to be surprised at anything beyond the next barely visible stage.

In Wilber's previous book on social evolution, *Up from Eden* (1983), consciousness is seen as the driving force behind all aspects of social evolution. He seems to assume that consciousness is evolving up the chain, and that at certain historical moments it progresses, causing social and material changes as it goes. However, he provides no explanations for why consciousness evolved from one stage to the next at the times in history it did. This leaves us with no real understanding of the driving forces behind social evolution. In his latest book, he broadens his approach to include social and material realities, and there is some indication that the planned sequel to this book may deal with driving forces in other realms.

Dialectics and Dissociation. Wilber's model is dialectical, but in a different sense than mine. He assumes that the evolution of consciousness moves in a straight line up the ladder and only allows for a dialectical process within each stage of evolution. Each stage emerges from the previous stage and then is able to take the previous structures of consciousness as objects that can be perceived and operated on [mediation].

Thus they are "preserved," but the exclusive reliance on them is "negated" in the development of the next higher level, which has its own emerging properties. Thus there is an emergence and then an integration.

If the separation goes too far and the integration doesn't happen, then it becomes a dissociation, producing problems. This far I agree with him. However, he doesn't seem to consider the possibility that there might be a cumulative and increasing dissociation involving many stages of evolution, which is what I believe has actually happened. He only says that at each stage there is a possibility of the healthy transcendence or an unhealthy dissociation. These are certainly the options at any stage, but it seems to me that it is possible to move on to higher levels without resolving the dissociations of lower ones. This is what has happened in social evolution, and I also believe it happens in individual development, where a person can mature in some ways and become a highly functioning adult, but still have major unresolved issues from childhood that can involve dissociation and repression of lower levels of consciousness.

Wilber's model agrees with the need for integration today; in fact, he calls the next level of social evolution the "centaur" stage, which involves integrating the body and the consciousness of the pre-Modern stages. He understands that the Modern era has now "clearly moved into the beginning stages of dissociation," and that integration is needed. However, as far as I can tell from his model, this integration happens as part of the development of each new stage, and so the integration of the body and earlier stages should be the culmination of the Modern stage's development and not the hallmark of a new stage. My guess is that Wilber intuitively understands that there has been a more fundamental dissociation and therefore a profound need for integration, and that is why he calls the next stage centauric. However, his model doesn't seem to include a larger dialectical movement involving many stages.

As a result of this, Wilber doesn't seem to sufficiently recognize the fundamental importance of reclaiming and integrating the ground qualities in surmounting the current crisis. He gives lip service to the current problems of dissociation but seems to be most interested in the advancement of the emergent quality, reflexive consciousness. I also believe he is unduly critical of people and movements that are committed to reclaiming the ground qualities. While I agree that it is important to integrate these qualities, not just reclaim them, I believe we should applaud those people and groups who have held the ground qualities for society and are now bringing them back. They are doing us a great service.

Pre-trans Similarities. His model provides no explanation for the interesting fact that the stages below the mental level (today's adult consciousness) have many similarities to the stages above the mental level. For example, an infant or a psychotic individual or a member of an indigenous tribe may experience a sense of union with their environment in ways that have some similarities to the experiences of advanced mystics. This has led some psychoanalytic theorists to postulate that the mystics are poorly developed or even crazy. Wilber understands these similarities and has coined the term "pre-trans fallacy" to elucidate why many theorists have confused the early levels of development (prepersonal) with the advanced (transpersonal) levels.

Despite Wilber's concept of the pre-trans fallacy, his model doesn't explain these pre-trans similarities, except by saying that they both go beyond rational consciousness. But this is not an explanation unless there is something special about rational consciousness. After all, there are no similarities among stages that are both before and after, say, mythic consciousness. In my model, these similarities are explained by the fact that there is a high degree of participatory consciousness in both early and advanced development. Both infants and indigenous peoples have greater participatory than reflexive consciousness. (I don't mean to imply that indigenous people are like infants. There is only this broad similarity.) In a normal adult in modern society, reflexive consciousness is high and participatory consciousness is suppressed. In the advanced mystic, participatory consciousness is again highly developed, but now it is integrated with an even higher development of reflexive consciousness.

Comparison with Washburn's Model. Michael Washburn (1988, 1994), building on Wilber's ideas, has presented a model for the development of consciousness that does explain the similarities between the prepersonal and transpersonal states. Washburn's model deals with the development of consciousness during the life span of an individual. He proposes a dialectical model in which there is an interplay between the developing ego of the person and something which Washburn calls the *dynamic ground.* This is a reservoir of instinctual/spiritual energy which is deep and powerful but not organized or coherent by itself.

In the person's very early years the dynamic ground is active, but as the person develops, it is suppressed by the emerging ego. In mature spiritual development, the ego learns to become open and flexible and serves as a channel and organizer for the dynamic ground. In psychotic people or others with poor development of the ego, the dynamic ground can burst through with damaging effects. This dialectical model explains the similarities between prepersonal and transpersonal states because they both represent the activity of the dynamic ground, related to in different ways by the ego.

Washburn also proposes that as a person moves into higher spiritual consciousness there is a temporary regression as the dynamic ground bursts through. Though this is certainly true for some people, it does not seem to be a universal phenomenon, and many people are able to develop spiritually without this regression. This has weakened the acceptance of Washburn's model. I think this is unfortunate because the basics of his model help us understand the profoundly dialectical nature of human development. Washburn's model is consistent with mine in that his "dynamic ground" is similar to my participatory consciousness, and the ego is, of course, related to reflexive consciousness, at least up to the Modern, rational stage.

XIX

CONSCIOUS PARTICIPATION

Unlike the social and material realms, in the consciousness realm, solutions to the planetary crisis are indirect. Changes in this realm can't directly promote ecological health or eliminate oppression. They affect our social structures through the way people think and feel about themselves and the world. However, this realm is no less important or influential; the influence is simply less direct and obvious.

The consciousness realm is crucial to the process of social change because it is the realm in which it is easiest to promote change incrementally on a one-to-one basis. In the social realm, it takes the involvement of a great number of people and significant social power to affect *any* economic changes, for example. Similarly, in the material realm, it would take a social consensus to change the way society supports and develops technology. However, in the consciousness realm it is possible for individual people to change their consciousness in healthy directions, and therefore consciousness movements can build gradually. This means that a movement can build significant momentum without having to be large enough to change major policy decisions.

Because of this, in some ways the consciousness realm is ahead of the other realms. Many of the consciousness solutions I discuss below have already been adopted by a great number of people. In the other realms, a social movement must attain far greater influence in society as a whole before any changes can happen, so many of the social and material solutions are still in the proposal stage.

As in the other realms, I will be looking at not only solutions that involve the integration of ground and emergent qualities, but also solutions that involve an advance in the emergent quality. These are especially important in the consciousness realm since individuals can more easily forge ahead of societal norms.

INTEGRATIVE SOLUTIONS

First let's look at integrative solutions in the graphic for the consciousness realm (figure 19.1).

Figure 19.1 Consciousness

The integrated situation, *conscious participation,* means having the aliveness and meaningfulness of participatory consciousness while using your ability to reflect, criticize, and make conscious choices. It means being able to step back from your participation and ask critical questions about what it really means, whether anything is missing, whether you are being manipulated, and so on. It means retaining your individuality and making choices about your participation. It also means having the vision to see that reality is indeed a meaningful, participatory whole. This integrating structure for the consciousness realm is a structure of consciousness rather than a social or cultural structure.

Modes of Intelligence. Recent research suggests that human beings have at least seven different kinds of intelligences (Gardner 1983). Modern society places such an emphasis on reflexive consciousness that our school systems value only verbal and logical intelligence. The other five—musical, visual, interpersonal, intrapersonal, and kinesthetic—which mostly represent participatory consciousness, have largely been ignored. As a psychotherapist I notice that most people who first come to therapy have very little training in dealing with their emotions or their inner world. Their socialization in Modern society has emphasized the rational mind exclusively.

The split brain research of recent years has identified that the left side of the brain performs such functions as logical and verbal reasoning while the right side handles visual, musical, artistic, emotional, and other more intuitive, participatory modes. Based on this evidence, Sim Liddon (1989) concludes that there are two basic modes of mental processing, which he calls "linear" and "holistic," corresponding to the left and right sides of the brain respectively. In today's world, with such a strong emphasis on only one side of our consciousness, we have lost the richness and aliveness of the other. We need to develop an integral consciousness that includes all forms of intelligence and both sides of the brain.

Activity. One can also look at the complementary qualities of the consciousness realm in terms of activity. In participatory consciousness, activity tends to be spontaneous and flowing, coming from instinct, feeling, and impulse. In reflexive consciousness, activity tends to be deliberate, planned, and structured. Actions are chosen rather than happening spontaneously. Neither of these is good or bad in itself. Spontaneous, instinctual action can be alive and exciting if it is appropriate to the situation. If it is dissociated from conscious choice, it may become impulsive and inappropriate. Choice and planning are necessary for the success of many activities, but if this deliberate mode is dissociated from all flow and spontaneity, then life becomes dull and stilted. The ideal is an integration of the two modes where you can act and express yourself spontaneously and also be consciously in charge of your actions. Sometimes you may integrate these two modes in the moment, and sometimes you may choose one or the other according to the needs of the situation.

Revitalization. In chapter 13, I discussed the loss of meaning, empathy, and vitality in today's world, and how this affects both the quality of people's lives and contributes to our social and ecological crises. When people realize the emptiness of their lives and seek to deal with the resulting pain, they often try to revitalize themselves through psychotherapy, self-help groups, holistic health, spiritual disciplines, and other approaches. Increasing numbers of people are involved in these pursuits; enough that I think it is appropriate to speak of a consciousness movement. In addition, people are coming alive through reconnecting with nature, conscious community, and engagement in artistic and creative endeavors. These are signs of the return of participatory consciousness and the reawakening of our lost vitality and sense of belonging.

When this happens on a broad enough scale, it will not only bring personal satisfaction to people but also realign the value system of our societies. Then public policy can be guided by compassion for the suffering of others, by a sense of interconnection with the human race and all of life, and by deeper purpose and meaning. When people are able to satisfy their real needs for intimacy, creativity, and spiritual connection, then they won't need to pursue substitutes such as power, money, and status. This will provide the personal and psychological support for social efforts to build a healthier economy, government, and business world.

However, as we regain the lost ground quality of participation, we must remember not to disparage the emergent quality of reflexive consciousness. In reconnecting with the body and the emotions, we don't want to throw out the intellect. In psychotherapy this can lead to deep catharsis without insight and therefore no real personal growth. In regaining a sense of spiritual belonging, we don't want to lose our critical ability, or we may become trapped in a cult. In regaining our empathy for others, we don't want to lose our individuality and our assertiveness. As always we need to integrate the complementary qualities, leading to *conscious participation.*

Spiritual Integration. In the Ancient and Medieval eras, the dominant worldview saw the consciousness realm as the underlying reality and the material world as derived from it. One result of this world-view was that the most advanced spiritual seekers were often monks and nuns who gave up sexuality, family life, and sometimes even personal autonomy on their path to spiritual realization. They surrendered those worldly things that were seen as a hindrance to spiritual development.

The Modern era reversed this world view, producing the idea that the material realm is the only thing that is real, and consciousness is just an epiphenomenon. In today's transition, we are seeing an integration where the more advanced spiritual approaches include those aspects of material life that were relinquished in stage 4. Spiritual aspirants are now allowed and even expected to integrate their spirituality with sexuality, raising a family, having a career, social action, and a full life in society. In this way, the spirituality arising in stage 6 involves an integration of spiritual and material realities.

Regaining Empathy. As I discussed earlier, in our Modern dissociated way of comprehending the world, we tend to reduce everything to objects. We see the natural world as "resources." We see other people as opponents to be beaten. We see our bodies and minds as mechanisms to be manipulated. This is what enables us to wage high-tech war without seeing the human consequences and to destroy our natural environment without feeling the loss.

We need to recognize that we share the world with other people and creatures who are alive and feeling and connected to us. We must regain our feelings and our empathy, so that we can experience the richness of a rain forest and feel for a victim of Third World oppression. We need to experience the aliveness of our bodies and the depth of our minds. It helps to know that our "enemies" are people, too, with families and faiths, with hopes and fears and dreams.

However, again we don't want to throw the baby out with the bath water. We don't want to lose our reflexive abilities as we regain our aliveness. We need to empathize with victims of oppression and also perceive the causes of that oppression, so we can be effective in stopping it. We need to love the earth and also understand how to create an ecological economy. We need our hearts and our minds.

ADVANCING REFLEXIVE CONSCIOUSNESS

In addition to the integration of participation and reflexive consciousness, reflexive consciousness is advancing, providing additional impetus into stage 6. However, before exploring this, let's review the evolution of reflexive consciousness from the beginning. Remember that reflexive consciousness means emerging from being embedded in a worldview that you were not able to see because you were too close to it. The classic example is the fish that doesn't realize it is in water. Throughout social evolution humanity has gone through a series of emergences from being embedded in various ways of thinking and being. In each case, we advanced by becoming more aware of an aspect of out experience that wasn't seen before, and therefore moving away from an exclusive or unexamined reliance on this way of being and embracing a larger and more inclusive one.

Table 19.1 illustrates this process by indicating the major emergences in each stage of social evolution as explained so far in this book. The meaning of the stage 6 terms is explained afterwards.

Table 19.1 Embeddedness and Emergence

Stage	Emerged from embeddedness in	Emerged to
2	Blood ties	Mythic tradition
3	Natural cycles	Initiative and power
4	Unexamined action	Morality
	Mythic parochialism	Universality
	Realm fusion	Separate material and spiritual realms
5	Faith in authority	Autonomy, rationality, scientific method
	Society	Individuality
6	Mechanistic thinking	Systemic/dialectic thinking
	Science	Multiple modes of understanding
	Unexamined inner experience	Psychology
	Fixed identity	Spirituality

In developing table 19.1, for simplicity I have placed each emergence in only one stage, the one most significant for it. However, keep in mind that in many cases there was a more gradual emergence over a number of stages. For example, individuality emerged gradually over stages 3, 4, and 5, but in the table I place it in stage 5, where the largest jump in individuality occurred.

Systemic Thinking. Modern science in its more extreme dissociated form tends to be atomistic and reductionistic. It assumes that the way to understand reality is by analyzing it into parts and reducing it to the lowest level of these parts. It views reality as a machine that can be understood mechanically.

If we try to understand the human body by reducing it to chemistry and anatomy, we miss out on the complex physiology of our body's systems. For example, the immune system has no anatomical location; it is spread throughout the body. What makes it a system is the way its parts work together functionally to fight disease. For a long time, scientists didn't recognize its existence because it couldn't be discovered mechanistically. Today as researchers are uncovering some of the complex interactions between the mind and the body's ability to heal itself, some are speculating that there may be another physiological system, which they call the "healing system," that has yet to be recognized (Dreher and NcNeill 1993). To move into stage 6 we need a way of thinking that recognizes the intrinsically relational, interconnected, participatory nature of things (Capra 1982).

Some of the newest and most exciting developments in science are ecology, general systems theory, chaos theory, and complexity, all of which view reality as an interconnected whole, where the relationships between the parts of a system are even more important than the nature of the parts (von Bertalanffy 1968; Gleick 1987; Lewin 1992; Waldrop 1992).

Complexity is an especially promising development because it is an attempt to reverse the long-standing trend toward specialization and create a truly generalist science (Waldrop 1992). It attempts to see common patterns in the emergence of higher orders of complexity in a wide variety of social, biological, and physical sciences.

> The other viewpoint is complexity, in which there is basically no duality between man and nature. . . . It's a world view that . . . is becoming more important in the West—both in science and in the culture at large. . . . There's been a gradual shift from an exploitative view of nature . . . to an approach that stresses the mutual accommodation of man and nature. What has happened is that we're beginning to lose our innocence, or naiveté, about how the world works. As we begin to understand complex systems, we begin to understand that we're part of an ever-changing, interlocking, nonlinear, kaleidoscopic world. (Waldrop 1992, 333)

Thus we are emerging from an exclusive reliance on disconnected, mechanistic models of reality, and embracing more inclusive models.

Dialectical Thinking. In the early phases of humanity's attempt to understand the world rationally and experimentally, we used static models. In the latter part of the Modern, developmental and process models have become increasingly important, the most famous being Darwin's theory of evolution and Freud's developmental theory of psychology. Later psychological theories have emphasized process even more (Perls, Hefferline et al. 1951). This has moved our mode of thinking in the direction of understanding process and change, rather than simply cataloging existing structure.

Further steps in this direction have come through the introduction of dialectical thinking, where you understanding that development is not necessarily linear, but often progresses through conflict and contradiction. Dialectical thinking also recognizes that seeming opposites can be reconciled by moving to a greater level of understanding which includes both sides of the conflict. Wilber (1995) suggests that the stages of consciousness evolution are related to Piaget's stages of cognitive development in children, with the stage of formal operations related to our Modern scientific, analytical consciousness. A further step is toward dialectical thinking.

> Numerous psychologists . . . have pointed out that there is much evidence for a stage beyond Piaget's formal operational. It has been called "dialectical," "integrative," "creative synthetic," "integral-aperspectival," and so forth. (Wilber 1995, 258)

Our Modern destructive use of technology has been sanctioned by our view of nature as simply a machine whose parts are static and separate from each other. In this perception, domination of the natural world makes some sense. A truer view of reality, emerging through systemic and dialectical thinking, is encouraging us to align ourselves with nature rather than exploiting it, and helping us understand how to begin repairing the damage we have done.

Psychology. Each step in advancing reflexive consciousness has been based on a deeper examination and understanding of our inner processes. In stage 4, for the first time human beings examined the ethical and moral consequences of our actions. This was one of the factors in the development of the higher religions. In stage 5, for the first time we explored how we know what we know, and what makes knowledge valid. This resulted in Modern science. In the twentieth century, for the first time we are examining not just one aspect, but the entire inner world of consciousness, our emotions, motives, thinking processes, conflicts, perceptions, and so forth. This has resulted in psychology.

Of course, methods for exploring inner process have existed since ancient times, including the very sophisticated psychology of Buddhism, but now inner exploration is becoming widespread. During most of psychology's century of life, it has been confined to academia and professional psychiatry, but within the last thirty years popular psychological and spiritual movements have become widespread among the population as a way of understanding personal life and seeking happiness.

Psychotherapy has moved from an arcane procedure for the "mentally ill" to a common way of bettering one's life. There is great interest in spiritual development, personal growth, New Age pursuits, and self-help groups, especially the 12-step method of recovery from addiction. This interest in consciousness has also spread to churches, schools, and corporations. For the first time in history the inner life of the average person is being examined and explored in detail. This is a clear indication of the advancing of reflexive consciousness as we move into stage 6.

Integrated Psychology. Some methods of psychotherapy and personal growth are primarily intellectual. Cognitive-behavior therapy (Ellis 1962; Beck et al. 1979), many forms of counseling, much of the practice of psychoanalysis—these methods reflect on inner experience, but do it through a primarily mental approach. The person (or their therapist) develop theories about their inner conflicts, covert meanings, distorted belief systems, and so on. This can be very helpful, but it perpetuates the dissociation of ground and emergent qualities.

The more integrative approaches are those that work directly with inner experience—felt emotion, body sensation, reliving childhood memories, altered states of consciousness—for example, Gestalt therapy (Perls et al. 1951), psychodrama (Moreno 1956), bio-energetics (Lowen 1975), interactive group therapy (Earley in press) and other humanistic, somatic, and transpersonal approaches to psychotherapy. These bring participatory consciousness directly into the therapy or personal growth process, usually forming a more advanced integration with reflexive consciousness. The danger is that some practicioners of these approaches engage in reverse splitting, denigrating the intellect in favor of felt experience rather than working for an integration.

Awareness and Meta-Comments. Thus far we have been examining large advances in reflexive consciousness, as we move from one stage of evolution to the next. Let's now look at smaller ones that happen in our everyday lives as we grow in small increments in our reflexive ability. Each time you become aware of something about your way of feeling or acting in the world and integrate that awareness into your way of being, you are increasing your reflexive consciousness. For example, suppose you become aware that when you feel threatened by someone, you tend to judge them harshly in your mind. Before this awareness, you only knew that you didn't like or approve of certain people, but now you realize that this feeling of disapproval is really a defense against feeling threatened. This is an emergence, an increase in reflexive consciousness. Beforehand you were embedded in your judgments. Now you have emerged from this embeddedness and can reflect on your process of defending yourself.

Similarly, in the process of communicating with someone or with a group, it is possible to emerge from embeddedness in the process and reflect on what is going on. This is sometimes referred to as making "meta-comments," because you are making comments on the comments. For example, suppose you and a friend are trying to decide something but you feel confused and not sure of what the issues are. Then you emerge and reflect on your process and realize that you are both trying overly hard not to hurt or offend the other, with the result that neither of you is really saying what you want, and the result is confusion. You explain this understanding to your friend, and then the two of you can stop being so "nice" and move ahead with clarity in your decision making. This is an example of reflexive consciousness. You emerged from embeddedness in the process and formed a mediated relationship with your experience using concepts.

IDENTITY

I will now explore in more detail solutions to the planetary crisis in four subrealms of consciousness—identity, morality, epistemology, and meaning.

First I will explore the subrealm of identity, which begins with the dialectic between individuality and belonging.

The ground quality is *belonging,* which means the experience of being part of and embedded in your group or community. With belong-

Figure 19.2 Identity

ing people gain the greater part of their psychological well-being and identity through their membership in a group, and their self-esteem may be strongly dependent on the esteem of the group. There are shared values and a feeling of intimacy and caring. Belonging also implies a sense of oneness with the natural world and/or the larger spiritual reality. The emergent quality is *individuality*, which means that people derive a sense of well-being and identity through their personal qualities and accomplishments. They are able to make choices about morals and lifestyle and to shape their own lives according to personal preferences and values. I have shown how individuality was fostered by many of the social changes brought on by increasing social structure. Individuality is an aspect of reflexive consciousness because the concept of the "self" is the prime mediator between the person and their experience and because conscious choice is so crucial to individuality.

Individuality without belonging, and especially without community, results in social *isolation*. People experience little in the way of satisfying connection with others. There is no sense of being connected to or cared for by anyone. There is no tradition or coherent set of values to rely on. Belonging without individuality results in *merging*. To the extent that a person is merged with a group, their uniqueness is suppressed, ignored, or undeveloped. The person has no sense of autonomy or individual power. They don't think for themselves; they are not in touch with their own desires and values. Conformity is the unwritten rule. The extreme of this in today's world is the cult. The healthy goal is an integration of individuality and belonging, which I will call *conscious belonging*.

The Model. I have decided to include this subrealm in the model even though its overall trajectory in social evolution is not unambiguous. In most ways it seems that there has been an increase in individuality throughout social evolution. Many writers characterize stage 1 and 2 peoples as having little individuality and being almost exclusively group oriented. There was a clear increase in individuality from stage 3 to 4, and of course, individuality in the Modern era is even more prevalent. In addition, *belonging* is a crucial component of participatory consciousness, and there is no doubt that belonging has been gradually lost during social evolution. In all these ways this subrealm does fit our social evolutionary model. The one exception is that there is evidence from anthropology that some early tribal peoples had considerable individuality and autonomy (Barnouw 1963, 139–57; Robarchek 1989).

Notice the similarity between *belonging* in the consciousness realm and *community* in the social realm. This is because they are really just two different perspectives on the same phenomenon. Every human quality has two aspects, an inner and an outer—one that can be observed in the world and one that is experienced internally. The consciousness realm deals with the inner aspect of things. Almost every phenomenon in either the material or social realms also has an inner aspect and therefore a mapping onto the consciousness realm. An inner aspect of community is the experience of belonging to a group. An inner aspect of natural living from the material realm is the experience of belonging to the natural world.

Conscious Community. The integrating structure is *conscious belonging*, one aspect of which is conscious community, where individuality and intimacy go hand in hand, where closeness in a group is not dependent on suppression of differences. In conscious community, differences are expressed directly and then worked through or used constructively. Each person's unique individuality and autonomy is respected. This is the explicit goal in psychotherapy groups, and should also be the goal for couples, families, work groups, and all small and large group situations.

In attempting to achieve this in today's world it is important to remember that we are trying something relatively new. Community is part of our heritage from the past, but many tribal and small-town communities did not respect individuality. They certainly didn't respect racial and cultural diversity. "As tightly knit and stable as most old-style communities were, they were also homogeneous, suspicious of outsiders, socially and economically stratified, emotionally stifling, and limited in opportunities for personal and professional development" (Shaffer and Anundsen 1993, 6).

We need to learn from our ancestors and from indigenous peoples about how to live in community, but some of what is needed must be invented in the present. The integration of community and individuality is one of the tasks of stage 6.

Choosing Community. There is another meaning to the term "conscious community"—the community that is chosen by its members. In the past people didn't choose to be in a community, they were born into it. They were born into a religion, a culture, or a village, and that was their community, whether they liked it or not. Today in the industrialized nations, much of this kind of community has been destroyed, but our innate need for community is as strong as ever. Consequently people are beginning to create their own communities, this time by voluntary association rather than by the accident of birth.

There are many interesting trends in this direction. There are conscious residential communities as chronicled in *Builders of the Dawn*

(McLaughlin and Davidson 1990), and there is a new movement toward "co-housing," which combines community with privacy and less expensive housing. Perhaps the largest movement toward conscious community is through informal and professional networks, neighborhood salons, and various personal growth and self-help groups. Many of these don't yet provide a complete sense of community, but they represent steps in that direction. *Creating Community Anywhere* (Shaffer and Anundsen 1993) is an excellent resource on the community movement.

Community is not only a basic human need. It also is what enables us to collaborate effectively, not just in small neighborhoods, but in organizations, economies, nations. One of the crucial factors that will determine whether humanity can survive the current planetary crisis is how capable we are of working well together to make the vast changes that are necessary—whether we can see our common interests and cooperate in resolving our conflicts. In this way, community is critical to our movement into stage 6.

Creating Tradition. Robert Bellah (1985) reminds us that shared tradition is also an important part of community. Much of the fragmentation of this transition time in the industrialized world derives from the diminished ability of our traditions to guide us and provide us with a sense of purpose and belonging. We easily become isolated consumers struggling to substitute status and wealth for the loss of our roots.

However, tradition can also be stifling at a time when we desperately need to be open to radical change. Therefore as part of developing conscious community, we need to create new customs that are meaningful to us without being constricting. In doing this we can choose from our own or others' cultures, and in the process, each community can experiment, create, and gradually develop what is most significant for it. In addition, as nations and as a world we need to develop new traditions and values that we can all share in some way. Of course, any globally shared values must include the appreciation of diverse traditions.

Global Identification. A more advanced integration of belonging and individuality is global identification. This means you identify with the human race as a whole and link your welfare with that of all of humanity. This involves a wider circle of belonging formed by an advancing individuality.

Consider the following: Where are we going? What changes should we make in the way we live? What is in our best interests? When we ask questions like this, who is the "we" being referred to? If it is humanity as a whole, then these are examples of global identification. If the "we" is the United States or the West or black people, for example, then our identification is more limited and therefore more prone to divisiveness. This is not to say that it is inappropriate to think in terms of nations or ethnic groups, but without a larger global identification as well, this can cause problems.

Let's look at an example from the early 1980s. One of the biggest difference between the "doves" of the peace movement, and the "hawks" of the defense establishment was a difference in identity. The hawks would say, "We must defend ourselves against the Russians." The doves would say, "We are acting crazy, building enough weapons to destroy ourselves 50 times over." Notice the difference in identity in these statements. The "we" for the hawks was the United States. The "we" for the doves was humanity. If you looked at the arms race from a strictly national point of view, it didn't look so unreasonable; the Russians looked pretty dangerous. However, if you looked at nuclear build-up from a global point of view, it indeed looked insane.

Notice that the issue of global identification is not simply a cognitive one. It is also an emotional and spiritual issue. Anyone can think about humanity or the planet as a whole. The question is whether we *identify* with the whole, especially when making important decisions. When we decide whom to vote for, or whether to support a war, or how important it is to preserve the rain forests, do we consider the whole world, or only our country, our group?

Looking at this through my model of social evolution, global identification is dependent on an integration of the emergent qualities of advanced reflexive consciousness and intersocietal structure with the ground qualities of empathy and belonging.

Global identification doesn't necessarily mean altruism; it can mean enlightened self-interest, realizing that our best interests are served by looking after the whole. If we each take actions that benefit only ourselves in the short run, we will destroy the world in the long run. (And today the long run isn't very long.) However, we can only see this if we have global identification, if we realize that our interests intertwine with the fate of humanity as a whole. It is quite common for people to be altruistic without global identification, to help others or work for a cause larger than ourselves without thinking globally. We might be dedicated to helping poor people, or people with AIDS, or people from our ethnic group or gender. These attitudes are quite admirable, but they don't constitute global identification.

Expanding Identification. When you identify with a group (family, ethnic group, country, race, religion, profession, gender, etc.), you are concerned about the well-being of that group. You want it to do well.

Often your self-esteem is tied to your perception of the value of (and success of) the group. This is because self-esteem accompanies identity. At the individual level, as part of your identity, you have a self-image and a feeling of how valuable you are. It is crucial for psychological well-being to have positive self-esteem, and this depends not only on your perception of your own value but also the value of groups you identify with. It means being proud to be a woman or a Jew or an American. How many wars have been fought to save face or national honor?

Global identification means identifying with humanity as a whole. It means that your self-esteem is tied to the success of the human race. You are concerned with how well humanity is succeeding at ending war or living in harmony with the natural world, for example. This attitude naturally promotes cooperation rather than competition.

Global identification means expanding our individual identities to encompass all of humanity. Each of us expands our sense of identity in identifying with groups we are a part of, but too often this expansion stops short of the whole. In addition, we often put rigid boundaries around our larger identifications, the groups we identify with. For example, a person with rigid boundaries may identify with his or her country but not trust foreigners, or value being a Christian but hate Jews. Our goal must be to respect and be considerate of people who are outside those groups we identify with. We need to have soft boundaries with our identifications. This allows us to expand to the point where we identify with all of humanity.

Conscious Belonging. In today's world, many of us are also isolated from a sense of belonging to nature and from a larger spiritual connection. Our early ancestors had a profound experience of belonging to the earth and participation in the ways of nature, which gave meaning to their lives. This is being revived today through interest in indigenous and earth-based religions, especially the various forms of shamanism, and through the popularity of the idea of the planet as Gaia, the earth goddess.

There is also a great need today to integrate a feeling of belonging to the cosmos and participating in the larger reality. For example, there is a tremendous interest in Buddhism, Hinduism, and other Eastern religions because they provide for some people a way to recover that ultimate sense of belonging to the whole that has been lost in the Modern era. These traditions provide important aspects of an integrated consciousness, but they are religions of stage 4, when individuality was not well developed, and consequently most of them do not respect the importance of autonomy. Some demand complete obedience to a guru without any choice on the part of the spiritual aspirant. This was evidently appropriate when these religions were developed during stage 4, but it is not today.

A religion for stage 6 must provide for the development of the belonging we have lost without compromising the individuality we have gained. The stage 4 spiritual paths too often devalue the self and individuality. Since the ego often blocks the way to spiritual openness, they consider it a mistake which needs to be relinquished. Instead, we need spiritual disciplines that recognize the value of healthy individual development. Some Western teachers of Eastern religions are modifying the original teachings to make them more appropriate for Western students and for modern sensibilities about autonomy, sexism, and other issues. Some spiritual teachers are developing new understandings which include the value of individuality. A. H. Almaas (1987) has developed a stage 6 spiritual approach that includes the development of what he calls "personal essence" in an overall path of spiritual realization.

Regaining a sense of belonging to the earth and the cosmos will help us relinquish our enchantment with consumption, power, and other vitality substitutes, and learn to align ourselves with nature and the highest human good. This is crucial to making the social and technological changes needed for stage 6. Conscious belonging will help us do this without losing the creative vigor of our individuality and autonomy.

Spirituality. Though the spiritual adepts of stage 4 generally achieved their enlightenment or union with God through a highly experiential process, the vast masses of people received their religion at the mythic level, as dogma, and didn't involve themselves in spiritual growth. This is beginning to change today, with the widespread popular interest in spirituality. Hopefully this will continue into stage 6 in the form of a higher development of reflexive consciousness.

If we look carefully into the experience of spiritual growth, it can be seen as a further advancement of reflexive consciousness. Remember that the progression of reflexive consciousness involves looking ever more deeply at our inner experience. Ken Wilber expresses it nicely:

> The more one can go *within*, or the more one can introspect and reflect on one's self, then the more detached from that self one can become, the more one can rise above that self's limited perspective, and so the less egocentric one becomes . . . and the more one can thus embrace a *deeper identity* with a *wider perspective*. (Wilber 1995, 256–57)

In my view, the essence of spiritual growth is the turning of reflexive consciousness even deeper into the psyche by focusing our attention on the experience of identity itself. What does it mean to identify myself with my body, my mind, my personal history? Who am I really? What happens when I die? Who dies? Is the self a permanent object? What about larger identities—with humanity, with nature, with God, with a larger ground of being? Though these questions can be explored intellectually, true spiritual development involves exploring them through concentrated awareness of our inner experience. Through this exploration, we emerge from embeddedness in a fixed identity with our body and local self, and move into larger, more flexible and fluid identities. Therefore spiritual development constitutes an even more advanced level of reflexive consciousness, which is at the same time thoroughly integrated with participation.

Spiritual growth is far more than just an interesting individual matter. It forms the basis for much of the personal qualities that will be desperately needed for accomplishing the move into stage 6. According to Elgin (1993), the next stage of consciousness evolution will be characterized by a witness consciousness, allowing the detachment needed for global communication and reconciliation. There are a host of other attributes crucial for navigating the coming historical transition which can be the fruits of spiritual development: Empathy and compassion for those who are different from ourselves; the ability to let go of attachment to ego needs and act for the good of the whole; humility; open-heartedness; and an identification with all of humanity, nature, and the cosmos.

While it has been common for people to become narcissistically engrossed in their own personal or spiritual growth and ignore the wider world, there is a growing movement of people and organizations with a strong spiritual base who are actively working toward a resolution of the planetary crisis. In fact, I believe this nascent movement offers our best hope for the future.

MORALITY

Integrative Solutions. In the subrealm of morality, the ground quality is *relational morals*, where morality is governed by empathy for those close to you or whom you care about. The emergent quality is *principled morals*, which flow from universal principles. In stage 6 both of these qualities need to evolve and to be integrated with each other.

If you have relational morals without larger principles, then your morality usually applies only to your own people in a *parochial* way. If

Figure 19.3 Morality

your morals are handed down by a tradition rather than chosen through a reflexive process, they can easily become *dogmatic.* Principled morals dissociated from relational empathy tend toward *detached morals,* which have little effect on real personal interactions.

An important task for stage 6 is to redevelop the ground quality of empathy, our ability to feel with others, as a basis for our morality. Then in integrating this with principled morality, we need to expand our empathy beyond people we know who are similar to us. We need to be able to empathize with Third World peasants, Polish shopkeepers, and tropical rainforests, for example. I will call this integrating structure *global empathy.* This uses our improved reflexive consciousness, our sense of intersocietal connection, and our expanded moral principles, and combines these with a heartfelt relational empathy, which is rooted in our most deeply felt spirituality and sense of meaning in life, not just based on the religious traditions of our upbringing.

Systemic Morality. Just as systemic thinking is an advance in reflexive consciousness, principled morals need to advance beyond principles that protect the rights of the individual to *systemic* principles. We must be able to perceive the world as a many-leveled system, with individuals in families embedded in communities, and these contained in bioregions, ethnic groups, nations, humanity-as-a-whole, and the earth. Our morality needs to recognize the importance of each of these levels. For example, we need a morality that recognizes the importance of community, including each person's rights and obligations (Etzioni 1993). We also need a morality that includes voluntary limits on consumption for the sake of ecological stability.

In addition, we need to be able to see the systemic connections in our world, so that our moral choices can be based on these more encompassing realities. For example, take the simple principle of not harming other life forms such as found in traditional Buddhism. It is no longer adequate to adhere to this moral principle in the old fashioned way by not eating meat or killing insects. We in the industrialized nations cause more serious harm to life forms simply by participating in our economy with its far-reaching effects on the environment. Furthermore there may be more important ways to promote the well-being of animals than refraining from killing, such as working to preserve and restore their habitats.

This new level of morality is illustrated by the abortion issue. In the usual debate, both sides focus on the protection of individual rights—the right of the fetus to life or the right of the woman to control of her body. And, of course, these are very important. However, with our planet seriously overpopulated, there is another and even more important consideration. Though society should do its best to eliminate the need for abortion, we must recognize that to outlaw it would exacerbate population growth, compounding a problem that is threatening to destroy our civilization. We must look at this moral issue from a systemic as well as an individual perspective.

Global empathy and systemic morality will help us to have compassion for the suffering that is happening in the world today, not just that which is happening around us, but the destruction of animals, forests and ecosystems, the poverty and oppression of billions, the great waste of human potential. This will also allow us to view this suffering from a large enough perspective that we can be intelligent in our attempts to change it. This kind of morality combines concern with vision.

Nature and Morality. Some people these days suggest that the natural world should form the basis for an advanced system of morality, that the human race can learn from nature's respect for diversity and interconnectedness (Bookchin 1982). While it's true that we have important lessons to learn from nature's ways, it is a form of reverse splitting to simply romanticize nature and ignore important realities.

For instance, ecosystems do not respect the fate of individual organisms or care about suffering. Predators must kill great numbers of individuals during their lifetimes just to live. A healthy ecosystem doesn't minimize suffering and death. Many species have large numbers of their young die before reaching adulthood as part of a process of selecting the healthiest to continue the line. Concern about the life and health and suffering of individual organisms is a *human* ethic, and one we should be proud of, even though we have yet to actualize it very well.

Of course, we must avoid the opposite extreme of portraying nature as "red in tooth and claw." At the beginning of the Modern era, when much of our effort was focused on conquering nature, the prevailing view was that nature and indigenous peoples were "wild" and "savage" and that we needed to bring the benefits of civilization to the wilderness and these "primitives." As discussed in this book, indigenous peoples are often more ethical than "civilized" people, and there is evidence of a great deal of cooperation in nature along with competition and destruction. This outmoded negative image of nature is as misguided as the current romanticizing of nature. The natural world is beautiful as it is, but it is both creative and destructive. Human nature at its best has its own beauty, and human morality has its own unique strength, which is different in important ways from that of the rest of nature.

Morality Based on Expanded Identity. As we develop spiritually, not only our morality but our sense of identity can expand to include the human race and the natural world. From this place, people naturally act in ways that are moral, not because of principles, but because they are simply acting to take care of their larger "self." (Macy 1990) This is one of the main teachings of the deep ecology movement. Joanna Macy writes: "The conventional notion of the self with which we have been raised and to which we have been conditioned by mainstream culture is being undermined. . . . It is being replaced by wider constructs of identity and self-interest [which are] coextensive with other beings and the life of our planet" (Macy 1991, 183).

Deep ecologists are fond of pointing out that we don't have to be moral to avoid harming our foot to benefit some other part of the body. So if we identify humanity and the earth as our larger self, we will naturally want to nurture and protect all of the planet. This morality is based on an advancement of the emergent quality, reflexive consciousness.

EPISTEMOLOGY

Let's study the evolution of our mode of understanding reality as a subrealm of consciousness, which can be called epistemology.

Figure 19.4 Epistemology

The stage 5 method for understanding reality has been science, which is based on reflexive consciousness and involves rational understanding of empirical data. It has been purged of participation so completely that it has become *detached* and therefore limited in its ability to study many aspects of reality. Our current model of science assumes a completely independent and objective observer, whose bias shouldn't affect the outcome of an experiment. This approach has been extremely effective with the purely physical aspects of reality, though modern developments in subatomic physics have demonstrated its limits. Modern science has had much more difficulty in studying human reality, social and psychological, because it is so participatory. The attempt to use objective experimentation in these areas has led to distortions of the subject matter.

The ground quality in this subrealm involves understanding reality through the subjective rather than the objective. In earlier times we understood our world through intuitive and participatory modes, for example through identification with animals, ritual, and living with the land. We understood others through empathy. We understood the body through reading subtle energy flows. We understood life through art and religion. In the Modern era, these modes are seen as superstitious and inaccurate, and they are denigrated or relegated to second place in our social priorities.

Of course, these participatory methods of understanding can also be one-sided. Used without rationality they can result in *impressionability,* where a person uncritically accepts others' interpretations of reality and his or her experience. This blind faith, often accompanied by dogmatism, distorts reality in a different way.

Doubting and Believing. A crucial difference between ground and emergent forms of epistemology is illustrated by Peter Elbow's ingenious distinction between the "doubting game" and the "believing game" (1973, 147–91). The doubting game is best illustrated by Modern science. You test whether something is accurate or valid through the use of skepticism. You try to prove it wrong; you look for contradictions and errors. This works very well for the physical sciences, but there are many situations where a doubting attitude distorts what is being tested. It you want to test the effects of confidence on the immune system, for example, an attitude of doubt will erode confidence, therefore altering what is being tested. Of course, you can attempt to avoid this through double blind studies, but these have their own problems and can't be used in many real life situations.

The believing game is particularly well suited for consciousness questions. In this game, you provisionally assume that something is true and then see what the results are in your life. For example, if you want to see if your mental attitude affects your medical state, you could provisionally assume that it does, work on changing your attitude, and see if your health improves. Notice that this is very different from blind faith, where you uncritically assume the truth of something. In the believing game, you try out a belief for a while and then critically ask what its effects have been. Of course, our original ground quality in stage 1 was blind faith, impressionability. However, the believing game includes both participatory and reflexive consciousness. And in stage 6 we need to use both the doubting and believing games.

Table 19.2 summarizes the differences between participatory and reflexive modes of knowing.

Table 19.2 Participatory and Reflexive Ways of Knowing

Participatory	**Reflexive**
Intuitive	Factual
Artistic, religious	Scientific
Subjective	Objective
Emotional	Rational
Believing	Doubting

Integration. For an integrating structure we will need a form of science that includes an understanding of the scientist as a *participant-observer.* This has already crept into quantum physics and has been a part of the social sciences from the beginning. Many of the most important issues before us today cannot be understood without a recognition of psychological, spiritual, and cultural realities that are not completely objective. These issues can't be studied with a reductionistic approach to science involving a completely divorced researcher experimenting with isolated variables. In order to properly deal with these issues we must have a participatory science, a science that includes methods that can be applied to problems that are inherently meaningful, interconnected, and multileveled. The Institute of Noetic Sciences has been on the frontier of the development of such an approach to science (1993).

Society also needs to give more validation to ways of knowing reality other than science. There are too many crucial aspects of life that can't yet be fully understood with science, even the best science. Much of psychology, medicine, spirituality, social relations, and economic and political realities are simply too complex and subtle for science in the near future. Art, religion, and the humanities have always provided understanding of these other aspects of life. These ground quality modes need to regain the importance they have had in the past. However, we need to integrate them with our Modern skeptical, reflexive consciousness so we can critically evaluate the answers they produce. We need to have the advantage of our spirit, emotions, and intuition without the danger of being trapped in dogma.

Advancing the Emergent Quality. In addition to integrating the ground quality, we also can advance the emergent quality, reflexive consciousness. Going back to the beginning of stage 5, notice that the introduction of the scientific method involved a deeper reflection on our mode of understanding reality. This resulted in a particular way of knowledge (science) that was very successful and useful. Now as we see the limits of exclusively relying on this mode, this can take us to a deeper level of reflection on our inner process of knowing and therefore another level of emergence. This time we are emerging from a reliance on just one mode of knowing to a recognition that there are many different ways of knowing and of validating knowledge, each appropriate for different subject matters and situations. Thus stage 6 consciousness is moving toward multiple modes of knowledge.

MEANING

This subrealm deals with how human beings discover deeper meaning and purpose in our lives.

Figure 19.5 Meaning

I have discussed previously how meaning is intimately connected with *participation* and belonging. It seems that the sense of meaning or higher purpose in life comes from feeling part of something larger than yourself, such as a cause, a group, an ideal, nature, or the spiritual whole, which gives your life meaning through participating in its intrinsic value. For example, it might involve a concern for other people that grows out of a sense of community and common humanity. As our experience of participation has been suppressed, we have largely lost touch with a sense of life purpose, our lives have begun to feel *meaningless,* and we have made money and superficialities our goals. In addition, our societies have lost direction and purpose, contributing to the current crisis.

However, meaning does not come from participation alone; it also depends on *understanding,* using your reflexive ability to critically evaluate your experience and make rational sense of life. If you have an intense experience of participation without the ability to critically evaluate the experience, you are likely to accept whatever *dogma* accompanies the experience. If it occurs in a religious context, you may become a true believer. If it happens in a political context, you may become a fanatic. Remember that Hitler played on people's emotions and sense of belonging. Without the reflexive ability to evaluate and understand your experience, you can be swept along by something that might be destructive for you or others. In moving to stage 6, we need *critical participation* in the search for meaning in our lives, individually and as societies.

In addition, in the identity subrealm if you can integrate participation and belonging with individuality, it means that you don't sacrifice yourself for a higher cause, but instead find ways to contribute that are simultaneously satisfying to you and helpful to others or society.

As people develop spiritually, they sometimes experience a spiritual calling that imbues their lives with meaning. This is a case of advancing reflexive consciousness integrated with participatory consciousness allowing a person to access a deeper part of the psyche that is often hidden from awareness.

My Experience with Life Purpose. I've had a good deal of professional experience with the issue of life purpose, working with people therapeutically and running workshops on the topic. A significant portion of my self-help book *Inner Journeys* (Earley 1990) involves psychospiritual exercises for finding your life purpose.

An important part of my own personal growth has been discovering and actualizing my life purpose, which is about contributing what I can to mastering the planetary crisis and building a healthy global society, hence this book. This sense of purpose comes from a spiritual place in me that is deeply participatory. Despite all the logical reasons I know about the importance of fundamental social change, my purpose comes primarily from my heart. I feel that I have a calling to help resolve the current planetary crisis and therefore advance the great process of social evolution.

UNDERSTANDING SOCIETY AND SOCIAL TRANSFORMATION

Let's look at the implications of advancing reflexive consciousness for the understanding of social realities? In *New World, New Mind* (Ornstein and Ehrlich 1989), the authors point out that our instinctive emotional reactions to danger aren't adequate for recognizing the gradual, insidious ecological perils that are now threatening us. Humanity evolved biologically in such a way that we are prepared to see the danger of an advancing tiger but not the approaching disintegration of our environment. Let's look at this insight through the lens of the model of social evolution I am developing. Our participatory consciousness isn't adequate to give us good information for action in the Modern world because our environment is so vastly different from that in which we biologically evolved. Therefore we need a highly developed reflexive consciousness, integrated with participation, to understand our predicament and act accordingly.

Our reflexive consciousness has developed to the point where humanity has some understanding of how society operates and changes. Society may now, for the first time, have enough wisdom in this area to make a fundamental change in what drives social evolution. Until recently societal survival has been the primary driving force in social evolution. We haven't been able to make societal choices that were really aimed at promoting our well-being because we were too caught up in military and economic competition and the need to feed our growing population. Now, however, we are beginning to see the larger picture, to know enough to direct social evolution consciously rather than having it be driven unconsciously. This gives us the opportunity to create a global society that is truly healthy and fulfilling for all its members and for the earth. This will be required for us to surmount the current crisis and move on to stage 6.

SUMMARY

Table 19.3 summarizes these recommendations for the consciousness of stage 6.

Table 19.3 Stage 6: Consciousness Solutions

Realm	Integration	Advancing Emergent or Integrated
Consciousness	Integral consciousness conscious participation & revitalization	Systemic/dialectical thinking, experiential psychology & spirituality
Identity	Conscious belonging, community	Global identification, spiritual identity
Morality	Global empathy	Systemic morality, morality based on expanded identity
Epistemology	Participant/observation	Multiple modes of knowledge
Meaning	Critical participation	Spiritual calling

What would a world of stage 6 consciousness be like? I see people having closeness and community in their lives without giving up their individuality or their right to cultural experimentation. People make moral decisions based on a deep empathy with each other and the natural world and a larger understanding of the systemic consequences of our actions in an interconnected world. In this world, scholars have a deeper understanding of the physical world, human nature, and society, coming from new participatory forms of study and more advanced process and dialectical thinking.

Everyone is interested in expanding and revitalizing their lives in a variety of ways—through physical, emotional, and spiritual healing, through relationship and community, through reconnecting with the earth, through art and ritual. However, these are not pursued blindly but rather with a critical intelligence. There is an integration of the mind and the heart, not only in individual lives but also in our culture. People have a sense of higher purpose in their lives, and many are dedicated to restoring our natural habitat, actualizing a new healthy culture and society, or helping those who have been hurt during the painful transition to stage 6. There is a common societal purpose, inspired by a spiritual vision of a better life for all people and a sense of belonging to the human race, the earth, and the cosmos.

XX

THE SOCIAL REALM

In chapters 16 and 17, I explored solutions in the power realm. Now let's look at other aspects of the social realm that need integration in solving the planetary crisis.

COMMUNITY AND BUREAUCRACY

One of the tragedies of the Modern era is the increase in bureaucracy and the corresponding loss of genuine human contact. This is a direct outgrowth of the pervasiveness of social structure and the loss of community. I have already discussed community in the context of individuality and belonging in the last chapter; now let's look at its relationship to bureaucracy. I will delineate a subrealm of the social realm that deals with this.

Figure 20.1 Organizations

Bureaucracy comes from the triumph of social structure over community in the social realm. In most business settings and even in churches and schools, impersonal bureaucracy has become the norm. When community is suppressed in favor of mediated transactions, then everything is done by the rule book and people are treated as objects, as if they were no more than the role they play.

It is interesting to note that formal bureaucracy was originally instituted in order to limit favoritism, corruption, and advancement based on "old boy" networks. These abuses of community in organizations were so rampant that a highly mediated form of social structure was introduced to keep them in check. Of course, now things have gone too far in the other direction, but it is instructive to see that community can be abused as well as social structure.

Integrative Solutions. Only in small *simple groups*—communities, organizations, societies—can people exist without much social structure. In larger groups a lack of social structure results in *ineffectiveness*, a failure to accomplish important tasks needed for the welfare of the group. Thus in medium to large organizations we can't avoid social structure, but we can attempt to integrate it with community and personal connection. Let's call this integrating structure *community within organization.* One way to accomplish this is to recognize the value of the personal side and to set aside time to nurture it. This has been brought into business by management consultants under the name of "organizational development." It must become the corporate norm that human and relational needs are attended to. Time needs to be set aside for employees to enjoy each other and work through personal conflicts. The current popularity of self-managed work teams is moving things in this direction.

It is also important for corporations to develop some real community with their customers instead of simply treating them as sources of money. Companies have always wanted loyal satisfied customers, and the best way to do this is to develop a relationship with the consumer group that goes beyond advertising. This would help the company to be more in touch with the true needs of its customers and allow ecological and democratic businesses to educate their patrons in these areas. The resulting corporate community might even include all the stakeholders of the company—employees, managers, stockholders, customers, the local community where the business is located, and business associates in other corporations.

In addition, we customers also need to learn to relate in a human way to all the people we meet in business contexts—storekeepers, cab drivers, repairmen, sales reps, and so on. People relate in this way in small towns, and we need to find ways to bring this human touch into our lives in the large cities and suburbs where most of us live. This may require a reorganization of the structure of our urban spaces so that we live in smaller, more self-contained units that naturally promote community.

Organizational Intelligence. At a deeper level, we are beginning to see that the most effective organizations are actually those that have developed an organizational structure that promotes community, empowerment, initiative and creativity. These organizations have the most committed employees, the best communication, and the highest levels of creative problem solving. We might call this group or organizational intelligence. In the end, integrating the ground and emergent qualities is necessary for the emergent quality to advance further.

SPECIALIZATION AND COORDINATION

As social structure evolved over time, societies differentiated into sectors, such as education, the military, religion, and so on. Originally these functions were all performed by everyone or by a leader or governing group. However, during the course of social evolution, each function became the province of a different segment of society. Over time these sectors specialized even further into finer and finer subdivisions. This has resulted in academic and occupational specialties that deal in more and more depth with smaller and smaller aspects of reality and society.

I can represent this as the subrealm of function (figure 20.2).

Figure 20.2 Function

The emergent quality is *specialization*, as just discussed. The ground quality is *coordination*, which characterized society at the beginning of social evolution. The original societies were specialized only by gender and age, and each person was of necessity a generalist, being able to perform almost all the functions necessary for survival and well-being. Thus these simple societies naturally had good coordination. It is only in simple societies or other *simple groups* that there is a situation of coordination without specialization.

With the growth of social structure and specialization, societies develop a need for ways to coordinate the different sectors in their overall functioning. The natural coordination of stage 1 needs to be replaced by an organized coordination in later stages. At the very least there must be a ruler or president who deals with the whole picture. However, this is a minimum; in Modern society we really need much more in the way of coordinating structures and people who have a broad understanding of the overall picture.

Fragmentation. In today's world, the lack of coordination has resulted in a situation of *fragmentation*, where there are many specialists who have a great deal of detailed information and expertise but little understanding of where their specialty fits into the whole. There is a joke about specialization: As we specialize we come to know more and more about less and less, until eventually we know absolutely everything about nothing. This unfortunately has a ring of truth to it.

Overspecialization often leads to a situation where there is a great deal of very high quality work done on the wrong problems or with faulty assumptions. For example, the United States has very talented economists creating detailed economic models that are based on such misleading ideas about society and economic behavior that they provide little help with the real world. This is because economics has become so specialized that its practitioners have little knowledge of psychology or ecology, two areas that are crucial to it. Thus standard economic theory assumes that material input sources and output sinks for economic processes are inexhaustible (Daly and Cobb 1989). It also makes naive psychological assumptions about people's economic behavior. Modern society has specialists in many areas who are operating in such a narrow range that they have little understanding of the relationship of their specialty to the whole of society. Consequently many destructive decisions are made.

Overspecialization also contributes to the dissociation of our time. For example, originally everyone participated in artistic and creative endeavors as a natural part of life, such as the creation of tools or community rituals. Today art is specialized so that most people don't participate in anything artistic while certain people are full time artists who carry all the creative impulses for the society. This leads to a deadness in the average person and a tendency toward eccentricity or emotional disturbance in many artists.

Specialization in Context. What integrating structure does the world need in this subrealm? At an individual level, we need to regain the well-roundedness we had in earlier times, when people had access to many sides of themselves. We need to be artistic and logical, knowledgeable about people and machines, interested in science and literature. In addition to delving deeply into one area, we all need to be generalists.

At a societal level, we need *specialization in context.* We need people who are aware of the larger context in which they are operating. Besides being experts in their own specialties, people need to be familiar with other related specialties and to grasp the dynamics of human nature and society. In addition, each sector needs to employ some generalists—people who are well versed in the connections between areas and have a larger perspective on the whole. Generalism has long been the goal of liberal education, but with our increasing emphasis on economic competitiveness, individually and nationally, it has fallen by the wayside. Today students are more likely to choose business or engineering rather than liberal arts in order to ensure their prospects of making a good living.

Specialization in context can be illustrated by my own choices. My area of specialty is group psychotherapy. To be effective as a group therapist, I need a general knowledge of psychotherapy and psychology. To understand people and the context of their lives and struggles, I also need to know something about spirituality, philosophy, literature, relationships, social class, and the current planetary crisis. This makes me a specialist in context. In addition, in writing this book I have educated myself as a generalist, studying a wide variety of disciplines to put together an overview of our current situation in the context of human history.

Our current societal problems are so broad and interconnected that most helpful solutions can only come through a broad general understanding of many different areas.

CHANGE

The change subrealm deals with how social change occurs. This is a crucial issue today because we are in the midst of a major historical transition, and change is especially rapid. This subrealm deals with the speed of change and the flexibility or resistance to change in technology, social structures, and consciousness.

Figure 20.3 Change

The Rate of Change. In this realm, the ground quality is *tradition,* which means that the society is oriented toward maintaining its cultural values, technology, and ways of living. New ways of doing things are frowned on, and what is admired is the tried and true. There is a sense of shared values and worldview. *Innovation* means an openness to developing and experimenting with new ways of thinking and living. This quality has gradually emerged throughout social evolution. Not only has society changed considerably over the span of human history, but the *rate* of change has been increasing. You can see this by examining the time span for each successive era in table 20.1.

Table 20.1 Time Spans of the Eras

	Era	Dates	Length
1	Upper Paleolithic	35,000–8000 B.C.	27000 yrs.
2	Neolithic	8000–3000 B.C.	5000 yrs.
3	Archaic	3000–500 B.C.	2500 yrs.
4	Ancient/Medieval	500 B.C.–1500	2000 yrs.
5	Modern	1500–2000	500 yrs.
6	Next	2000–	

These figures are only a gross indication of the fact that the rate of technological and social change have been increasing throughout social evolution.

In a society that has tradition without innovation, there is *rigidity*, where people cling to the old ways no matter what. Novelty is avoided at all costs, and the need for change is often denied. Such a society might do well in a quiet historical period with little turmoil or challenge, but in today's world, rigidity is a recipe for disaster. When a society has innovation without the steadying influence of appropriate traditions, it leads to *reckless experimentation,* such as happens in the development of new technology without understanding its societal consequences.

In the Modern world, one of the reasons we are moving away from tradition is because of our loss of community. Tradition is closely tied to community, and as community is suppressed, tradition loses some of its influence. This has both good and bad consequences. The waning of the importance of tradition has left many people without moral or spiritual guidelines, contributing to the rootlessness, commercialism, and power hunger of our time. However, the decline of traditional rigidity may aid us in the current crisis when we strongly need flexibility and innovation. Therefore we must find ways to restore community without returning to the narrow customs of our past.

Conscious Use of Tradition. One way of integrating the ground and emergent qualities is by making conscious use of existing traditions without being bound to any one. Let's call this *conscious tradition*. For the first time in history we have available to us cultures from all over the world and from many previous eras. People are drawing from these traditions as they experiment with ways of moving into the next era.

Some people are consciously choosing to embrace aspects of their own traditions in creating healthy cultures (Spretnak 1993). A person may choose to adopt a different tradition because it provides an antidote to problems with his or her heritage. Many people are selecting aspects of various traditions in creating a lifestyle for the next era. They are using tradition consciously as a springboard for innovation. This is one of the most promising developments for the future.

Sanctioned Innovation. An advancement in the emergent quality that also includes an integration of the ground quality is *sanctioned innovation.* This means having traditions that encourage innovation. For example, the field of scientific research is specifically organized to encourage innovation. To be successful as a scientist you must do original research, and the most honored scientists are those who make the most radical contributions. There are, of course, even in this field, examples of blind clinging to tradition, where scientists refuse to consider new evidence that might require modification of their cherished views of reality. However, the traditions of the field do encourage innovation. "Modernism" is a movement in the arts that explicitly values innovation.

A third example of sanctioned innovation comes from the corporate world, where companies must be oriented toward flexibility and change in order to survive and flourish in their highly competitive situation. Especially in the 1990s, successful corporations need to be able to introduce new products very quickly, anticipate short-term trends in their industry, reorganize their companies, and be fast and innovative. They have been forced to transcend their bureaucratic sluggishness in order to succeed. This is one of the reasons that the corporate world has potentially much to offer in this time of historical transformation.

Modern society faces an interesting dilemma. The institutions with the most ability to be innovative (corporations) are those that do not care about society and have a very short term perspective. The institutions with the least flexibility (government) are those that are supposed to care about the interests of society as a whole. One of our tasks for the next era must be to make corporations more accountable to society as a whole and to make government more innovative. We need to find ways to build into our structures of governance much more innovation and orientation toward change.

In stage 6 more than in earlier stages, we need flexibility and sanctioned innovation in our social structures, our technology, and our attitudes and values. For example, this could include a mode of governance that integrates mainstream politics and political activism. At a personal level it might involve people in life-long learning, periodic changes of career, and personal growth and development. Society might have a sector that looks toward the future and plans for change.

Until recently, our models of social and material reality have been static. We have not recognized the dynamic process nature of reality, and this has led us to create technology and social structures that are static, that don't include in a deep way an understanding of process. With the advancement of developmental and dialectical thinking in the consciousness realm, we will soon be ready to incorporate these understandings into both our technology and our social systems.

Appropriate Innovation. So far I have been talking about tradition versus innovation in the Modern era and what is needed for the next era. However, the world is now in a special situation. We are in a time of profound change from one era to another so we need a high degree of innovation. We are undergoing such a profound transformation of every aspect of living, that this degree of change couldn't possibly be included under any sanctioned conception of innovation. We must be ready to examine and, if necessary, alter our most fundamental ideas about reality and society. Only this level of willingness to change will allow us to move into the next era.

One of the greatest barriers to fundamental change is that it necessarily will disrupt many existing arrangements and vested interests. Many people will have to find new jobs or even new careers. Many corporations and governmental institutions will have to significantly revamp their ways of doing things. In promoting the changes that are needed at this time in history, we must acknowledge the disruptions that will occur and find ways to help the people and organizations that are affected. This will make them less likely to resist the necessary changes.

However, rapid innovation is not enough; society needs *appropriate* innovation. We certainly don't want an unconscious acceptance of change for change's sake or the "new is better" attitude that we see in the yearly changes in fashions and automobile models. Even genuine innovation is not sufficient. We already have considerable real innovation in science, technology, and business, but much of it is oriented toward supporting the status quo. We have innovation in biotechnology, genetic mapping, nuclear fusion, marketing, management, and other areas, but most of it simply continues our current suppression of the ground qualities and therefore isn't likely to help us move into a healthy stage 6 world.

Even though tradition is the ground quality in the change realm, by now at the end of the Modern era, the emergent qualities have become our traditions in most areas. Therefore the innovation we most need involves regaining the ground qualities and creating new ways to integrate them with the emergent qualities.

CROSS-REALM INTEGRATION

Let's explore appropriate innovation in the model by including other realms in our analysis. For example, nuclear fusion is the result of sanctioned innovation in science and business, and therefore it represents an integration in the change subrealm, but in other realms it represents dissociation. In the material realm it is technology dissociated from natural process, and in the power realm it encourages unnecessary centralization and therefore power imbalance. Thus an activity can't be properly evaluated according to its status with respect to change alone. It must also be analyzed in conjunction with the other realms involved.

This is not unique to change. Any activity must be evaluated according to all the realms it touches. For example, there are personal growth organizations and spiritual groups that represent true integrations of reflexive and participatory consciousness, but promote dependence in their participants and authoritarianism in their leaders, thus being dissociated in the social realm. It is also possible for an organization to use advanced methods of democratic decision making in causing ecological destruction, thus being integrated in the social realm and dissociated in the material realm. An integration in one realm makes it more likely that there will be integration in others, but it doesn't guarantee it.

In fact, the realms are somewhat arbitrary ways of dividing up reality, so in evaluating an organization, person, method, or movement, we must consider how integrated or dissociated it is in all its aspects.

SUMMARY OF SOLUTIONS

Table 20.2 sums up the recommended solutions presented in each realm and subrealm and table 20.3 completes the chart of social evolution.

Table 20.2 Solutions in Each Subrealm

Realm	Integration	Advancing Emergent or Integrated
Material	Ecological technology & industry, population stabilization	Computer/information technology
Politics	Improved democracy	Cooperation
Economics	Democratic & ecological economy	

Realm	Integration	Advancing Emergent or Integrated
Intersocietal Politics	Federalism	World governance
Intersocietal Economics	Fair trade, subsidiarity, guardianship of economy	World economy
Culture	Cultural pluralism	Cultural freedom
Gender	Gender equality	Gender role freedom
Organizations	Community in organization	Organizational intelligence
Function	Specialization in context	
Change	Conscious tradition, appropriate innovation	Sanctioned innovation
Consciousness	Integral consciousness, conscious participation & revitalization	Systemic/dialectical thinking, experiential psychology & spirituality
Identity	Conscious belonging, community	Global identification, spiritual identity
Morality	Global empathy	Systemic morality, morality based on expanded identity
Epistemology	Participant/observation	Multiple modes of knowledge
Meaning	Critical participation	Spiritual calling

Table 20.3 Social Evolution

Era	Qualities	Material	Social	Consciousness
1 Paleolithic		Hunting & gathering	Family, band	Magic, animism
2 Neolithic		Horticulture, herding	Village, chiefdom	Myth: Goddess
3 Archaic		Agriculture, bronze	City, early state	Myth: gods & heroes
4 Ancient/ Medieval		Gradual advance	Historic empire	Religion, philosophy
5 Modern		Industry	Democracy, capitalism	Science, autonomy
Current Crisis		Population/environmental crisis	Economic colonialism	Loss of vitality, empathy, meaning
6 Next Integrative		Ecological technology & industry, population stability	Pluralism, federalism, democratic/ ecological economy, fair trade	Conscious participation & revitalization
6 Next Advancing		Information technology	Cooperation, world governance	Systemic/dialectical thinking, psychology, spirituality

XXI

POSITION ANALYSIS

Now that I have laid out the model and discussed societywide solutions to the planetary crisis, it is time to apply the model to a more detailed analysis of what each person and group can contribute to resolving the crisis.

RELATIONSHIP BETWEEN THE QUALITIES.

First let's look at the relationship between the ground and emergent qualities, and how it develops over time. In examining this, keep in mind that the qualities are abstractions that come into existence through people, groups, values, social structures, and institutions. I will call these *representatives* of the qualities. For example, if a person is strongly oriented toward technology and the intellect, then I would say that person *represents* the emergent qualities.

Pure Ground Quality. In stages 0 and 1 of social evolution, the emergent quality exists only to a small degree, so the ground quality is all that is important. I will call this a *pure ground quality*. As the emergent quality evolves over time, the ground quality in a particular society can remain pure only if the society in question is isolated from those societies that are developing emergent qualities. Today the pure ground quality is represented by those few isolated hunter-gatherer societies discovered by anthropologists in this century.

Evolution of the Ground Quality. If the two qualities are in contact in a society, which is usually the case, then at each stage of social evolution the ground quality evolves as well as the emergent quality, and the relationship between the qualities evolves. In the early stages the ground is dominant and the emergent quality is just trying to establish itself.[1] The qualities may be opposed and dissociated from each other or they may

1. Of course, a quality can't try to establish itself; it is an abstraction that has no will. This phrase means that the representatives of the quality try to establish it. I will occasionally personify qualities in this way as a shorthand way of referring to the representatives of the quality.

be relatively integrated. In later stages the qualities are usually dissociated from each other; the emergent is dominant and the ground is trying to keep from being suppressed. Today the ground has been thoroughly suppressed and is now beginning to return.

As the emergent quality evolves, the ground quality will change because of having to deal with it. The ground quality will absorb some of the emergent quality, or oppose it, or both. Those people or groups representing the ground quality will be affected by those representing the emergent quality and need to take a stance toward them. For example, as technology develops, those people who retain a way of life dedicated to natural living will do this either because they have no access to technology, or because they choose not to use it, or because they use it in natural ways. In all of these cases, the ground quality is no longer pure. Even those who have no access to technology know that there is something others have that they are missing.

Once the emergent quality begins to dominate, there are frequent ground quality movements attempting to keep it alive or bring it back. Eugene Taylor (1993) chronicles ground quality movements in the consciousness realm throughout American history. Riane Eisler (1987) and Murray Bookchin (1982) recount the history of ground quality movements in the gender and power realms.

Suppression of Ground Quality. In today's world with the emergent qualities ascendant, the ground quality is pushed into the background and society is largely dedicated to the emergent quality. This happens in two ways:

1. The ground quality can be suppressed through *splitting*. This means that a set of values and ideas develop that appreciate the emergent quality and denigrate the ground quality. The ground quality may be seen as evil or shameful or inconsequential or, in some way, second rate. Under these circumstances, for the ground quality to be integrated, there must be a change in cultural values. For example, until recently in Western society in the consciousness realm, emotion and intuition were maligned. They were seen as the province of women, inferior beings who couldn't use logic and rationality as they should. This is now beginning to change as society starts to recognize the value of emotional understanding for psychological health and the value of intuition for achieving understanding that is not accessible through rational channels.

In working to undo splitting, the development of self-esteem and group-esteem among ground quality representatives is very helpful. The more they can learn to feel good about themselves, their group, and the qualities they represent, the better chance they have to espouse those qualities in the larger society.

2. The ground quality can be suppressed through *social dynamics*. This means that the increasing prevalence of the emergent quality has the social effect of decreasing the ground quality even if there is no splitting ideology that disparages the ground quality. For example, community has been disrupted by social mobility, the market economy, and other forces associated with social structure, even though society doesn't have an ideology that devalues community. In the case of suppression through social dynamics, solutions are likely to emphasize institutional, economic, and political changes rather than changes in values.

Response of Ground Quality Representatives. When a ground quality is suppressed, people and groups who represent the dissociated ground quality can respond with submission or assertiveness:

1. Being *submissive* means they accept their secondary role in society and may even believe negative ideology about their quality. Thus a person whose strengths are emotion and intuition may feel inadequate because he or she isn't as good at the rational thinking that is valued by society.
2. Being *assertive* means that they value the ground quality for themselves and refuse to accept their secondary place in society. They may actively espouse the value of their way of living and try to convince others of the dangers of overreliance on the emergent quality. For example, some people have promoted a return to the land to live in a more intimate relationship with nature.

DISSOCIATION OF THE QUALITIES WITHIN THE POPULATION

Now let's return to a discussion of the suppression of the ground quality, today's situation. The ground and emergent qualities are dissociated from each other, which means that they are divided among the population and institutions of society. Some people and groups represent the emergent quality, others represent the ground quality, and very few represent both in an integrated way. For example, in the consciousness realm, men tend to represent the emergent quality, being more oriented toward rational, logical, linear thinking and individuality. Women tend to represent the ground quality, being more emotional, intuitive, and oriented toward relationship. Of course, these are only general statements about the averages among men and women. There are many men who are emotional and intuitive and many women who are rational and logical.

Dominant groups in Modern industrialized societies usually represent the emergent qualities, and oppressed groups often represent the ground qualities. In fact, it is fair to say that the oppressed groups *hold* the ground qualities for society. Since the ground qualities have been suppressed, the groups in power may denigrate them, so it is up to oppressed groups to keep these qualities alive. Of course, oppressed groups don't ordinarily do this purposely. They simply represent the ground qualities because that is who they are; their culture values the ground qualities. However, in social evolutionary terms, oppressed groups serve the function of preserving the ground qualities during eras when they are suppressed in the rest of society.

Oppressed groups don't always represent the ground qualities. This must be analyzed on a case-by-case basis. For example, in the material realm, men are more technologically oriented but women aren't necessarily more connected to nature. In the social realm, whites represent social structure because they are so involved in the structures of society, but oppressed ethnic groups aren't necessarily more oriented toward community. Some of them have retained a strong community orientation in their cultures, and therefore they hold this quality for society, but not all.

Most of the institutions in Modern society represent the emergent quality. For example, the medical profession is strongly oriented toward machines, surgery, and drugs (technological living) rather than natural or systemic forms of healing (natural living), and it ignores the doctor-patient relationship and the strong influence of the patient's state of mind on disease (participatory consciousness).

The ground and emergent qualities also tend to be divided up among societies, also along power lines. Thus the industrialized countries are oriented toward the emergent qualities, and the Third World is oriented toward the ground qualities. In addition, some Third World societies represent previous stages of social evolution rather than a Modern ground quality.

Looking at this from a long-term evolutionary point of view, those groups representing the emergent qualities have helped society to evolve, and those groups representing the ground qualities have held those qualities so they could be integrated when society was ready for a further step in evolution.

Dissociation within People. These characterizations I am making are only rough approximations. Some members of the dominant group will actually represent the ground quality and some members of oppressed groups will represent the emergent quality. Even as individuals we don't represent only one quality. We all have both ground and emergent qualities within us. In a historical time of dissociation, these qualities within us will tend to be dissociated from each other. For example, our intellect will dominate and our emotional life will be suppressed and devalued, or vice versa.

It is the dissociation that really causes the problem. In psychotherapy parlance, dissociation means that two different parts of a person are kept separate from each other, so that they don't work together. One may be suppressed entirely in favor of the other, or each may function in its own realm with no communication. For example, some people are more intellectual than emotional, but this isn't a problem if they are capable of tuning into their emotions and using them to guide their lives when appropriate. In dissociation, they suppress their emotions and avoid dealing with them. On the other hand, some people are more emotional than intellectual, but that in itself isn't a problem. The difficulty comes from not using their minds to organize and understand their emotions. Another example of dissociation involves religion; a person might be in touch with their religious side when in church on Sunday, but live an unspiritual life of competitiveness and greed during the rest of the week.

Dissociation with Groups. Today's problems come not just from dissociation within individuals but also within groups and societies. There will always be some groups that emphasize the ground quality more than the emergent or vice versa, but in a healthy society these two tendencies within a group would work together. For example, an environmental group might be very strongly oriented toward natural living in its policy actions (ground quality, material realm), but to be effective it would also need to know how to deal with the power structures of the society (emergent quality, social realm). A group such as this that used emergent qualities in the service of ground qualities would be integrated.

Notice that in this example I have crossed realms. This shouldn't be surprising. Remember that the realms are somewhat arbitrary subdivisions of reality which I am using for convenience in constructing this model.

Representing Previous Stages. A person or group can also represent a previous stage of social evolution. Each stage of social evolution is characterized by a certain relationship or balance between the ground and emergent qualities. As the leading edge of evolution moves on to a new stage, there are many groups and societies that don't make the transition for a few centuries or even longer. This is especially true for groups that don't have much contact with the leading edge societies. For example until recently most of the Third World was in stage 4, with parts of

Africa in stage 3 or even 2. There have even been scattered discoveries of isolated stage 1 societies surviving to the present.

Even within a stage 5 society there will be people and groups that represent stage 4. In today's world there are still large remnants of stage 4 cultures, since the transition to stage 5 occurred only about 500 years ago. For example, fundamentalist religious movements—Christian, Muslim, Jewish, Hindu, or other—are stage 4 representatives. Stage 5 has been so far the shortest stage of social evolution, so in moving on to stage 6 there is still a significant stage 4 presence to deal with.

POSITIONS

I will now explore how to analyze the position of any person, group, movement, or society with respect to the model. This will help us see how that representative could contribute to a solution to the planetary crisis. Today there are five broad positions:

Dissociated emergent quality
Dissociated ground quality
Integrated quality
Previous stage of social evolution
Indigenous society

I will discuss each of these in turn.

Dissociated Emergent Quality. The dissociated emergent quality is, of course, preeminent in today's industrialized societies, represented by the majority of the population, and especially by successful people and most of society's institutions. In the material realm, this quality is *artificial living*, Example representatives would be engineers, computer programmers, car racing fans, TV addicts, and anyone who loves technology, works with it, or uses it heavily (unless they use technology integrated with natural living). In a sense this is almost all of us. In the consciousness realm, this quality is *detached consciousness*, represented by scientists, intellectuals, and people who places their primary faith in rationality and live primarily through cognitive processes rather than more participatory modes.

In the social realm, the dissociated emergent quality is represented by bureaucrats and government and corporate employees, and people heavily involved in the market economy, which is again almost all of us, except those who are strong in community. People with more money and power in society tend to be especially strong in this quality, but poor people who are involved in society through employment or welfare also represent this quality to the extent that they are lacking in community.

At first glance you might assume that oppressed people represent the ground quality in the power realm, but this is not usually true. The ground quality is *power distribution*, and most poor people do not represent power distribution unless they are struggling to gain power for themselves or their communities. Most poor people are just as immersed in the social structures of society as wealthy people, and therefore they too represent the emergent quality. Therefore, to represent the emergent quality properly in the power realm, there must be two positions, one for dominant and one for oppressed groups. An example dominant representative would be a corporate executive, and an oppressed group example would be a poor working person.

Most people and groups who represent the emergent qualities have the most power in society, and therefore, if they are flexible enough to embrace the ground qualities and integrate them, and possibly also to advance their emergent qualities, they can play a pivotal role in helping society move to stage 6.

Dissociated Ground Quality. This position involves people who embody the ground quality in their lives in a way that is not integrated with the emergent quality, with the exception of those representing a previous stage of social evolution. In the material realm, examples of ground quality representatives might be old-fashioned family farmers or people living in rural areas. These people may live in a relatively natural way because of being far from the paved-over cities and suburbs or because they make their living from the land.

In the social realm, the ground quality might be represented by people living in small towns or ethnic groups that retain a strong sense of community. In the consciousness realm, the ground quality might be represented by people whose personal strengths are in the intuitive and emotional areas, rather than the cognitive area. In the power realm, the ground quality, power distribution, might be represented by people who are cooperative in their personal interactions and promote equality in the groups they are involved with.

As I mentioned, some ground quality representatives are submissive and accept their secondary, inferior place in society. However, if they learn to value themselves and champion the ground quality they represent, they can help society to integrate what has been lost. I discuss this further in the next chapter.

Integrated Quality. The integration of the ground and emergent qualities is most helpful in advancing social evolution. Remember that integration doesn't necessarily mean manifesting both qualities all the time. It can mean actualizing the quality that is most appropriate for the situation. This was discussed in chapter 14. Often with a person or group who represents an integration of the qualities, there is an emphasis on one quality or the other, so I will give two sets of examples, one emphasizing the ground quality and one the emergent quality.

Ground Quality Emphasis. First I discuss ground quality representatives who not only value the ground quality but also integrate it with significant aspects of the emergent quality. An example in the material realm would be a modern organic farmer who uses a permaculture philosophy in his or her work. This person might emphasize the ground quality of natural living but be willing to use technology in creative ways in the design of an agricultural system.

In the social realm, community (ground quality) is encouraged by the co-housing movement and the growing movement toward salons and discussion groups. This is done in a way that is integrated with the existing social structure (emergent quality).

In the consciousness realm, an example would be new forms of experiential psychotherapy, which emphasize emotion, immediate experience, intuition, and altered states of consciousness (ground qualities) and explore these through reflexive awareness and insight while maintaining an interest in theory and understanding psychological process (emergent qualities).

In the power realm, this position would be exemplified by Nelson Mandela and the African National Congress in South Africa, who fought for decades to end apartheid and give blacks equal power (ground quality) and then entered into a collaborative arrangement with the white ruling party to frame a new constitution (emergent quality) to achieve that end.

Integrated representatives that emphasize the ground qualities contribute a great deal to social evolution. They bring back the ground quality in a healthy way that includes the emergent quality, and they are more likely to succeed because this can be more easily accepted by the existing society.

Emergent Quality Emphasis. Once one realizes how destructive it is to have the ground qualities suppressed, it is tempting to assume that the only way to contribute to social evolution is through bringing them back. However, this is not true. It is crucial to remember that our problems today are not because of having too much of the emergent quality, but rather because of its dissociation from the ground quality. People and groups whose strengths are in the emergent qualities have just as much to offer if they can integrate the ground quality into their work and their lives.

In the material realm, an integration with an emphasis on the emergent quality might be represented by ecological engineering. An example would be the work of John Todd of the New Alchemy Institute (1993), who has devised "living machines" for waste disposal consisting of marvelous combinations of microorganisms that break down waste products, including toxic and even nuclear wastes. This is highly advanced technology (emergent quality) that is built on following nature's ways (ground quality).

In the social realm, this position would be represented by managers and organizational development consultants who understand the value of community and healthy interpersonal relationships in the functioning of corporations. Their emphasis is on corporate viability (emergent quality) and part of their method relies on community (ground quality).

In the power realm, this position might be represented by an alternative economist like Herman Daly who worked for the World Bank at the pinnacle of society's hierarchy (emergent quality), yet who promotes an approach to economics that emphasizes community and self-reliance (ground quality) (Daly and Cobb 1989).

In the consciousness realm, this position might be represented by this book, which is a highly abstract intellectual treatise (emergent quality) that promotes the importance of aliveness and participation (ground quality) and is informed by decades of exploration of my own psychological and spiritual inner world.

Integrated representatives that emphasize the emergent quality tend to have more influence and credibility in society, so they have a better chance of being taken seriously and of being able to introduce the ground quality into existing social structures. And of course, the emergent quality is needed just as much as the ground quality in any healthy society. In fact, the emergent quality often needs to advance even further as part of moving to stage 6, and emergent/integrated representatives are in the best position to foster this.

Previous Stage. Some societies as a whole are still in previous stages of social evolution. For example, many Third world countries are largely in stage 4 in that they are primarily agricultural, with feudal and/or community oriented social arrangements and a stage 4 religious consciousness. They usually have a small stage 5 urban industrial component.

These societies embody a unique problem and opportunity in moving into stage 6. On the one hand, they have further to go in social evolutionary terms, and some groups that actively espouse their stage 4 way of life can present serious obstacles to evolutionary advance. For example, Muslim fundamentalist movements in the Middle East seem intent on moving backward in areas like women's rights, religious freedom, and cultural pluralism.

On the other hand, these societies have an opportunity to move directly from earlier stages to stage 6 without much of the destructiveness of stage 5. Some far-seeing individuals in these societies who have personally moved into stage 6 may be able to help their people skip some of the mistakes of stage 5. For example, they may be able to avoid our dependence on heavy industry and move right into the information age, and they may be able to design their industrial products and processes for ecological sustainability from the start. Those of us in the industrialized world who are experimenting with stage 6 may be able to provide them helpful models. Stage 4 cultures have retained some of the ground qualities that need to be integrated as humanity evolves, so if they don't hold rigidly to their current stage, they may move more gracefully into stage 6.

Most importantly, they may help the rest of the world to make the transition. For example, some of the less dogmatic of the Eastern religions, such as Buddhism, are providing stage 5 Westerners with aspects of stage 6 consciousness, such as an understanding of interconnectedness and nonattachment. In the material realm, some stage 4 healers, for example in China, retain a sophisticated knowledge of herbs and acupuncture. These are useful to society as we create a form of stage 6 medicine that is more natural and holistic.

There are small encapsulated segments of modern societies that remain in stage 4, such as the Amish in the United States. More widespread are certain people and groups that represent stage 4 in one realm but not in others, such as the Christian fundamentalists who retain a stage 4 consciousness but embrace stage 5 technology and social structure. In Britain, the aristocracy and their servants maintain a stage 4 social system within a stage 5 society.

In holding to their old ways in the face of a Modern society, stage 4 groups tend to be more reactionary than helpful. These groups often try to cope with the disintegration of stage 5 society by clinging even more tenaciously to stage 4 rather than advancing to build a stage 6 society. It helps to understand that this desperate holding on to the past is their way of dealing with a very threatening situation.

Indigenous Society. Indigenous societies usually represent stages 1 or 2. However, most of them are actually a mixture of stages because of partial assimilation to the dominant society in which they are embedded. Pure stage 1 and 2 societies are rare today, represented by the few indigenous groups that have remained isolated.

Indigenous societies have much to offer the world in helping us through this transition to stage 6 because they have held the ground qualities in a relatively pure form. They have earth-based forms of consciousness, which can aid us in regaining a reverent attitude toward the natural world which promotes ecological practices. In addition, they often have sophisticated knowledge of healing herbs which can be of use in holistic approaches to health.

Their greatest task is to preserve their traditions against the press of Modern life so that their richness of ground quality living is not lost to us. The pure indigenous societies especially need to have their land protected from encroachment because this is a common way of destroying their cultures. With their cultures intact, they can then make their own choices, as groups and individuals, about how much, if any, of the dominant stage 5 culture they want to integrate with their native culture.

The partially assimilated groups, such as Native American tribes, are struggling with loss of their cultures because of the enticement of their young people by Modern technological wonders and impoverishment of the spirit on the reservations, leading to alcoholism. They need help in finding ways to successfully assimilate to American culture without discarding the richness of their native traditions. This is their version of the task of integrating ground and emergent qualities.

Table 21.1 shows these example positions. In the power realm I have included examples for dominant and oppressed groups.

Table 21.1 Example Positions

Position	Material	Social	Consciousness	Power
Dissociated Emergent	Engineer, agribusiness	Bureaucrat	Scientist, intellectual	Dominant: corporate exec Oppressed: poor worker
Dissociated Ground	Rural dweller, family farmer	Small town, ethnic community	Intuitive, emotional person	Cooperative person
Integrated, Ground Emphasis	Organic farming, permaculture	Co-housing, salons	Experiential psychotherapy	African National Congress
Integrated, Emergent Emphasis	Ecological engineering	Organizational development	This book	Alternative economists
Previous Stage	3rd World village	Amish	Fundamentalist	Dominant: aristocrat Oppressed: servant

I could add more columns to this chart representing subrealms such as culture, gender, and intersocietal power. However, this should be enough to demonstrate how position analysis can be used to understand the situation of a person or group with respect to social evolution. It is worth noting that a given person might be in one position in one realm and a different position in another. For example, someone might be a scientist (emergent, consciousness) who also loves to hike in the wilderness (ground, material). This could be an example of integration or dissociation depending on how the person lived with these differences.

Low in Both Qualities. You might assume that every person or group must represent either the ground or emergent quality. However, it is possible to be low in both qualities. For example, in the material realm the poor who live in the burgeoning slums of Third World cities have neither the advantages of modern technology nor a meaningful connection with the natural world. In the social realm many of the homeless of the United States are unable to participate in the social or economic life of the nation and are also alienated and without community. In the consciousness realm, a person might have little education and intellectual ability (reflexive consciousness) and also be caught up in the Modern detachment from emotions, spirituality, belonging, and creativity (participatory consciousness).

People who are low in both qualities have difficult lives indeed. They are often struggling just to survive and are happy to gain any amount of either quality. Having been shut out of the socially prevalent emergent qualities, they can probably contribute most to social evolution by attempting to develop their ground qualities.

Gender. To avoid confusion, let me point out that gender comes into play in two different places in this model. In the power realm, gender is explicitly defined as a subrealm related to the ways that power inequality is based on gender. Thus in this chapter, if we looked at the subrealm of gender, men would represent the dominant group and women the oppressed group.

Gender also is important in the consciousness realm (and to a lesser extent in the social realm) because the emergent quality (reflexive consciousness) is so often associated with men and the ground quality (participatory consciousness) is so often associated with women. Thus people are expected by society to have certain personal qualities based on their gender, which may or may not correspond to their true selves. I will explore this further in the next chapter.

XXII

EVERYONE HAS A PART TO PLAY

PERSONAL QUALITIES

Position analysis is exciting to me because it allows us to see how each person, organization, or movement stands in relation to social evolution. It provides the basis for understanding how each one can contribute to or resist the great need of our time—advancement into stage 6. In this chapter I look more deeply at the positions people can take as representatives of the ground or emergent qualities, and how changes in their personal lives can play a part in social evolution.

In order to do this, let's look at the *personal* side of the complementary qualities. The ground and emergent qualities, as the model defines them, apply to society as a whole, especially in the material and social realms. For example, social structure defines a quality of a society, not an individual. In this chapter I will explore what personal qualities are associated with the ground and emergent qualities, and especially with the integration of the qualities, in the material and social realms. In the consciousness realm, this has already been done because consciousness qualities apply to both individuals and societies. For example, reflexive consciousness can characterize a person or an entire society.

In the discussion below I emphasize those personal qualities that correspond to the ground quality or the integration of the qualities because that is what we need most in today's crisis.

Material Realm. The ground quality in the material realm is natural living. One personal quality that is closely associated with natural living is a feeling of connection with the natural world. This especially comes from an appreciation of being in nature—taking a walk in the woods, working in a garden, being rooted in a piece of land or a bioregion. This *earth connection* is built into us. Humans evolved in intimate communion with nature, and we have a profound need for it. Evolutionary biologists have proposed the "biophilia hypothesis," which says that human beings have a deep, genetically based emotional need to affiliate with the rest of the living world (Wilson and Kellert 1993). In many Modern people this is repressed or hidden, because of our living in artificial surroundings enticed by so many vitality substitutes. In order to access this need, we may have to tap into what Theodore Roszak calls the "ecological unconscious" (1992). When we are related to the earth in this natural way, it is easy to understand the urgency of our ecological problems.

A second personal quality that promotes natural living is *plentitude.* This term was first defined in this way by Lewis Mumford and discussed at length by Roszak (1992, 252–62). Plentitude is an attitude toward material consumption and happiness. With this attitude you recognize that personal fulfillment does not come primarily from material goods, and therefore you pursue the good life through other means—spirituality, community, creativity, love. You limit your consumption partly because you know it is required for the health of the earth and partly because you have other interests. However, you are not ascetic or unnecessarily frugal. You allow yourself to have whatever will genuinely give you pleasure and help you grow as a person. If this occasionally happens to involve material consumption, that's OK. Voluntary simplicity (Morris 1993) is a similar idea, with perhaps more emphasis on frugality.

Personal qualities that promote the emergent quality in the material realm, technological living, are *technical ability* and a *love of technology.*

Power. In the power realm, the ground and emergent qualities were chosen in such a way as to elucidate the historic societal evolution of power. They don't represent very well the dialectic of personal qualities in this area. Therefore I present in figure 22.1 a new graphic that does this.

Figure 22.1 Power

Figure 22.1 must be interpreted a little differently from the others of this nature. The two complementary qualities, assertiveness and receptiveness, are not ground and emergent qualities with respect to social evolution. However, they *do* define the appropriate complementary qualities that must be integrated for a person to have healthy power relationships.

Assertiveness means being able to exercise your personal power to accomplish what you want. You have the initiative and courage to start things and take risks, the creativity to overcome obstacles, and the endurance to see a job through to completion. You have the charisma and force of personality to stand behind your ideas and persuade others. *Receptiveness* means being in tune with what others think and want. You can meld your desires and coordinate your efforts with those of others. You don't need to have more than your share of the limelight or influence.

Receptiveness without assertiveness becomes *compliance*, giving in to the will of others rather than standing up for your desires and opinions. It can lead to a state of *powerlessness*, where you feel unable to affect your world to make it what you want. Of course, compliance and powerlessness can be forced on people by a political or social system independently of their personal qualities.

Assertiveness without receptiveness means looking out for yourself without considering the feelings or needs of others, leading to competition and domination. If everyone is assertive without being receptive, this leads to a situation of *competition*. If some aren't assertive, then it leads to *domination* of the weak by the powerful. This situation is sometimes referred to as "power over," to distinguish it from "power with," which is the integrated situation. When there is an integration of assertiveness and receptiveness, it leads to *cooperation*. You are able to stand up for yourself and work together with others. You are looking out for the good of the whole as well as your own interests.

Notice that the complementary personal qualities, assertiveness and receptiveness, do not necessarily correspond to the complementary societal qualities in the power realm, social structure and power distribution. Assertiveness is not only associated with social structure; it is also an important component of power distribution. Someone who is assertive may use that ability to climb the power hierarchy in society or to fight for equal power distribution. Similarly, someone who is receptive might use it to become a cog in the social machine or to encourage cooperation in society.

Culture. In working toward cultural pluralism and gender equality, there are two personal qualities that are helpful. *Self-esteem* is closely associated with the ground quality, liberation. It means feeling good about yourself and having a positive self-image. This is a very important psychological issue for many people that applies to far more than the issue of culture. I bring it up here because it is particularly helpful in overcoming cultural and gender oppression. This is because oppression frequently becomes internalized causing members of oppressed groups to feel inferior. This can be ingrained deep in the psyche even when people know intellectually that it isn't true. In developing self-esteem and pride in their culture or group or gender, people take a significant step toward liberation.

Another crucial quality in this realm is *appreciation of diversity*. When we are confronted with people from another culture with different ways of dressing, speaking, behaving, and seeing the world, it can be very threatening. Not only is it difficult to understand and communicate with them, but we might have to reconsider our world view if we take them seriously. Therefore, it is easier to dismiss them. The first step in overcoming this attitude is to learn tolerance, where we realize that they have just as much right to their way of life as we do.

However the most helpful response goes beyond tolerance to appreciating the other culture. What can we learn from them? Maybe their food or music is exotic and interesting. Maybe we will be forced to grow personally in order to relate to them. Maybe their religion has something that is missing from ours. This is not an attitude you can force. You can only work toward becoming open and experimental enough that you are intrigued by the newness and challenge of a different culture. This sentiment truly promotes cultural pluralism.

Many of the same issues also apply to gender. It is becoming popular today to recognize the ways that men and women differ in patterns of communication and relationship, as well as the more obvious differences in outlook and preferences. It can be very beneficial to learn to appreciate the strengths of the opposite gender.

In order to have gender role freedom and/or cultural freedom, you must have the ability to emerge from gender or cultural roles, think for yourself, and create ways of being that uniquely fit you. I will call this person quality *role freedom*.

The Social Realm. *Relatedness* is a personal quality that is associated with the ground quality, community. It means being interested in and giving priority to personal relationships in one's life—family relationships, love relationships, friendships, and community. People who are high in relatedness may even define themselves in terms of the quality of their relationships rather than status or achievement. Relatedness is similar to the consciousness quality of belonging.

The personal qualities associated with the emergent quality in the social realm, social structure, are too numerous to explore in any detail. I have mentioned some under power and gender above. Others might include *organizational ability* and *leadership*.

Change. This is a time of rapid change, when it is crucial to flow with social evolution rather than clinging to our current way of doing things. Therefore *flexibility* is a personal quality that is enormously helpful in moving on to stage 6. This means the ability to let go of old ways of living that no longer work, even if they are deeply conditioned in us. As flexible people, we embrace the positive changes that are emerging in society, and lead by personal example in some areas. We are willing to examine our attitudes and habits and beliefs, to see if they are really the best for us and the world. We are also willing to take risks, to upset our lives if necessary, in order to experiment with new ways of being.

Included in this is the ability to tolerate dissonance and disagreement, to handle not knowing answers, to live with ambiguity and uncertainty. When moving into new areas, we must be able to live with these uncomfortable mental states, at least for a while until clarity arises. For example, we will need to experiment with different forms of cooperative political process until we discover what works best in various circumstances. In doing this, we need to be open to what is most effective, rather than having preconceived notions and attachments. To take another example, in order to be able to work with people who are different from us, we need to be open to the possibility that some of our cherished ideas may need modification, that people with different ways may have something to teach us.

Consciousness. All the qualities in the consciousness realm that I have discussed are already personal qualities, so I will simply list them here. People representing the ground quality are often *intuitive*, *artistic*, *creative*, *emotional*, and/or *spontaneous*. In addition, *empathy* is a crucial personal ground quality that seems to cut across a number of realms. Empathy is the ability to feel what other people are feeling. When someone else is in pain, empathy leads to compassion. At other times it leads to appreciation. Empathy aids us in being cooperative, in respecting the autonomy of others. It helps us to appreciate cultural and gender differences. It promotes international understanding, leading to peaceful ways of resolving conflicts. To have empathy with animals and with the natural world promotes ecological practices.

People representing the emergent quality tend to be *intellectual*, oriented toward *rationality*, and/or *organized*. In addition, *vision* is a personal emergent quality that is important for moving into stage 6. This means the ability to see the larger picture, to have a fresh perspective on things, to look beyond our concrete daily life and see larger meanings and connections. Vision means you are not locked into a narrow way of perceiving things, so you are perhaps able to see the global picture, or the historical and evolutionary viewpoint, or you can encompass both scientific and spiritual perspectives. This helps with international understanding and global consciousness. It aids in understanding the planetary crisis and knowing how to be effective in making a difference. If vision is integrated with heart, it brings wisdom.

I have already discussed the personal qualities associated with the advancing emergent or integrated qualities in the consciousness realm. They include *global identification*, *systemic* and *dialectical thinking*, and an orientation toward *psychology* and *spirituality*.

This discussion of personal qualities is neither complete nor carefully constructed theoretically. That would be the work of another book. It is summarized in table 22.1. In those cases where the integrated quality is primarily an integration of the ground and emergent qualities listed, I specify "both."

Table 22.1 Personal Qualities

Realm	Ground	Integrated	Emergent	Advancing
Material Realm	Earth connection, plenitude	Both	Technical ability, love of technology	
Power	Assertiveness, receptiveness	Both	Assertiveness, receptiveness	Cooperation
Culture & Gender	Self-esteem	Appreciation of diversity		Role freedom
Social	Relatedness	Both	Organizational ability, leadership	
Change			Flexibility	
Consciousness	Intuition, empathy, emotionality, spontaneity, creativity	Both	Vision, rationality, intellectuality, organization	Global identification, systemic/dialectical thinking, psychology, spirituality

PERSONAL POSITIONS AND LIFE CHOICES

Let's look at the various positions people manifest in their lives and how they relate to social evolution. From this it is possible to analyze how the life choices we all make can contribute to or work against the resolution of the planetary crisis. There are three different types of positions.

Types of Positions. People's *given* positions are the positions that are handed to them because of the place and circumstances of their early lives. This includes their gender, race, ethnic or religious group, nation, and the socioeconomic status of their family. It also includes how they are socialized during their upbringing. For example, people who are born and socialized to be white, middle-class, American males generally have, and are expected to have, the personal emergent qualities, such as intellect, personal power, and technical ability. In addition, this group is situated socially in a way to make it easy for its members to make the best use of these personal qualities and to achieve power, social standing, access to the benefits of technology, and so on. On the negative side, they are also most likely to end up alienated from community, relationship, and participatory consciousness.

People's *natural* positions reflect those personal qualities, strengths, and talents that are innate and natural to them. For example, people who are naturally artistic and emotional have a natural position of the ground consciousness quality. People who are born with a high degree of technical ability have a natural position of the emergent material quality. People's natural positions reflect who they really are independent of the circumstances of their birth.

People's *chosen* positions are the positions that they may choose as adults in the process of creating their own lifestyle, values, and worldview. Of course, these choices will be influenced by their given and natural positions and may be constrained by social, political, and economic factors beyond their control. A crucial factor in people's sense of place in life and future development is whether their given and natural positions coincide or conflict.

GIVEN POSITION: EMERGENT QUALITY

Emergent Status Quo. Let's look at people whose given position is an emergent quality, such as the white American males I mentioned above. They are likely to develop at first in a dissociated way, with their ground qualities suppressed so they fit into the privileged social niche available to them. Those who don't ever see beyond this will remain in this position and contribute little to our advancement into stage 6.

Developing Ground Qualities. However, some will be encouraged to reevaluate their lives because of tragedy or failure. They may realize that their given lifestyle is meaningless or that the emergent qualities are destructive for society. Then they may choose to spend time developing their ground qualities. For example, a man's wife might leave him, thus prompting him to go into therapy to develop his emotional side and his ability to be intimate. Failure in business might allow certain people to become aware of an interest in backpacking and connecting with nature or to feel a keen need for community in their lives. Others might have experiences that promote their concern for oppressed people or the environment.

Which people choose this route will be affected by their flexibility and self-esteem and their general psychological well-being. It takes a considerable amount of resilience to be willing to make such profound changes in their lives, to give up security in risking something new and unknown. It is much easier to let go of a dissociated position if they feel good about themselves and generally secure as people. This applies not just to people in the "given emergent" position, but to all the positions explored in this chapter.

One option for people who are changing is to focus intensively on ground qualities rather than emergent qualities in their lives. Some may become disgusted with the power structure and drop out to make a life of plentitude for themselves in the country, living simply, consuming little, and focusing on their relationship with nature. Others may devote themselves full to time to art. Others may leave their suburban lives to join a residential intentional community. A corporate manager may quit to become an environmental or community activist. Men may become disenchanted with their rigidity and isolation, and focus on developing their feminine qualities of emotional openness, caring, and intimacy.

Each of these is a courageous and important step. It gives the people a chance to develop the other side of themselves and to bring these needed ground qualities to society.

Emergent Reversal. However, let's ask if the people do this in a way that rejects the emergent qualities. In their life in the country, do they spurn all technology? As artists, do they completely abandon the rational mind? As community members, do they reject all structure and organization? As activists, do they hate the establishment, or can they form alliances and work cooperatively? In the cases where they reject the emergent quality, I call this an *emergent reversal.* This kind of radical turnaround can be valuable, but it may go too far. We need both emergent and ground qualities to make a healthy society.

Emergent Integrating Ground. Some people with a given emergent quality may recognize the importance of the ground qualities and devote themselves to integrating them into their lives and society. As I discussed in the last chapter, such an integrated position has a better chance of contributing to stage 6. Three possibilities come to mind:

1. Given emergent representatives may make a dramatic turnaround as above without rejecting the emergent qualities. For example,

some will learn about permaculture or develop community-enhancing social structures; others will develop their empathy along with their assertiveness.

2. They may remain in the emergent position and work for change from there. For example, some will stay in their corporate jobs and support ecological policies. Others may continue as college professors and teach about the value of ecology or community or spirituality.
3. Emergent representatives can also contribute by developing their emergent qualities further, into stage 6, which naturally will involve some integration of ground. For example, scientists may become interested in studying their field in a more holistic, process, or interdisciplinary way. Engineers might become engaged in developing advanced intelligent or ecological technology. Corporate executives might begin to promote the latest nonhierarchical management structures.

Sometimes an emergent reversal happens first, as people reject their background, and then when they have developed their ground qualities, they decide to integrate the emergent qualities. For example, this happened in the men's movement, when at first many men rejected masculinity because they could see how the distorted image of maleness they had grown up with was destroying their lives and the world. Then they realized that they had thrown the baby out with the bath water, and they needed to reclaim the positive aspects of being male, the emergent qualities they had lost. This was the impetus for the popularity of Robert Bly and his concept of the deep masculine (Bly 1990).

GIVEN POSITION: EMERGENT
NATURAL POSITION: GROUND

In the above discussion, I explored what happens to people with a given emergent position, but I didn't specify their natural position. Now let's consider people whose given position is emergent who are naturally strong in the ground qualities. Some might be emotionally or spiritually sensitive or artistic. Others might be naturally drawn toward cooperation rather than power, or intensely interested in farming, or devoted to animals. This creates a conflict between their given position and their natural position. Unless they had very understanding parents, they may feel different and inferior and have trouble with low self-esteem. There are a number of choices in dealing with this.

Dissociating Ground. Some people may try to deny their natural tendencies and play the role that society has dealt them. They can dissociate themselves from their natural ground qualities and try to make a life for themselves using their social position rather than who they really are. This is likely to lead to frustration, a sense of being a charlatan, or a feeling of boredom and malaise. They will certainly not contribute to the changes needed now in society, and they may even become active oppressors of others as a way of denying their ground qualities and propping up their own self-oppression.

Emergent Reversal or Integration. On the other hand, some may recognize their true nature and take ownership of their ground qualities. This will be a joy for them and an important aspect of their personal growth. When they realize their natural qualities they may rebel against their background and reject the emergent qualities that were foisted on them. This would lead to an emergent reversal as I described above. This reaction is understandable. Such people certainly need to be free to develop their natural talents, but they will have a better chance of helping society to evolve if they don't reject their emergent heritage. They have an opportunity to use their given position in life to bring to society the ground qualities that are their natural strength. They can use their social position or influence to foster the ground qualities in others and to advocate for them in institutional and societal settings.

Most importantly, they are in a natural position to integrate the ground and emergent qualities. For example, in the power realm, someone might be born into a wealthy, powerful family (emergent), but be naturally oriented toward cooperation (ground). This person would be in an advantageous position to promote cooperative social structures in society.

Advancing Emergent. In the consciousness realm, people with natural ground qualities are often psychologically or spiritually open. If they are born into a well-educated family and subculture that also tolerates their openness, this would give them enough of the stage 5 emergent quality, rationality, to make integration easy. Then they would be able to advance the emergent quality even further by focusing on personal and spiritual growth and perhaps leading others in this way.

As the emergent quality advances from one evolutionary stage to another, different people may become its leading representatives. For example, when we moved from stage 4 to 5, the leading representatives in the consciousness realm changed from religious leaders to scientists and philosophers. There was certainly some overlap, since many of the early scientists were also highly religious or spiritual, but mostly the lead shifted from one group to another.

Today this is also happening. The lead in consciousness is shifting from science (at least the traditional physical sciences) to psychology, spirituality, and other human sciences. This doesn't mean that there isn't still important work to be done in the physical and biological sciences, and of course, some of the lead in consciousness will be taken by scientists who are skilled at systems and dialectical thinking. However, my (perhaps biased) guess is that stage 6 consciousness will be led by the human/social sciences and experiential psychology and spirituality.

GIVEN POSITION: GROUND QUALITY

Ground Submissive. Let's consider people whose given position is the ground quality. These could be women whose upbringing stressed empathy and intuition. They could be people born into an ethnic group with close community ties or onto a family farm. These people are given a position that is not valued by society. The most important question is whether they accept this negative view of themselves and their heritage. Do the women value their orientation toward empathy and intuition or do they feel inferior because they haven't been trained to be more assertive or intellectual? Do people born into community appreciate it or do they feel trapped and denigrate their cultural group for being "backward"? Do rural people value their connection with nature or do they long for an affluent lifestyle?

An important factor in this choice is self-esteem. People with a given position of the ground qualities generally have to struggle with low self-esteem because society doesn't value their heritage, though this can be ameliorated by having loving parents and a close community. If their self-esteem is not high, they may devalue their ground-quality background. They may submissively accept society's depreciation of them and their people, and therefore not bring their ground qualities to society in a way that can foster social change.

Ground Reversal. People who devalue their ground qualities may even discard those qualities and their heritage. They may attempt to develop their emergent qualities and become successful on society's terms. Women may discount their intuition and caring and try for success in the corporate world on traditional male terms. People born into community may reject their cultural group and try to assimilate and become a mainstream American. People born on farms may move to the city and become eager consumers. In some cases, they may even become contemptuous of the ground qualities, especially in other people from their background.

People trying to make such a *ground reversal* will have a tough time unless the emergent qualities are natural in them. They will struggle with hidden self-esteem issues because they have rejected an important part of themselves. And as long as they devalue their ground quality background, they won't contribute to the changes that society needs at this time.

Ground Assertive. Those who have high self-esteem are likely to value the ground qualities for themselves and even for society as a whole. They may encourage others to develop these qualities. For example, some may teach classes in psychic development or parenting. Others may write novels extolling the virtues of their ethnic community or the natural world. These assertive ground representatives can contribute a great deal to social evolution by educating us about the advantages of the ground qualities.

Critique of Reverse Splitting. However, those who have not integrated the emergent qualities may advocate a dissociated perspective through reverse splitting, where they denigrate the emergent qualities, thereby diminishing the potential value of their contribution. It is important to understand the possible shortcomings of an unintegrated assertion of the ground qualities. Let's examine those people and groups who have advocated the ground qualities in a dissociated way .

In the material realm this would include people who advocate a back-to-the-land philosophy and extol living in intimate connection with nature, such as Thoreau and John Muir. It also includes writers such as Edward Goldsmith, whose new book *The Way* (1993) promotes an ecological worldview that romanticizes stage 1 societies and the natural world. He takes a radical, judgmental position that sees only the harm that has come from our Modern science, technology, and way of life, and none of the benefits. He seems to espouse a return to the life of indigenous peoples as a way of solving our environmental problems.

An example in the social realm would be the hippie communal living movement of the 1960s, which advocated dropping out of society to concentrate on developing community. They made little or no attempt to integrate their insights and experiments with "the establishment," mainstream social structure. There was a naiveté about the movement that didn't understand the difficulties of communal living or deal with how to build a large society on this basis.

The Romantic movement is an example of a dissociated ground quality representative in the consciousness realm. The Romantic poets and artists extolled the virtues of participatory consciousness as a reaction against the hyperrationality and deadness of Modern consciousness, but they made little effort to integrate the two. A current example would be people who uncritically accept everything that is said about spirituality by the popular channeled entities of the New Age. These people value the intuitive, spiritual side of consciousness but some don't use their rational faculties to think through and evaluate what is being said.

In the power realm, Murray Bookchin comes to mind (1982). As an advocate for "social ecology" he presents an interesting, effective critique of oppression and hierarchy in society, and advocates a radical egalitarian perspective. However, he doesn't seem to recognize the difficulties in coordinating large groups of people. His solutions point only to small-scale egalitarian communities without dealing with how to extend this to a world of 6 billion people. Another example from the power realm would be the Black Muslims and other black separatist movements that have made important steps toward liberation but without an understanding of the value of cultural pluralism or cultural freedom.

Dissociated ground representatives can be very helpful at certain times. They assist us in realizing the value of the ground quality, and they hold that quality for society until the time is right for it to return. Thoreau and the Romantics certainly served this function during the Modern era. Now that it is time to integrate the ground quality, society can learn from the assertive ground quality representatives who experimented with new ways of living that emphasized the ground qualities. The hippies and Black Muslims and the New Age movement learned much of value from their experiments and brought it to public attention in a way that shook up the entrenched system.

However, in nurturing the transition, we must beware of reverse splitting and an exclusive emphasis on the ground quality and instead learn how to integrate it with the emergent quality. Otherwise the ground quality will remain marginal and be unable to transform society in the way it must. In addition, a healthy society needs integration; the ground quality is *not* adequate by itself. It wouldn't be wise or possible to give up civilization to be hunter-gatherers again. It wouldn't work to live as nations separated by color. We need our intellect as well as our emotions and spirit. To move into stage 6 we need to regain the ground qualities in an integrated way.

Ground Integrating Emergent. The most evolved possibility for ground quality people is to assertively recognize the value of their given ground quality and also integrate the emergent quality into their lives. For example, the intuitive woman might develop her intellect so that she could help rational people to understand the value of intuition. The rural person might become an innovator in developing a sustainable technology of forestry. The community person could become an organizer of community-based worker-owned businesses or an advocate of cooperative approaches to social change. Thus by integrating the emergent quality with the ground quality, these people develop a synthesis for moving into stage 6.

In the examples I have given so far, the integration has been within a given realm. For example, the woman integrated her intuition with her intellect within the consciousness realm. However, the realms aren't really separate, so important integration can happen across realms as well. For example, the intuitive woman might become a consultant teaching intuition in corporate settings, thus integrating the ground consciousness quality with the emergent social quality.

GIVEN POSITION: GROUND
NATURAL POSITION: EMERGENT

Let's look at people who are born into a ground position with natural emergent talents. This could be a person born into an oppressed ethnic community who has the natural talent to become a corporate executive. It could be a person raised on a family farm who has an interest in science and engineering. It could be a woman from a traditional family who has strong intellectual capacities.

These people are not likely to stay with their given position. The biggest danger is that they might do a ground reversal, discarding their background and fully embracing the dissociated emergent quality where their talent lies. However, these people have an exciting opportunity to integrate the qualities, since they have one in their background and one in their genes. They could develop their natural emergent abilities to the fullest, while retaining their understanding of and affinity with the ground qualities of their birth. This would allow them to make an important contribution to stage 6.

GIVEN POSITION: OPPRESSED

In the power realm, the ground quality is power distribution. When it is suppressed, the emergent quality of social structure affects people in two very different ways, depending on their social and economic class—whether they are part of an oppressed or dominant group. Those who belong to a dominant group have already been included in the previous discussion. Here I look at the situation for those whose given position is oppressed—members of the working class or the poor underclass.

Natural Position Receptive. Those whose natural abilities in the power realm run in the direction of receptiveness rather than assertiveness are not likely to change their oppressed status on their own. They could become part of a movement toward liberation through cooperating with those of their people who are naturally more assertive.

Natural Position Assertive. Those whose natural abilities run in the direction of assertiveness, initiative, and self-esteem have some chance of escaping their oppressed status. Thus a powerful woman might become a successful salesperson. A poor person or person of color who has talent, self-esteem, and a drive to succeed might become a teacher, a physician, or a corporate executive. However, this is far from the norm. It takes luck and proper guidance to manage such an achievement. In addition, oppressed people with significant assertiveness may simply become gang leaders or drug dealers, using their power in destructive and self-destructive ways that simply reinforce their oppression and the oppression of their group.

Oppressed Reversal. Some oppressed people who are successful in escaping from their oppressed position may simply enjoy their new dominant position without making use of the special understanding they have because of their background. The may ignore or even denigrate people from the same circumstances who haven't managed to escape.

Oppressed Integrating. People from a given oppressed position who have natural assertiveness have the potential to contribute to societal evolution in two ways. One option is to stay in their oppressed position and fight for power for themselves and their people. For example, they might become community organizers or civil rights activists. The danger is that they may only fight against the existing social structure. This can be of great help in keeping oppression from becoming really harsh, but it isn't helpful in making fundamental changes in society. They can be most effective by making an effort to promote social structures that are intrinsically egalitarian and non-oppressive. This way they are integrating the ground quality, power distribution with the emergent quality, social structure.

For example, if oppressed assertive people are fighting for cultural or gender liberation (ground quality), it is helpful if they also appreciate cultural or gender differences (integrated). In this way they won't become lured into separatism or reverse racism or sexism, but instead will work for pluralism and gender and cultural freedom as well as liberation.

The second option for oppressed assertive people is to escape domination first, establish themselves in a powerful position, and then dedicate themselves to power distribution and the emancipation of their people. They will have power at their disposal to accomplish this, and they will know how to work with established societal structures, so they are likely to achieve something that will be sustainable. The danger is that they will become part of the established power structure, lose touch with their roots, and forget about helping others to gain their share of the power.

GIVEN POSITION: PREVIOUS STAGE

Let's now explore the options for people whose given position represents a previous stage of social evolution. This would include people born into fundamentalist communities in the United States or people born into peasant villages in the Third World.

Submissive. Some previous stage representatives will retain their given culture because of being unable to advance into the Modern world, for either personal or societal reasons. An example would be Third World peasants who are unable to gain power to develop materially.

Assertive. Some will retain their given culture because they value it and believe it to be as good as or better than Modern society. If this is done in a closed way, if they reject all aspects of stage 5 and any prospects for stage 6, then they will not only fail to contribute to our evolving into stage 6, they will actively block it. This is the situation with many fundamentalists. Their position is often taken out of fear. As our society goes through its transition into stage 6, many aspects of stage 5 are breaking down, causing trauma and suffering and danger. A healthy response to this is to recognize that stage 5 no longer works and to begin moving on to stage 6. However, some people, out of fear, interpret the demise of stage 5 as proof that stage 4 was really right all along, and they cling to it or regress to it in an attempt to find security in the chaos of the transition. This, of course, only makes matters worse.

The personal quality of flexibility is an important key to what happens when people are confronted with this choice. Those who are comfortable with uncertainty and change, or can at least tolerate it, may choose to let go of the past and move on. They may have the courage to think for themselves and venture into territory where there are no clear authorities. Those who can't tolerate ambiguity and fear anything new will cling all the harder to the fundamentalisms of the past that offer ready-made answers for everything.

Previous Stage Integrating Next Stage. Another possibility is that people may retain their stage 4 culture because they value it, and remain open to the possibility of integrating aspects of their culture with the emerging stage 6 culture. For example, the Buddhist monk Thich Nhat Hahn has brought aspects of his spirituality to the West while remaining open to its being integrated with Modern psychotherapy (Hanh 1993).

In the case of Third World oppressed people, there is little chance that they can move ahead as individuals within their own societies; there are too many social limitations on them. They must advance as cultures or societies. As I mentioned in the last chapter, the world's greatest hope is that they will retain some of the valuable ground qualities of their cultures and integrate the worthwhile aspects of our emergent qualities. This way they may be able to skip some of the mistakes the industrialized societies made in stage 5. In the material realm, this is called *sustainable development.*

Other Possibilities. Stage 4 people may reject their culture and adopt stage 5 emergent qualities (not helpful), or alternatively adopt stage 5 ground qualities (better), or an integration of the two (best). All these choices will be affected by their natural position and how much it matches or conflicts with their given position.

PRINCIPLES OF POSITION ANALYSIS

There are many options other than the particular ones I have explored here. People can represent the emergent quality in one realm and the ground in another. They can go through a number of stages in their lives. People are profoundly affected by groups and organizations and movements they join. Many are also constrained by the limitations of the power position they have in society. Others are deeply affected by psychological trauma in childhood. I have presented these possibilities not as an exhaustive list, but rather to illustrate how to use the model to analyze and understand a person's positions and choices in life.

Everyone has resources that can be helpful in advancing to stage 6. We have resources from both our given and our natural positions. We may have societal status and power or an understanding of the effects of oppression. We may embody natural or socialized ground qualities that are needed by society for integration. We may possess emergent qualities that can be enhanced by integrating the ground, or we may have advanced stage 6 emergent qualities that society needs. Our task is to find a way to integrate the ground and emergent qualities in ourselves and to help others and society to do the same. Position analysis helps us to see clearly where we stand and how we can best be of aid in this great step in the unfolding of our species.

MY STORY

Consciousness Realm. I will describe my own life trajectory as an example of this process. My given position in the consciousness realm was reasonably oriented toward the emergent quality. I was born into a middle-class suburban home, with Irish Protestant parents who valued education (reflexive consciousness) and success. I am also naturally oriented toward the emergent quality of stage 5 because my greatest talent is my verbal-logical intelligence. However, I also have a good natural dose of the ground quality in my emotional, empathic, and interpersonal abilities, especially the capacity to empathize with people's emotions. In addition, I have a natural talent in the stage 6 emergent qualities because of my ability to inquire deeply into my psychological and spiritual experience with awareness and insight.

Until my early twenties I focused completely on the verbal-logical side of myself. I had no emotional or psychological awareness as a child, which is fairly unusual for someone who later becomes a therapist. I did very well in school, getting a Ph.D. in computer science, teaching at UC Berkeley, and developing a national reputation in my subfield of research. However, I became very interested in relating to people in more intimate ways, so I joined an encounter group and became deeply involved in the cultural aspects of the 1960s in Berkeley. This led to my own personal therapy, and then to becoming a therapist professionally. Despite my love of computer science and my success at it, I found that I didn't want to dedicate my life to something that was used primarily in bureaucracy and the military, which was true of computers at the time. The therapy I pursued was highly experiential, involving intense emotional and bodily experiences, and thus I immersed myself in the ground quality, participatory consciousness.

During this process I discovered that I could relate more easily to women, especially when talking about my new-found interest in feelings and intimacy. I lost interest in friendships with men and focused my energy toward women during my twenties and early thirties. At this stage in my life I was engaged in an emergent reversal. Though I retained some interest in psychological theory, I focused strongly on "losing my head and coming to my senses." I had subtly rejected the emergent quality in favor of the ground. This was a fairly common pattern for men of that time who were involved in the human potential movement.

In my late thirties and forties I reintegrated the emergent quality. I realized that I had rejected the male side of the human race and myself with it, and I began to reown and value the positive aspects of masculinity. I also realized that I missed doing serious intellectual work, so I became interested in studying psychological and social theory. I am now incorporating more of a theoretical perspective into my work as a group therapist and trainer, while I retain my love of experiential therapy. I also developed an interest in spirituality which has grown and deepened over the years.

This book, of course, is an abstract work of theory, representing reflexive consciousness, both stage 5 rationality and the more advanced systemic and dialectical thinking. In addition, the book is informed by my own experiential psychological and spiritual work over the years, not only in content but also in spirit, thus embodying an integration of the ground quality plus advanced emergent consciousness qualities. My current position would be characterized as emergent integrating ground and advancing.

Material Realm. I love working with computers and I have a high degree of technical ability in this area, so my natural position in the material realm is the emergent quality, technological living. I grew up in the 1950s during the Sputnik era, when young Americans were encouraged to go into science to keep up with the Russians. Therefore, given my aptitude, I naturally studied computer science and worked in the field during my twenties, making my given position also emergent quality. However, my slowly growing social conscience and interest in my inner life pushed me toward a different career. Meanwhile, living in Berkeley during the 1960s and early 1970s, I discovered hiking and backpacking and a deep love of the natural world, igniting a development of the ground quality, natural living. This has substantially influenced my worldview and choice of recreation and vacations, but I still feel frustrated that I haven't yet succeeded in being able to live in more of a rural setting. I feel a profound sense of peace and connectedness when I am in nature, and I long to move out of the city and suburbs so I can enjoy this full time.

My income as a therapist is reasonably high, so I haven't yet been forced to consider a life of material simplicity or plentitude for financial reasons. Even though I don't spend extravagantly on material items, I feel a nagging guilt over the energy and resources I do consume just by living an upper-middle-class lifestyle. This is a part of my personal evolution that is not settled yet. In the material realm I would characterize myself as emergent quality that is partly dissociated and partly integrating ground.

Social Realm. I grew up with a fair measure of organizational and leadership ability. This was encouraged in school, and my academic success helped me to feel confident and powerful in intellectual and work situations. Thus in the social realm I had the emergent quality both naturally and given. In contrast, I was very shy in social and dating situations, though I had normal friendships in childhood and adolescence.

When I became involved in therapy and group work in my twenties, I discovered a hunger and excitement about relationship, intimacy, and community. My ground quality, though underdeveloped, was yearning for expression. Over the years I have improved this side of myself through therapy, by working on my love relationships, and through participating in activist and personal growth peer groups that provided a sense of community. Today I have a wonderful marriage with a great deal of love and closeness, but I still lack a full experience of community in my life. This is partly because I have moved across the country and partly because of personal limitations that I haven't yet worked through. I still put more energy into pursuing professional success than into developing friendship and community, though I am now trying to integrate the two. Thus I would characterize my position as emergent quality that is partly dissociated and partly integrating ground.

PART FOUR

THE LARGER VIEW

In part four I place the study of social evolution within a larger inclusive framework for evolution in general (chapter 23). This leads to the possibility (chapter 24) that our next step may be a move to a new level of evolution, which I call global consciousness or conscious evolution. Chapter 25 concludes with an overview of the model and its implications for the meaning of life and our immediate future.

XXIII

SOCIAL AND GENERAL EVOLUTION

In this chapter we examine how this model of social evolution relates to evolution in general. Biological evolution has been studied extensively. How is social evolution related to it? Is there a larger understanding of evolution that includes both biological and social and perhaps more as well? This is a highly abstract theoretical chapter and that can be skipped by the reader not so inclined.

AN INCLUSIVE FRAMEWORK FOR EVOLUTION

General Systems Theory. General systems theory has explored these questions and produced some provisional answers that help to place my model within an overall understanding of evolution. General systems theory was developed as a way of understanding the commonalties among the different sciences—physical, biological, and social (von Bertalanffy 1968). It creates the very general concept of a "system," and then studies the properties of systems in general.

A *system* is any collection of entities that interact in such a way that they can reasonably be viewed as a functioning unit; there is enough stability over time and coherence in the way the parts relate. Systems exist at all levels of reality; atoms, molecules, cells, organisms, institutions, and societies are all examples of systems. A molecule is a collection of atoms that function as a unit. An institution is a collection of people that function as a unit. A collection is not a system if it doesn't cohere in this way. For example, the set of all people in the United States with red hair is not a system, because they don't function together in any meaningful way.

The Containment Hierarchy. The parts of a system are also systems. So each system is a *holon* (Koestler 1978), which means that it is both a part and a whole. It consists of subsystems and is also a constituent of at least one supersystem. Thus a cell consists of subsystems called molecules and it is also a member of a larger system called an organ or organism. This leads to a hierarchy, in which the higher systems contain smaller systems, and they contain still smaller ones, and so on. It seems that reality is naturally structured hierarchically in this way. I will call this a *containment hierarchy* to distinguish it from a hierarchy of status and control such as in the armed forces or a hierarchy of preference such as Maslow's hierarchy of needs. Hierarchies of status and control are often used as instruments of oppression in the social realm, but containment hierarchies do seem to be the natural order of reality. Figure 23.1 sketches the general form of a containment hierarchy.

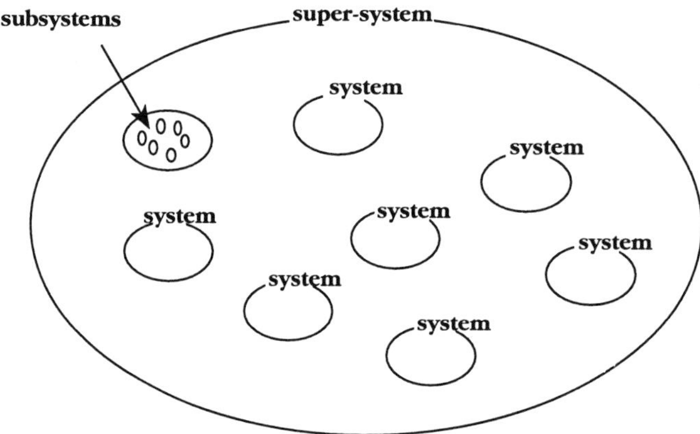

Figure 23.1

Evolutionary Trends. The most common general definition of evolution, biological or social, involves *complexity.* More evolved systems are defined as those that are more complex, more differentiated. This means they have a greater number of subsystems which can be interconnected in more ways or they have a greater number of different kinds of subsystems which have a wider variety of modes of interacting. For example, a human brain has more cells with more possible connections than the brain of a mouse.

System theorists have investigated the unfolding of the physical universe from the beginning of time until the present and noticed a trend that moves from small, simple systems toward larger, more complex ones (Laszlo 1987). This includes physical, biological, and social evolution. This doesn't mean that all systems necessarily become more complex or larger. Some have stayed the same for millions of years. Some even regress in evolutionary terms. However, over time systems have continued to appear that were more complex than what preceded them. These can usefully be considered as more evolutionarily advanced. This doesn't mean that there is an evolutionary tendency that requires any particular system to evolve in a certain way. It is an acknowledgment of the long term trends.

Not all evolutionary theorists agree with this idea. In fact, some biologists believe that there is no particular direction to evolution at all, only adaptation by natural selection. Since I agree with the evolutionary viewpoint of general systems theory, I will build on its insights in this chapter.

Systems theorists have noticed a number of other system properties associated with evolution:

1. *Hierarchy level*. Systems at higher levels of the containment hierarchy are more evolved. Thus a multicellular organism is more evolutionarily advanced than a single celled organism, and a society of organisms is at a still higher level.
2. *Increasing speed*. Evolution has increasingly moved faster. The evolution of the physical universe can be measured in hundreds of millions or billions of years, biological evolution in hundreds of thousands or millions of years, and social evolution in hundreds or thousands of years. And social evolution itself is speeding up, as mentioned earlier.
3. *Autonomy*. More evolved systems tend to be more autonomous with respect to their environment. They have more degrees of freedom, they are more determined by their own inner workings than by the systems that contain them, and they have more ability to respond adaptively and creatively to changes in their environment. For example, a human being has more freedom and choice about how to deal with an unusually cold winter than a robin does.

COMPLEXITY AND AUTONOMY

Let's look at some of these evolutionary properties in more detail. Most interesting for our purposes are complexity and autonomy.

Complexity is a well-accepted measure of evolution. It is the result of the differentiation of a system into a variety of kinds of subsystems with different ways of interacting with each other. Thus the human body is differentiated into an endocrine system, an immune system, a nervous system, and so on, and each of these is differentiated further into organs, and each of these into cells. The more differentiated a system is, the more complex. Where a simple water molecule has just two hydrogen atoms and one oxygen atom, a complex protein molecule contains a much larger number of atoms with different combinations and ways of bonding.

Let's look at differentiation in human society. One form it takes is the specialization of function into different sectors, occupations, roles, and subspecialties. Another is the stratification of society into different classes or castes, where the differentiation is according to status and power. A third is the proliferation of different religious and ethnic groups and cultures.

Autonomy is just as important as complexity, but not as widely recognized. To underscore its importance, I will review the ideas of some important systems theorists on autonomy: *The Tree of Knowledge* (Maturana and Varela 1987), which develops a systems approach to the study of cognition, sees autonomy as a primary characteristic of all living systems.

Ervin Laszlo notes that in evolution there is a movement toward less binding energy and therefore more degrees of freedom. This is a low-level form of autonomy.

> As we move from microscopic systems on a basic level of organization to macroscopic systems on higher organizational levels, we move from systems that are strongly and rigidly bonded to those with weaker and more flexible binding energies. . . . Protons and neutrons within the nucleus of atoms are bound by nuclear exchange forces, the strength of which is strikingly demonstrated in nuclear fission. Atoms within complex molecules are joined by ionic or covalent bonding and related weaker forces. The forces that join chemical molecules within organic macromolecules are weaker still, while those that bond cells within multicellular organisms are another dimension down the scale of bonding energy. (Laszlo 1987, 22–24)

In the biological arena, Gregory Bateson discusses three ways that organisms handle changes in the environment. "Adjusters" are organisms that allow the environment to impinge on their organism and then adjust to the result. An example would be cold-blooded reptiles, which allow their body temperature to change with that of their surroundings and then must adjust their activity level accordingly. "Regulators" handle impingements from the environment at their body boundaries. Thus warm-blooded mammals keep their internal body temperature fixed and regulate this through fur, sweating, movement, shelter, and so on. This gives them more autonomy with respect to the surrounding temperature. "Extraregulators" achieve control outside their bodies by changing their environment. Thus human beings wear clothes and build houses to control their body temperature, thus giving them even more autonomy. "In the broad picture of evolution . . . natural selection . . . favors regulators more than adjusters, and extraregulators more than regulators" (Bateson 1972, 361–63).

Arthur Koestler describes the evolutionary increase in autonomy as follows: "Generally we find on successively higher levels of the hierarchy increasingly complex, more flexible and less predictable patterns of activity with more degrees of freedom (a larger variety of strategic choices)" (Koestler 1978, 46).

At the human level, three levels of behavioral response can be distinguished.

1. *Instinctive behavior* is built in genetically, with adaptation happening only over the span of many lifetimes through biological evolution. There is no possibility of adapting to any recent changes in the environment.
2. *Learned behavior* changes through processes like conditioning or modeling, which gives us the chance to adapt to changes in our environment during our lifetime, as long as there has been enough time in the new situation for learning to have occurred. This gives us more autonomy.
3. *Conscious choice* allows people to choose our response according to the uniqueness of a given situation, even one that we may never have encountered before. This includes not only selecting from a given set of alternative choices, but also generating new possibilities for action. This gives us maximal autonomy through being able to respond most appropriately to circumstances.

Notice again that with these three types of behavior, the more evolved response patterns are the ones with more autonomy.

Adaptability. Complexity and autonomy are two sides of the same coin. The more internal complexity a system has, the more autonomy it has with respect to its supersystem(s). The complexity gives the system greater functional capacity in adapting to changes in its environment, and therefore greater autonomy.

I speculate that the reason evolution has led toward systems of greater complexity and autonomy is that these systems are more adaptable. Notice that there is a difference between a system being "adapted" and being "adaptable." A species or type of system will survive as long as it is adapted to its environment, meaning that it can remain viable and reproduce in those circumstances. However, if the environment changes, then the systems in it must either change or have enough built-in flexibility to handle the new environment. Otherwise they become extinct. This ability to adapt to a changed environment is called adaptability.

In any given ecological niche, a system type may be adapted without being adaptable, and therefore do well without being complex or autonomous. However, over time those systems that are the most adaptable will do best because they can survive the inevitable changes that will occur.

Complexity and Autonomy in Social Evolution. Let's look at complexity and autonomy in our model of social evolution. Here the system in question is the human society and its supersystems are the natural world and the system of all human societies. In all realms, the emergent qualities involve an increase in complexity and autonomy.

In the material realm, with the emergence of technology, our means of working with physical reality have become increasingly complex. Humans first used very simple tools and gradually evolved to the point where we now use very complex machines and computers. This has given our societies greater autonomy with respect to the natural world in that it has allowed us to protect ourselves better from weather and predators, feed more people, travel further and faster, etc.

In the social realm, social structure obviously involves an increase in the social complexity of a society. A more complex society is more able to trade effectively, secure resources, avoid being conquered, and so on. This gives it more autonomy with respect to the natural world and also in dealing with other societies.

In the consciousness realm, reflexive consciousness has permitted our thinking to grow in complexity, and this has supported the growth of technology and social structure. In addition, reflexive consciousness has given us conscious choice, a crucial aspect of autonomy.

WHOLENESS

Along with complexity (differentiation[1]) and autonomy, there is a third concept that is crucial to understanding the evolution of systems.

1. In the rest of this chapter I will use "differentiation" as a synonym for complexity because it is more appropriate for my purposes.

Wholeness indicates the tendency of a system to be coordinated as a coherent unit. Wholeness is necessary for the health of a system. If the differentiation of a system or the autonomy of its subsystems is strong enough that it disrupts the wholeness of the system, then its health and indeed its viability is threatened. Therefore, there is a crucial dialectical relationship between wholeness and both differentiation and autonomy, which I discuss below. I didn't include wholeness in the list of evolutionary trends because more evolved systems aren't necessarily more coherent, though there are certain evolutionary situations where wholeness does increase.

I have come to the conclusion that *differentiation, autonomy, and wholeness are the three basic tendencies of evolution*. Thomas Berry and Brian Swimme arrive at the same conclusion in *The Universe Story* (1992, 71), though they use the word "autopoesis" instead of autonomy and "communion" instead of wholeness. They consider these three to be "the governing themes and the basal intentionality of all existence."

Wholeness vs. Autonomy. Let's first look at the relationship between wholeness and autonomy. Arthur Koestler has defined this as a dynamic tension between the integrative tendency (wholeness) and the self-assertive tendency (autonomy) of systems.

> Every holon is possessed of two opposite tendencies or potentials: an *integrative tendency* to function as part of the larger whole, and a *self-assertive tendency* to preserve its individual autonomy. The most obvious manifestation of this basic polarity is found in social [systems]. . . . From the rights of the individual to those of clan or tribe . . . from ethnic minorities to sovereign governments, every social holon has a built-in tendency to preserve and defend its corporate identity. This self-assertive tendency is indispensable for maintaining the individuality of holons on all levels, and of the hierarchy as a whole. . . . At the same time the holon is dependent on, and must function as an integrated part of the larger system that contains it. (Koestler 1978, 57)

The right balance of tension must be maintained between these two tendencies, between the wholeness of a system and the autonomy of its subsystems, as shown in figure 23.2. On the one hand, if a system's wholeness is not strong enough, then its subsystems will not interact with each other in a coherent enough way to maintain it as a viable system. It will degenerate into anarchy or disease or dissociation. On the other hand, if a subsystem's autonomy is not strong enough, it will be swallowed up by its system and lose its viability in that way, as when a person becomes merged in a cult.

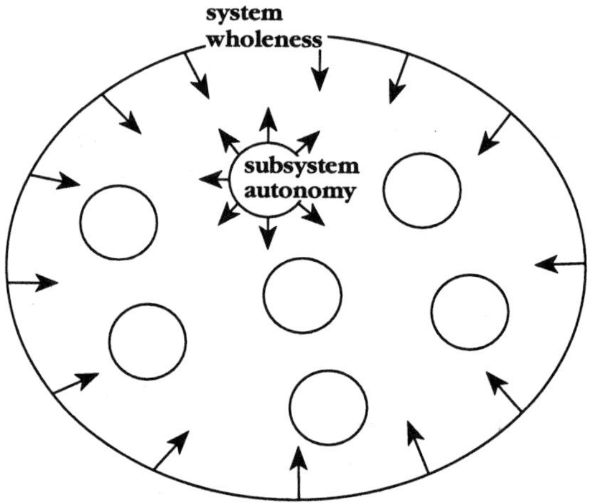

Figure 23.2

Wholeness versus Differentiation. There is also a dialectical relationship between wholeness and differentiation, shown in figure 23.3. A simple system has little trouble with wholeness; its job of coordinating its constituent subsystems is relatively easy because there are so few of them and so few ways for them to interact. As systems become more differentiated, new mechanisms of coordination must develop to keep the increasingly numerous and varied parts working together harmoniously. For example, very simple organisms don't need much of a nervous system, but as complexity increases there is much more coordination needed, so a large, complex central nervous system is required to do the job.

In social evolution, at least, it is possible for differentiation to significantly disrupt wholeness, as we discussed previously in chapter 20. Then the health of the system is in question. So as evolution proceeds, wholeness must be regained.

Wholeness in Social Evolution. During social evolution, societies have increased their differentiation (complexity) and their autonomy with respect to the natural world. As discussed above, the emergent qualities are characterized by a tendency toward differentiation and autonomy. In the process, wholeness has been diminished. Societies have become differentiated at the expense of their wholeness and that of their members,

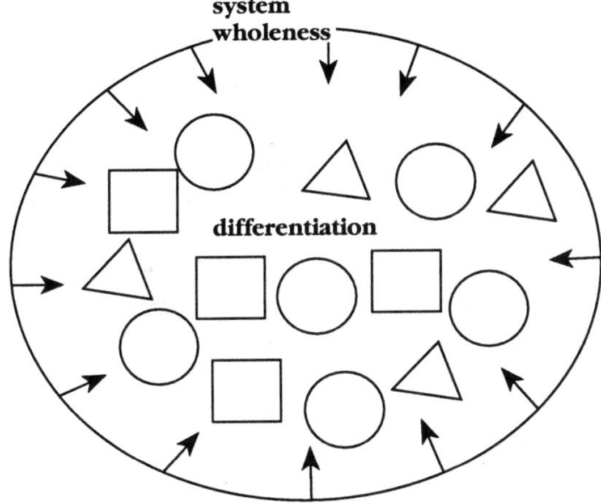

Figure 23.3

and societies have become autonomous from nature at the expense of their integration into the wholeness of the larger ecological system that contains them. Wholeness is really the essence of the ground qualities that have become suppressed as a result of social evolution.

In the material realm, society can be seen as a system and the natural world as its supersystem. Through the growth of our use of technology, humanity has gained a greater degree of autonomy from the effects of nature, but in the process we have disrupted our integration into the wholeness of the larger natural system to such an extent that our viability is threatened.

In the social realm, the increased differentiation of society into sectors and specialties, into classes and subcultures, has not been matched with a corresponding increase in coordination and cooperation based on the best interests of the whole. Therefore our choices as a society are often marked by battles for power or compromise between competing interests, so wholeness is lost. In addition, the increase in our social structure has destroyed the wholeness of community, one of our innate human needs. The additional coordination from our social structure has not provided enough wholeness to make up for what has been lost.

In the consciousness realm, our increasing autonomy, in the form of hyperindividuality, has caused fragmentation and alienation and therefore disrupted our integration into larger wholes—the earth, our human communities, and the larger spiritual reality. In this way, one can say that our external wholeness has been diminished. In addition, increasing differentiation in consciousness has resulted in the dissociation between reflexive and participatory consciousness, as exemplified by the split between reason and emotion. This is a disruption of our internal wholeness, and therefore contributes to psychological and even medical problems.

Therefore in the larger systems perspective, the return of the ground qualities can be seen as the regaining of wholeness (figure 23.5). The health of a system is determined by its wholeness. Evolution brings about an increase in differentiation and autonomy (figure 23.4), but if society doesn't develop more sophisticated coordinating and integrating mechanisms to maintain our wholeness, then health is diminished. Since that's what has happened so far in social evolution, our next task is regain our wholeness by integrating the ground qualities.

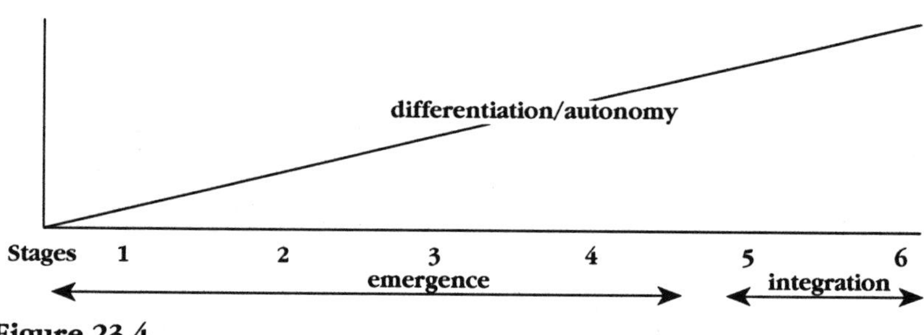

Figure 23.4

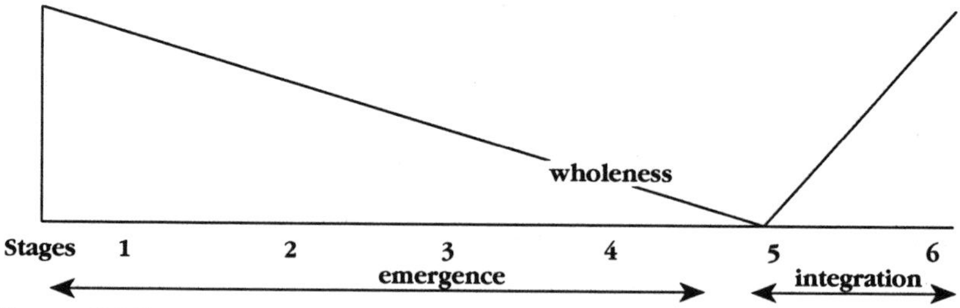

wholeness
Stages 1 2 3 4 5 6
emergence
integration

Figure 23.5

Biological Evolution. It is probably also true in biological evolution that wholeness can be disrupted by an increase in differentiation and autonomy. For example, suppose a new strain of a species is more autonomous with respect to its environment and therefore more successful in its drive to survive. Perhaps a predator can hunt in a greater variety of times and places and therefore becomes more successful at killing its prey. This new capacity might enable the species to unwittingly alter its environment in such a way that it could no longer survive in that environment. For example, the predator might kill off all of its prey species. In this way the increased autonomy might lead to the predator's lack of integration into the wholeness of the larger ecosystem, and therefore its demise.

In this example as in social evolution, there can be an opposition between increased autonomy and wholeness, thus opening the possibility of a dialectical process. Therefore although I am unfamiliar with theoretical biology, I speculate that the dialectical relationship between wholeness and differentiation/autonomy is not limited to social evolution, but may be a general property of evolution at all levels.

PERSONAL AUTONOMY

So far I have discussed societal autonomy, but what about the autonomy of persons with respect to society. This is related to power distribution in the social realm and individuality in the consciousness realm. In my understanding of *autonomy* at the human level, I include not only freedom from coercion and self-directed action, but also the development of all aspects of a person's potential.

Personal autonomy decreased from stages 1 to 3 with the advent of stratification and the Archaic empires, and then it increased in stages 4 and 5 with the growth of individuality and democracy. In stage 6 it would be helpful to promote even more personal autonomy while integrating community and connectedness. In systems terms, this means increasing the autonomy of the person with respect to the society while regaining the wholeness of society.

Systems thinking doesn't say anything definitive about what happens to the autonomy of the subsystems of a system as it evolves; there is no clear cut pattern. Therefore it isn't surprising that individual autonomy has varied during the course of social evolution. However let's ask whether one can expect a highly evolved system to promote the autonomy of its subsystems, as we would like stage 6 societies to do for personal autonomy.

System Intelligence. In order to explore this, let's consider the idea of the *intelligence* of a system as the ability of a system to promote its own well-being. The intelligence of a system will depend on the degree of its differentiation and autonomy as long as increases in them don't disrupt the system's wholeness. Therefore an intelligent system is high in differentiation and autonomy without losing wholeness. One can also ask how an intelligent system affects the wholeness of its supersystems and the autonomy of its subsystems.

It seems that a system that is intelligent in the long run will not only promote its own wholeness, but also its integration into the wholeness of its supersystem(s). Without this, the viability of the system itself is threatened, as Modern society is threatening its viability by disrupting its integration into the larger ecosystem.

I think that in the long run a system, in promoting its own well-being, will also promote the autonomy of its subsystems, as long as this autonomy doesn't disrupt the system's own wholeness. If the subsystems lose autonomy, then they lose their ability for self-directed action, and they must depend on the system to direct them. This puts a much greater burden on the system, requiring it to know a great deal of detailed information that is more available to the subsystems. Systems seem to function more effectively if such low level decisions can be made by the subsystems, leaving the system to concentrate on higher level coordination. For example, in the social realm this is illustrated by the problems with command economies and bureaucracies that limit the initiative of workers.

Holergy. There is another problem with low-autonomy subsystems. If the system controls everything from the top, then it is not likely to use all the talents of its subsystems. For example, in bureaucracies each person is given a single job, which generally uses only a small part of the person's potential. This is, of course, constricting for the person, and it also decreases the effectiveness of the system. By increasing the autonomy of the persons in an organization or society, there is a much better chance that they will maximize the use of their abilities, for their benefit and that of the organization.

Tom Atlee in "Collective Intelligence as an Approach to Transformative Social Change," has a term related to this, holergy, which he defines it in a parallel way to synergy: If *synergy* means the whole is greater than the sum of the parts, then *holergy* means that the part is greater than its role in the whole. To the extent that subsystems are autonomous, they are able to actualize their holergy.

So far in human social evolution, social structure has had mixed results in promoting personal autonomy, but since most of us value autonomy highly, we can design our social systems of the future in such a way as to explicitly encourage it. I believe that personal autonomy doesn't need to be in conflict with societal intelligence and, in fact, will probably enhance it.

A NEW HIERARCHICAL LEVEL

The normal situation in evolution is for differentiation and autonomy to increase and for wholeness to play catch-up. There is one situation, however, where this is reversed. That is when a new level in the containment hierarchy is being created. When a collection of systems that have been functioning relatively independently begins to coalesce into a super-system at a higher level, then wholeness increases, potentially at the expense of autonomy.

For example, at some point in the distant history of the universe, the most complex systems in existence were atoms. Then as matter cooled from the intense heat of the big bang, these atoms began to form bonds with each other to create molecules. Where before there was only a collection of atoms, with little or no wholeness, now there were bonded groups, with increased degrees of wholeness and perhaps less autonomy for the individual atoms. Similarly, at some point in evolution, the most complex forms of life were single-celled organisms. Then gradually some of them established symbiotic relationships with each other, and these eventually transformed into new multicellular organisms. In this process there was an increase in the wholeness of the groups of cells and potentially a decrease in the autonomy of the individual cells.

You might say that the systems gave up some autonomy to create the wholeness of a new larger supersystem, which then had greater autonomy with respect to the environment (figure 23.6). This is a sound evolutionary strategy because it increases the adaptability of the groups of systems.

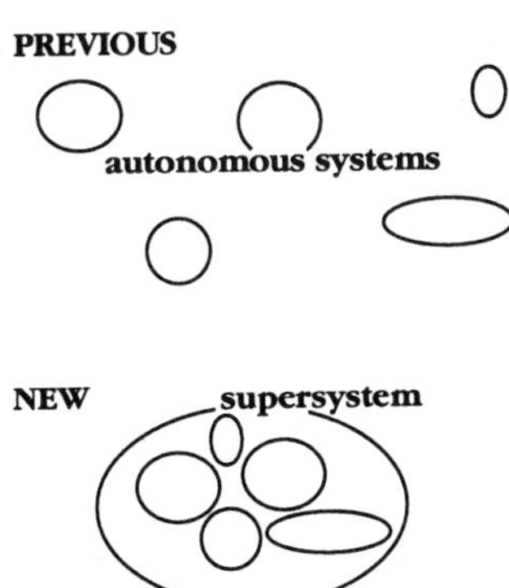

Figure 23.6

The Creation of the Global Society. In social evolution, humanity has also been in the process of creating a new hierarchical level. Our societies are systems that have gradually been coalescing into a supersystem called the *global society*. Because of this process, there have been two social evolutionary trajectories in the social realm. Besides the increasing differentiation of societies and the autonomy of society from nature, there has also been an increase in the wholeness of the world system of societies.

We have moved from a state of differentiation and autonomy to one of increasing wholeness. If we go back not to stage 1, but to stage 0, when we had just become human, there must have been little in the way of cultural diversity because the culture we had was genetically based. Then as humans multiplied and spread out over the globe, tribes became separated from each other, and as cultures changed over time, a wide variety of different cultures ensued. By stage 1, these were fairly autonomous from each other because they had little contact with each other.

As we moved into stages 2 and 3, societies were conquered and assimilated into successively larger units, and trade and transportation improvements fostered increasingly greater contact between societies. The global system of societies was increasing in wholeness. This process accelerated in stages 4 and 5 and presumably will culminate in a world society in stage 6.

Thus there have been opposing trends in the social realm. Even as societies were developing their capacity for autonomy, especially autonomy from nature, at the same time they were giving up autonomy to the growing wholeness of the global system. This second trend shows itself in the intersocietal realm, where the emergent quality is intersocietal structure (wholeness) and the ground quality is societal autonomy. This is the opposite of the other realms, as shown in table 23.1.

Table 23.1 Autonomy and Wholeness in Social Evolution

Realm	**Ground Quality**	**Emergent Quality**
Material	Natural living (wholeness)	Technological living (differentiation and autonomy)
Social	Community (wholeness)	Social structure (differentiation and autonomy)
Consciousness	Participatory (wholeness)	Reflexive (differentiation and autonomy)
Intersocietal	Societal autonomy (autonomy)	Intersocietal structure (wholeness)

A NEW TYPE OF EVOLUTION

Earlier I mentioned three types of behavioral response—instinctive, learned, and conscious—representing increasing levels of autonomy. These also correspond to three types of change—biological evolution, learning, and conscious choice—which occur over vastly disparate time scales and use different mechanisms:

1. Biological evolution happens by natural selection through genetics, taking place over perhaps hundreds of thousands or millions of years. This means that traits are selected that give the species the best chance of survival.
2. Learning happens through reinforcement, classical conditioning, modeling, and other psychological mechanisms over a person's lifetime. This means that behavioral responses are selected according to various criteria which presumably enhance the organism's survival.
3. Conscious choice happens in the moment. It means choosing a particular response according to what people decide is best for their well-being given the circumstances and their understanding of consequences.

Here the higher types don't supersede the lower ones; they augment them. Thus when a conscious choice is made, learned and instinctual influences may also be operating.

This analysis applies to individual organisms or persons. However, there is a similar typology for change in societies:

1. Biological evolution selects for social patterns of behavior that give the species the best chance of survival.
2. Social evolution happens through cultural symbols, values, technology, and way of living. As shown in this book, social patterns tend to be selected that give societies the best chance of survival in the short term, though this is now threatening the survival of all.
3. In today's transition, humanity has an opportunity to advance social evolution to a new type that I will call *conscious social evolution*, where social patterns are consciously chosen (not unconsciously selected) for their ability to promote personal and societal well-being (not just survival). This is depicted in table 23.2.

Table 23.2

	Person		Society	
Mechanism	**Process**		**Process**	
Genetics	Biological evolution	Selection of traits for survival	Biological evolution	Selection of social patterns for species survival
Learning	Learning	Selection of behavior	Social evolution	Selection of social patterns for societal survival
Consciousness	Conscious choice	Choice of behavior for personal well-being	Conscious social evolution	Choice of social patterns for personal & societal well-being

This indicates that the new social pattern that is evolving may be more than just stage 6 in social evolution. It may represent a new type of evolutionary mechanism. Remember that the inclusive framework for evolution recognizes physical, biological, and social evolution, each with a different mechanism of change. (Physical evolution isn't included in table 23.2.) The process may now be moving to a fourth type of evolution, where the mechanism of change is consciousness.

It is exciting to me to understand how our social evolution is really part of the larger story of the universe. There is a marvelous cosmic story progressing, which we are only beginning to glimpse, and our social evolution is an important part of this drama. In moving to stage 6 and creating a healthy planetary society we are not only saving ourselves from disaster and fulfilling our potential; we are also contributing to the larger unfolding of creation.

XXIV

GLOBAL CONSCIOUSNESS

As humanity moves into stage 6, perhaps our most important task is to take conscious charge of our social evolution. Until now our evolution has largely been driven by the parable of the tribes and population/environment constraints, both processes that are oriented primarily toward the survival of societies, not the well-being of people or communities or the earth. Now for the first time, our reflexive consciousness is evolved enough that we have the opportunity to consciously direct our evolution, and we face a crisis dangerous enough to force us to do that. But what exactly does it mean for a society (or a world) to consciously direct social evolution? Consciousness is a concept that usually applies to people, not societies.

Systems thinking has shown us that some important concepts can be applied to systems at many different levels of the containment hierarchy. Thus "autonomy" can apply to societies and cells as well as to persons. In the last chapter I used concepts such as "health" and "intelligence" to apply to systems in general, not just organisms or human beings. Gregory Bateson applied the concept of "mind" to systems in general.

> Bateson . . . proposed to define mind as a systems phenomenon characteristic of "living things." . . . Any system that satisfies [certain] criteria will be able to develop the phenomena we associate with mind—learning, memory, decision making, and so on. In Bateson's view, mind is a necessary and inevitable consequence of a certain complexity, which begins long before organisms develop a brain and a higher nervous system. He also emphasized that mental characteristics are manifest not only in individual organisms but also in social systems and ecosystems. (Capra 1993)

I discussed at the end of the last chapter how consciousness is the most evolved mechanism for increasing autonomy in a system. It gives a system the opportunity to respond to situations in the way that is most appropriate to the needs of the moment. Instinct, learning, or more primitive forms of autonomy don't have the same flexibility and creativity that consciousness has. It might be fair to say that consciousness is the form that autonomy takes in the most complex systems. Ken Wilber (1995) and others (Laszlo 1987; Berry 1990) have suggested that interiority (or consciousness in a different sense) is a property of all systems. Therefore there is no reason why the concept of consciousness can't be applied to groups, organizations, societies, and the emerging global system. It won't mean exactly the same thing as it does for a person, but it will be similar.

This chapter explores *global consciousness* as the hallmark of stage 6, the next step in human evolution.

WHAT IS GLOBAL CONSCIOUSNESS?

What exactly do I mean by global consciousness? It is a slippery concept, because "consciousness" has so many meanings. In this book I have used it to refer to the realm of the inner life and to mean being aware, rather than unaware or unconscious. My intended use of global consciousness is related but different from these. It is most closely related to "self-reflexive consciousness," the ability of human beings to be aware of themselves. This is the kind of consciousness that is characteristic of human beings, exists to a limited degree in the more intelligent animals, and is absent from the rest of the natural world.

Suppose that the entire human race were a single organism, a single creature. Would that creature be self-reflexively conscious? This is what I mean by global consciousness. Suppose that humanity as a whole wasn't a collection of organisms, but a single organism, let's say an enormous dinosaur. Suppose that humanity was an gigantic superorganism with five billion cells (humans) and various organs and body parts (perhaps nations, races, social movements, organizations). We then could ask whether this organism was conscious of itself.

By global consciousness I mean "collective global reflexive consciousness." The word "reflexive" refers to the ability of consciousness to reflect back on itself, the ability of a being to be aware of itself. "Global" refers to all of humanity. I use the world "collective" because I am referring to the consciousness of the human race *as a whole*, not a global consciousness that any of us might have as individuals.

Individual versus Collective Global Consciousness. I make a distinction between *individual global consciousness* and *collective global* *consciousness.* Individual global consciousness means the ability of a person to identify with humanity as a whole and to live and act accordingly. Collective global consciousness is the concept I am defining here. Collective global consciousness, of course, is dependent to a certain extent on individual global consciousness. The more people who are globally conscious, the better chance we have to achieve collective global consciousness.

However, collective global consciousness is not simply the sum of the individual global consciousnesses. Collective global consciousness is also determined by the larger configurations in the body of humanity, for example, multinational corporations, nations, organizations, ethnic and religious groups, communication networks. (These are analogous to configurations in the human organism such as the heart, the shoulder, the immune system, or the superego.) These groups may also be globally conscious to a greater or lesser degree, which I will call *group global consciousness.* Collective global consciousness is influenced by various groups' degree of global consciousness and how they interact with and contribute to the larger collective consciousness. This is summarized in table 24.1.

Table 24.1

Term	Definition
Individual self-reflexive consciousness	Individual aware of self
Individual global consciousness	Individual aware of humanity-as-a-whole
Group global consciousness	Group aware of humanity-as-a-whole
Collective global consciousness	Humanity-as-a-whole aware of self

Previous Studies. Planetary or global consciousness has been explored by Peter Russell (1983), Teilhard de Chardin (1965), and Sri Aurobindo (1970). Similar speculations have also been expressed in two classic science fiction novels—*Star Maker* and *Childhood's End.* In both these stories, humanity develops powerful telepathic powers and eventually merges into a single planetary mind. All of these authors seem to feel that global consciousness depends on the widespread advancement of individual consciousness, in the form of telepathy or higher spiritual consciousness. They see global consciousness as developing out of a mystical or telepathic union of all people.

Though I don't rule this out as a possibility, I wouldn't want to depend on it for the resolution of our present crisis. Widespread emotional and spiritual development would certainly help, but the kind of global consciousness that I'm suggesting happens at a different hierarchical level than individual consciousness.

Defining by Analogy. Collective global reflexive consciousness can be explored by analogy to individual self-reflexive consciousness. Let's look at what makes an individual self-reflexively conscious. I propose the following qualities:

1. Separateness
2. Identity
3. Observation of self (experience, behavior, and consequences)
4. Choice of action (based on these observations)
5. Understanding of dynamics underlying behavior

I will take each of these in turn, first understanding how each quality contributes to individual self-reflexive consciousness, then exploring the global analog in current society.

SEPARATENESS

Separateness refers to the ability of a person to experience him or herself as separate from the rest of the world. This quality develops during the first three years of human life. It has been studied extensively by developmental psychologists (Mahler, Pine et al. 1975). A baby is born having little or no sense experience of separateness from its surroundings, especially its mother, who is the main surrounding for the first few years. Then the child grows through a sequence of stages gradually developing a sense of itself as a separate being. This is largely complete by age three, although the development continues to a lesser extent all through childhood and adolescence.

By young adulthood, we have a fairly solid sense of ourselves as separate individuals, distinct from our family, our community, and the natural world. Separateness is an important component of individuality. Ideally we feel separate yet connected.

What about our separateness as a species? Collective separateness means feeling separate from the rest of life, from the natural world. Because of the emergent qualities of technology and reflexive consciousness, humanity certainly has achieved this aspect of global consciousness, but at the expense of losing the ground qualities of natural living and belonging.

IDENTITY

The second ingredient of self-reflexive consciousness is identity. This means recognizing yourself as a person with an ongoing existence who can be named and referred to. It is what allows you to say "I." You have a sense of what you are referring to when you say your name. Experientially, you not only feel separate from the world, you sense your uniqueness and on-going existence as a person.

The sense of identity also develops primarily during the first three years of life. Margaret Mahler (1975), a pioneering investigator in this area, uses the term "separation-individuation," referring to the twin processes of developing separateness and identity. She sees these as related but distinct developmental processes. As with separateness, the individuation process also continues later in life. In adolescence the search for identity is a major developmental task as described by Erik Erikson (1963).

Global Identification. What about our global identity, our identity as a species? This is something that we are only beginning to experience, and it is still quite tenuous. Before looking at our *collective* global identity, let's review our discussion of a person's *individual* global identification in chapter 19. This is an aspect of advanced reflexive consciousness which means the person identifies with the human race as a whole and links his or her welfare with all of humanity.

This same issue also applies to groups—organizations, institutions, nations. For any group, one can ask how much that group as a whole identifies with humanity instead of with narrower interests. For example, how much do our corporations and our nation-states identify with the interest of the whole world? I will call this *group* global identification.

This finally leads us to the concept I am aiming for—*collective* global identity: How much does humanity as a whole identify with itself? This is more than just the sum of the number of people with global identification. It is also influenced by the communication, organization, and power dynamics of the human race, especially by the degree of global identification of our powerful institutions. When humanity decides what to do about the ozone layer or global warming or war in Iraq, do we consider the whole world? Mostly these decisions are determined by the interests of those with the power—the industrialized nations and the multinational corporations—and their interests are rarely those of humanity as a whole. Often worldwide decisions are made through competition and balancing of the various interests with no one looking after the whole. Therefore our collective global identity is still fairly weak.

OBSERVATION OF SELF

The next attribute of self-reflexive consciousness is the ability to observe yourself. This includes observation of internal experience, behavior, and consequences of behavior.

Internal Experience and Behavior. This means the ability to stand back from yourself and recognize what you are feeling and doing. This ability is built upon our sense of identity and our cognitive and language capacities. It applies our reflexive consciousness to the self. It allows us to say such things as, "I am now getting tired." "I have been talking on the phone for the last hour." "I feel upset and angry." The ability to observe your behavior also includes the ability to generalize about how you usually behave, to develop some understanding about the kind of person you are. It means having a self-image. This enables you to say such things as: "I bought a lot of clothes this year." "I feel close to my sister." "I am a talkative person."

At a global level, reflexive consciousness means the ability to observe our actions and values as a species. It means being able to say things such as: "We are releasing X tons of carbon dioxide into the atmosphere every day." "Democracy is becoming an agreed-upon value around the world." "40,000 people die of starvation in the world every day." This observational ability relies on our modern communication, transportation, and information technologies and our reflexive consciousness. Through these means humanity now collects data on a wide variety of our behaviors and values—personal, social, economic, environmental. Then through our tradition of research and scholarship we analyze, correlate, and attempt to understand this information.

We have become relatively successful at observing our behavior and values. Until recently, this was done primarily on a national basis, but now more and more organizations such as the Worldwatch Institute observe and study our behavior at a global level. However, we are not yet disseminating this information so that it is widely known and appreciated. This can be considered a global analog to making it conscious at the individual level. Therefore we can say that this kind of observation is only partially conscious at the global level.

Consequences of Behavior. The next step in observing yourself is to observe the consequences of your behavior. You are aware of what you are doing, *and* you can see where it leads. A person might say, "I'm eating too many sweets at night, and as a result I'm getting a roll around my middle." Or, "I'm staying up late at night, and as a result I'm exhausted and irritable half the time." This involves the ability to live in extended time, which includes the past and the future. Anyone who has raised children is aware that this kind of self-observation is something that is a hard-won developmental task, which only begins to appear in adolescence. Even for many adults, it is sometimes hard to really see the consequences of our behavior. However, it is within our capacity; it is part of our self-reflexive consciousness.

At the global level, this kind of observation means being able to see the consequences of our actions as a species. "As a result of the carbon dioxide we are releasing, there is a global warming trend." "Our population growth is leading to major environmental and social problems." In this area, we need not only the data, but the ability to understand cause and effect and to project trends into the future. In many cases we don't have clear cut statistics, so we must try to understand trends and correlations that are not fully proved, where we can't know the consequences for sure. Personal values and political considerations creep in. When there is no room for question, as with the danger to the ozone layer, we tend to take our observations seriously. However, if there is any room for doubt, as with the issues of global warming and over-population, then influential people and groups deny the danger, calling for "more research," or simply ignore the threat. The denial comes from a focus on national, corporate, or other separate interests, from a lack of global identification. This then influences our choice of action.

In most circumstances, humanity has the information we really need to see the dangers ahead, but it isn't widely known or given the priority it deserves. Therefore I think our global consciousness in this area is only partial.

CHOICE OF ACTION

As individuals, once we have observed our behavior and its consequences, we can choose to act differently if we don't want the consequences. This means acting from a conscious understanding of the results of the action, not just from our immediate impulses and desires. This ability to choose is a basic of human nature, as has been recognized by existential and humanistic psychology (Bugental 1965). There are three aspects of choice of action—choice of short-term consequences, choice of long-term consequences, and choice of overall way of being.

Short-Term Consequences. If we are aware of short term consequences, we can say: "If I stay up late tonight, I'll be exhausted tomorrow, so I'll go to bed now." "If I express my anger at my boss, I might be fired, so I'll keep quiet." Like the other aspects of self-reflexive consciousness, this is an ability that gradually develops during the maturation process. Of course, even as adults, we don't always act from conscious choice, as has been demonstrated by modern psychological studies of unconscious motivation. This is most apparent in the widespread problem of addictions today. However, we have the ability to consciously choose our actions, even if we don't always exercise it.

At the global level, the ability to choose refers to our ability as a species to take actions to better our situation based on observations of our behavior and its consequences. It would include the ability to say, "The global economy is having certain difficulties, so we will cooperate on international bank actions to stabilize the dollar." "The world will be safer if Russia becomes stable, so we will aid them in restructuring their economy." In the last few decades we are beginning to be able to make these kinds of decisions about global issues with relatively short-term consequences.

Institutions and Action. The ability to take decisive action at the global level currently resides in our political institutions and our multinational corporations, but these are noted for self-interest, not global interest. Much of this power is vested in the political institutions of the nation-state, and too often these institutions are concerned primarily with the short-term interests of the nation's special interest groups or with national prestige, power, and "security." An increasing amount of this power lies in the hands of the large multinational corporations, which are almost solely concerned with their own short-term profit picture. For example, despite all the evidence of enormous danger ahead from global warming, the Bush administration stalled on taking action, probably because the changes required would have caused significant disruptions for many influential corporations.

The political institutions that have some global identification and outlook are the United Nations along with some nongovernmental organizations, but these have relatively little power. The most the UN can do is bring together the powerful nations and hope that they can agree on treaties that reflect a global orientation. Sometimes when the consequences are clear and immediate enough, the human race has been able to act. This has been possible because we now have enough global observational ability, some fledgling global institutions, and a degree of global cooperation. For example, the group of seven largest capitalist countries are sometime able to make economic decisions that take into account the short term improvement of the world economy. However, this ability is only recently gained, and sometimes even short-term consequences are sacrificed to competing national or corporate interests.

Choice of Long Term Consequences. As individuals, besides making choices based on immediate consequences, we can look farther into the future. We can practice "delayed gratification." For example, we can say: "Since I don't like gaining weight from eating too much, I choose to eat less." The weight loss won't show up tomorrow, but weeks or months later, so we need the ability to choose based on longer-term consequences. This requires a higher level of cognitive ability and a more mature emotional development.

At the global level this would include the ability to say: "We are seriously threatened by global warming, so we will make the changes necessary to reduce the release of carbon dioxide and other gases which cause the greenhouse effect." "Overpopulation is a major threat, so we will start a major campaign toward population stabilization." The consequences of global warming or overpopulation will not happen this year or next, so we must have more foresight to take them into account. (In the case of overpopulation, this is not strictly true. We are already suffering its effects, but it is a gradual, long-term process.)

Global Long-Term Choice. Our abilities are dangerously lacking in dealing with long term consequences. The institutions that currently wield power in the world are strongly oriented toward interests that are short term and nonglobal. Unfortunately, most of the issues that threaten us are global and long term. Perhaps "intermediate term" would be even more accurate, because they are issues with consequences in decades, not centuries. If we had centuries, the current danger would not be so great.

When an issue is clear cut, large sacrifices are not required, and the issue is not long term, then global cooperation sometimes now happens. This was the case with the danger to the ozone layer. There was a UN-sponsored meeting about the ozone danger in which the countries involved agreed to a certain reduction in their emissions of CFCs (chlorofluorocarbons, the gases that are primarily responsible for ozone depletion). Then when it became apparent, a few years later, that this decrease was not enough, they met again and agreed to a further reduction over the next decade. This illustrates the kind of action that the world should be taking on a wide variety of issues that threaten us.

Ultimately what we need is political institutions at the global level with our long-term global interests at heart that have the power to act on the crucial issues facing us. We need a much stronger UN or possibly even some form of world government with the power to make these decisions and enforce them. We need a closer connection between those institutions with global observational ability and identity and those with the power to act. There are a growing number of nongovernmental organizations and citizens' groups that may be gaining in power and influence. Many of them have a global and long-term perspective. If these groups network together and increase their membership and following, they may begin to provide a healthy form of globally conscious power.

Institutions and Global Consciousness. In exploring the question of global consciousness, it is interesting to notice which groups, organizations, and institutions perform the various functions I have been discussing. Here is a cursory summary:

Separation: Everyone
Identity: The UN and certain research and activist organizations
Observation and understanding dynamics: Research and academic organizations
Action: National governments and multinational corporations

Notice that the organizations with the power are not the same ones that embody global identification and observation. It is not necessary that they be exactly the same, but it is necessary that those organizations with global power identify globally and listen to the groups with observational ability. Of course, it is also crucial that the average person develop global identification and that our institutions democratically reflect this.

The above summary doesn't begin to cover the various organizations that perform some of the functions of global consciousness, now or in the future. That would be an interesting study in itself.

Before I discuss the third type of choice—the ability to choose one's overall way of being—I will discuss understanding dynamics, because this capacity is necessary for this most difficult kind of choice.

UNDERSTANDING DYNAMICS

Understanding Psychological Dynamics. The last component of individual self-reflexive consciousness is the ability to observe and understand the psychological dynamics behind our behavior. Whenever our behavior is motivated by something deeper than conscious choice (and this is much of the time), we can benefit from understanding what the underlying motivation is. Our perceptions are also strongly shaped by unconscious personal and cultural forces. Understanding dynamics includes everything from relatively simple surface perceptions and motivation to deep psychodynamic conflicts. It means the ability to say such things as, "I got irritated at you because I felt hurt by what you said." "I try to please you because I'm afraid you'll abandon me the way my mother did."

In one sense I hesitate to include this ability in the list, because it is clearly not necessary for a person to have this kind of self-awareness to be considered self-reflexively conscious. Many people live their entire lives without it. However, this is the most advanced form of self-reflexive consciousness, and it is important for global consciousness, so I will include it. Self-reflexive consciousness has developed very gradually over the span of human social evolution, and the ability to understand dynamics is the most historically recent of our self-conscious abilities. It is only in the last forty years that this ability has begun to be widespread among the population.

Since much of our perception and behavior is influenced by things we aren't entirely conscious of, whenever we can understand this influence, we have a greater chance of changing the behavior. Knowing why we act as we do, we can choose to act differently with a better chance of succeeding. Sometimes knowing the origins even changes the underlying motivation. This gives us a greater degree of freedom and choice.

Understanding Social Dynamics. At the global level, understanding dynamics means understanding the psychological, cultural, historical, economic, and political dynamics behind our behavior as a species. Here the psychological is just one of many areas we need to understand. In the global arena even more than the individual, humanity rarely acts from any conscious decision. Most of what we do and who we are is the result of complex social dynamics; often the result is something we wouldn't have chosen consciously.

An understanding of social dynamics gives us the ability to say things such as: "The main reason for massive hunger in the world is the lack of political and economic power in the hands of the poor." "It is difficult for us to reduce the environmental threats because our economic system requires continued expansion of consumption." Attempts to understand these dynamics come mainly from universities, think tanks, and independent scholars and theorists. It is the work of sociologists, political scientists, economists, political psychologists, and other social critics. Having this kind of understanding would help us deal with some of the really difficult problems we are now facing as a world.

Have we achieved global consciousness in this area? I think we have some understanding of our dynamics, but far from what we need. There is much we don't really understand, and there are enormous disagreements in this area about what the really fundamental dynamics are. Many thinkers are ensconced in various competing schools of thought that have ideological blinders to seeing the value of other schools. Even more dangerous is that our power centers are disconnected from our centers of understanding. Even where there is some agreement among the scholars, the politicians and corporations are not paying attention because their interests are not those of humanity as a whole.

CHOICE OF SOCIETY

Choice of Way of Being. At the individual level, you can go further than just choosing specific actions. You can also, in some cases, choose your overall way of being, the kind of person you want to be. If you realize that you procrastinate and lack discipline, you can work on changing your basic habits to become a more successful worker. If you realize that you are too rigid and constricted and lack joy in life, you can work on becoming spontaneous and expressive. These changes are not easy to make, but they are part of our human repertoire; they are an outgrowth of our self-reflexive consciousness.

In making these changes, it is a great help to understand the psychological dynamics that cause you to be the way you are. This would allow you to say things such as, "I am a workaholic because it was only by working hard that I could get my father's approval." Then you can set out to make deeper changes in your basic personality. This usually requires a persistent effort over a long time. This is the domain of the various psychotherapies and spiritual disciplines.

Choice of Society. Similarly, at the global level humanity needs to be able to choose not only specific actions, but also the kind of society we want—our values, our culture, our basic institutions. In fact, the current planetary crisis requires not only specific remedial actions, but a fundamental change in our whole way of living. As with individual change, this requires an understanding of the dynamics that have caused our society to be as it is. This book, of course, aims at increasingly this kind of understanding. We also need a better understanding of the dynamics of large scale social change.

To make this kind of choice, we must acknowledge that radical change is needed, and then foster serious public debate about the basic direction of our society. These discussions shouldn't be just about policy changes, but about fundamental issues such as our level of consumption, the urban breakdown of community, our consciousness, and all the other issues I touch on in this book. Most importantly, we need the courage and foresight to take action to transform our planet.

We are certainly far from globally conscious at the level of choosing our culture. At this moment we are barely able to take the remedial actions necessary to save ourselves from immediate ruin. Our leaders are certainly not acting out of a desire to make basic changes in our societies. The general population is beginning to become aware that something is seriously wrong, but most people don't understand the scope of the problem or the changes it requires.

GAIA AND EARTH CONSCIOUSNESS

In defining global consciousness, instead of asking if the human race as a whole is conscious, I could have asked if the planet earth is conscious. In an early section I asked "what if" humanity as a whole were an organism, but the earth may very well *be* an organism. James Lovelock (1982) has formulated a scientific hypothesis that the earth as a whole is a living organism, with most of the crucial attributes associated with living creatures. He was especially struck with the planet's homeostatic mechanisms which maintain the conditions for life. He named this the "Gaia hypothesis" after the Greek goddess of the earth.

The Gaia Myth. Along with the scientific merits of his work, he struck a deep chord in the planetary psyche. The Gaia concept has become extremely popular. Many people have been captivated by the idea that the earth is a living creature, perhaps even an aware being or a goddess. Everywhere you turn, the word "Gaia" is in use, referring to the living planet.

I would even suggest that Gaia is the emerging myth of the new planetary culture. Mythologists such as Joseph Campbell (1973) and Jean Houston (1987) teach us that each culture has a myth (or myths) that explains reality to its people. These myths define the larger context for people's lives, giving meaning and providing a guide for behavior. In this sense, the word myth means "guiding story," not "false story."

In our early Western history, people were guided by the Greek and Roman myths that we all studied in high school. Then the Christian myth shaped our civilization for over a millennium. More recently we have been guided by the Horatio Alger myth of the self-made man and the myth of unending scientific and technological progress. Mythologists are now speculating about the myths that may emerge to guide us through our current historical transition and give meaning to the new culture we must create.

I suggest that one of these may be the Gaia myth. This is not a myth in the usual sense, because there isn't a story accompanying the Gaia concept. Perhaps such stories will emerge as the myth takes shape, or perhaps it will remain in its current, more nebulous form. In any case, its popularity is unmistakable. Furthermore, it points to the crucial issue of our time—global consciousness.

Earth Consciousness. As Wilber (1995) points out, the scientific question of whether Gaia is an organism is a very different question from that raised by the Gaia myth, which tends to see Gaia as conscious in some sense. The scientific Gaia operates at the level of planetary geology, while consciousness operates at a much higher level of evolution. Asking whether Gaia is conscious is probably equivalent to asking the question of this chapter—whether the human race as a whole is conscious. It seems that if the planet were conscious, her brain and nervous system would consist of the human race and our information processing and communications systems. Of course, there is a deep organic intelligence to the natural world and the biosphere which is more fundamental than human intelligence. However, I am referring to consciousness here, and human beings and human society seem to be the only possible source for that. If Gaia is to become conscious, we are her means of consciousness.

If the earth is to become conscious through us, we must be identified with all the earth, not just the human race. We must not be dissociated from the biosphere. This means expanding our sense of individual identity even beyond humanity to encompass the natural world. Earlier I discussed expanding our identities and concerns beyond our ethnic groups and nations to include all of humanity. We are called on to expand even further, to feel our kinship with birds and trees, animals and insects, forests and oceans, to recognize that our fate is bound up with the health of the earth. This will help us to make the difficult ecological changes that are necessary for our survival.

Deep Ecology. We could rely on our cognitive understanding of ecological reality to motivate us to care for our environment, but if we also identify with the earth as a whole using our emotional and spiritual capacities, we are more likely to succeed. We need to move beyond global identification to earth identification, beyond global consciousness to *earth consciousness.* This is what is espoused by the "deep ecology" movement, which believes that animals and the natural world have value in their own right, not just as resources for the benefit of human beings.

Then our human global consciousness can be integrated with the underlying intelligence and dynamics of the earth, leading to collective earth identity and collective earth consciousness.

WHOLENESS

The Transition to Consciousness. Let's compare the issues humanity faces now in the transition to global consciousness with those which individuals faced during our prehistory in the transition to self-reflexive consciousness. The major issue that had to be faced in the development of individual self-consciousness was the development of appropriate cognitive and communication (language) skills to make individual identity and self-observation possible. These capacities were developed gradually over hundreds of thousands of years of first biological and then social evolution. Over this time we became intelligent enough to develop ways of naming and understanding objects in our surroundings, and then applied this ability to ourselves.

In the development of global consciousness, we already have sufficient global cognitive and communication abilities. The communication skills are represented by our communication and information technology, which started with writing and numbers, then moved to printing, and now includes telephones, computers, the internet, and the mass media. Our global cognitive capacities started with philosophy and the higher religions and now include our scientific, research, and scholarly traditions. These abilities have only become powerful and accessible enough to allow global consciousness in the last half century.

However, these cognitive and communication capacities are not enough to develop global consciousness. We also need *wholeness.* At the individual level, as we moved from animal to human, we needed only the right cognitive development; we were already whole as a result of our biology. Once we had the cognitive skills, self-reflexive consciousness followed. The human race is not very whole, not very well integrated. Though we are biologically integrated as part of the planetary ecosystem, we have extracted ourselves technologically and emotionally from our ecological base. We have developed societies that are not integrated with the earth and not integrated with each other. As a world, we are fragmented into competing nations, races, ethnic groups, and corporations. We have the cognitive capacities for global consciousness, but we aren't unified. Wholeness is the final step that is needed.

Spiritual Capacities. This wholeness will need to emerge from another set of capacities from the consciousness realm, especially empathy, compassion, vision, and interconnectedness. These attitudes will help us to realize that we are one, that all people and all life are our brothers and sisters. Today the fate of each person's ethnic group and country is intertwined with that of all people and the earth, but this is not easy for many people to see. When a person's psychospiritual capacities are developed, these understandings flow more easily.

At the global level, how are these spiritual integrative capacities manifested? Throughout our history these capacities have been the province of religion, but too often religion has also been divisive and warlike or has been concerned with the heavenly realm while ignoring the material plane. Today there are promising developments in traditional religion toward becoming more socially concerned, ecumenical, and earthy. In addition, the spiritual capacities of compassion and integrative vision are being developed in some of the popular consciousness movements of today as reflexive consciousness advances into stage 6. I have hopes that this will provide us with the planetary abilities that are needed for wholeness, allowing us to become globally conscious.

It should be clear now that I intend global consciousness to be more than just an interesting metaphor. I believe that it is just as valid to apply the concept of consciousness to a society as to a person. A society is simply at a higher level in the containment hierarchy, where we can't directly empathize because we are at the individual level. I believe that at this time in history we are in the process of forming the next level in the containment hierarchy—the global level—and developing its complexity and autonomy. Global consciousness is a crucial step in its evolution.

A VISION

What would the world be like if humanity were globally conscious? People everywhere would see themselves not only as French or Kurds or Hindus, but also as world citizens. They would identify their fate with the fate of humanity and the earth. Rather than having to win a war or an economic competition to feel successful, people would rejoice when humanity as a whole made strides forward. For example, we would feel successful when we could stabilize world population or eradicate hunger.

Globally Conscious Institutions. We would have well-funded, prestigious research and scholarly organizations studying all aspects of our global behavior and attempting to understand our social dynamics. The results of these studies would be widely disseminated and taken seriously by all world citizens, especially those in power.

We would have either a world government or a collection of planetary institutions that have the power to make and enforce decisions on those issues that are truly global in nature. These institutions would deal with war, world environmental issues, population and immigration, trade, development, and certain other issues that necessarily cross national boundaries. They would have global identification. They would serve the interests of humanity as a whole, not just those of the powerful nations. These global institutions would look after our long-term interests, rather than only being concerned with this year's economic results. They would be democratically run, so they truly reflected the will of the world's people and could not be used as instruments of domination and exploitation.

In addition, there would be a myriad of grassroots movements, nongovernmental organizations, and activist groups that care for various aspects of our global (and local) governance and our future. There would especially be groups concerned with our culture as a whole, our social institutions, our worldview, our way of life. One of our global values would be the celebration of cultural diversity. We would give birth to a richer and healthier world society through the creative interaction of many different viewpoints and traditions. Most importantly, we would advance into the future making conscious choices about who we want to be and how we want to live.

If a person becomes part of a larger organism, will he or she lose any individuality or freedom? No more than we already do to political oppression and economic exploitation. Human beings have been struggling against domination for five thousand years and have even made some headway recently. We must work to ensure that our global institutions are at least as democratic as our best nations, and in the long run strive to improve our overall level of democracy. In this way our global decisions will reflect the needs of the earth's people as individuals and communities as well as being attuned to the good of the whole.

A Conscious Earth. There are science fiction stories in which a computer becomes conscious. Perhaps because of its increasing size and complexity, there comes a time when the computer becomes aware of itself. Instead of being simply a machine that does what it is programmed to do in a mechanical, unconscious way, it wakes up and discovers that it can choose what to do. It develops relationships with human beings. It learns to program itself. It becomes like a person.

I am suggesting that humanity as a whole may now be approaching this turning point in our evolution, that Gaia may soon wake up. Just as human beings had to evolve a brain and then a neocortex in order to develop self-reflexive consciousness, Gaia must do the same. The earth has developed its neocortex in the human race and our technologies, and now humanity must develop the global social structures and institutions to play the role of coordinating system in the global brain.

XXV

CONCLUSION

FUTURE STUDIES NEEDED

This book provides a perspective on our current crisis through the lens of long-term social evolution. By seeing these trends, we know more clearly what forces are operating now and how to use and flow with these forces in working to create a healthy stage 6 world. In addition, there are also shorter-term trends operating today, which it would be helpful to comprehend:

1. Societies develop and change over time as a result of internal forces and contradictions and external impacts. In this book I have studied only the long-term evolutionary trends, not the principles by which particular societies change. This kind of study would be very useful in further understanding the forces operating today and how to surmount the planetary crisis.
2. Humanity is in the midst of a transition from one stage to another in social evolution. It would be helpful to study the transition process, how societies move between stages, maybe investigating how it happened in past transitions. This would give us guidelines about how to make the transition as rapid and smooth as possible.

We also need a much better understanding of how to effect and participate in social change, especially fundamental whole-system change as is happening now. What strategies are most effective for a person or an organization or a movement to use in what circumstances in promoting healthy social change? This is an urgent question that has received little systematic study.

SUMMARY

Evolution. Looking at the overall history of the universe, there is an evolutionary trend toward greater complexity and autonomy. This has led from physical matter to life to consciousness, from atoms to cells and organisms to societies and ecosystems. Over time the process has moved from physical evolution of inanimate matter to biological evolution of life forms to social evolution of human societies. This is a very exciting story, perhaps revealing something of the larger purpose of existence.

Evolution operates by the development of autonomy and differentiation and the gradual emergence of new levels in the containment hierarchy. In this process there is a dialectical relationship between these progressive forces and the health-conserving tendency toward wholeness. If differentiation and autonomy disrupt wholeness, then disease, dissociation, and perhaps destruction are the result.

Social Evolution. This has been the case in social evolution so far. To better control the world for our well-being and security, the human race emerged from being embedded in it and analyzed it. We differentiated and organized it and ourselves. This has led to great accomplishments in art and science and religion, humanitarian advances, and a deeper understanding of ourselves and reality.

However, in the process of developing these emergent qualities, we lost sight of the fact that reality is an organic, participatory whole that is vital and meaningful. We suppressed our aliveness and belonging; we disrupted our internal and external wholeness. This loss of our original ground qualities has led to tremendous suffering and oppression, a deadening of ourselves, and ecological destruction. Social evolution has produced both good and bad, but this is not surprising since it has been driven unconsciously by survival needs, not led by a conscious choice of our destiny.

The Next Step. We now need to bring back the ground qualities that have been suppressed and integrate them with the emergent qualities, so that both can develop further. We need to integrate our vitality with our understanding, our community with social structure, our technology with natural process. Then we will have regained our wholeness so it matches our complexity and autonomy. We will have a world where all people have the basics of life and a chance to pursue fulfillment free from war and oppression, a society that is dedicated to those things that are truly meaningful—love, community, creativity, spirituality, and connection to the earth.

We will advance in some way into stage 6 no matter what. The driving forces of the past, which led us toward technology, war, social structure, and rationality, are now operating in a different situation. We have now reached the limits of the capacity of the earth, and this changes everything. These forces will now push us toward an ecological society, whether we choose wisely or not. If we allow ourselves to be forced into this by circumstances, we will endure great suffering and destruction in the process. Our population may be decimated and the earth impoverished before we get to stage 6.

However, we now have the opportunity to choose wisely. Looking back on the process, it seems that there may even have been a necessary logic to the whole evolutionary dialectic, including our current crisis. Through it we have developed our emergent qualities, and therefore we have evolved to the point of being able to understand ourselves and what drives us, to understand social evolution. We have developed a capacity for technology and social structure that, if used properly, can allow us to take decisive action.

Globally Conscious Evolution. For the first time in our history, we have the chance to take charge of our evolution, to guide it consciously for personal and societal well-being. We must do this as a world society, an earth community, a globally conscious whole. This means advancing evolution to a new level in the hierarchy—the global society—and to a new type of evolutionary mechanism—consciousness. This is our great task at this time in the history of the universe, to take this next step in the ongoing story of evolution.

Note on Centers

This series is published under the auspices of the Center for a Postmodern World and the Center for Process Studies.

The Center for a Postmodern World is an independent nonprofit organization in Santa Barbara, California, founded by David Ray Griffin. It promotes the awareness and exploration of the postmodern worldview and encourages reflection about a postmodern world, from postmodern art, spirituality, and education to a postmodern world order, with all this implies for economics, ecology, and security. One of its major projects is to produce a collaborative study that marshals the numerous facts supportive of a postmodern worldview and provides a portrayal of a postmodern world order toward which we can realistically move. It is located at 6891 Del Playa, Isla Vista, California 93117.

The Center for Process Studies is a research organization affiliated with the School of Theology at Claremont and Claremont University Center and Graduate School. It was founded by John B. Cobb, Jr., Director, and David Ray Griffin, Executive Director; Mary Elizabeth Moore and Marjorie Suchocki are also Co-Directors. It encourages research and reflection upon the process philosophy of Alfred North Whitehead, Charles Hartshorne, and related thinkers, and upon the application and testing of this viewpoint in all areas of thought and practice. This center sponsors conferences, welcomes visiting scholars to use its library, and publishes a scholarly journal, *Process Studies*, and a quarterly *Newsletter*. It is located at 1325 North College, Claremont, California 91711.

Both centers gratefully accept (tax-deductible) contributions to support their work.

About the Author

Jay Earley offers groups and workshops in the San Francisco Bay Area relating personal and spiritual growth to social transformation.

Bibliography

Abraham, R., T. McKenna, and R. Sheldrake (1992). *Trialogues at the Edge of the West.* Sante Fe: Bear & Co.

Almaas, A. H. (1987). *The Pearl beyond Price.* Berkeley, CA: Diamond Books.

Anderson, W. T. (1987). *To Govern Evolution: Further Adventures of the Political Animal.* Boston: Harcourt Brace Javanovich.

———. (1990). *Reality Isn't What It Used to Be.* San Francisco: Harper & Row.

Atlee, T. (1991). "Transformational Politics." *Thinkpeace* 7.3: 1–5.

———. (1992). "Permaculture." *Thinkpeace* 8.1: insert.

Aurobindo, S. (1970). *The Life Divine.* Pondicherry, India: Sri Aurobindo Ashram.

Barnouw, V. (1963). *Culture and Personality.* Homewood, IL: Dorsey Press.

Bateson, G. (1972). *Steps to an Ecology of Mind.* Northvale, NJ: Jason Aronson.

Bellah, R., R. Madsen, W. M. Sullivan, A. Swidler, and S. M. Tipton. (1985). *Habits of the Heart.* New York: Harper & Row.

Berman, M. (1984). *The Reenchantment of the World.* Toronto: Bantam Books.

———. (1990). *Coming to Our Senses: Body and Spirit in the Hidden History of the West.* New York: Bantam Books.

Beck, A., J. Rush, B. Shaw, and G. Emery (1979). *Cognitive Therapy of Depression.* New York: Guilford.

Berry, T. (1990). *The Dream of the Earth.* San Francisco: Sierra Club Books.

Bly, R. (1990). *Iron John.* New York: Random House.

Bookchin, M. (1982). *The Ecology of Freedom.* Palo Alto, CA: Cheshire Books.

Bradova, V. (1993). "Participatory Democracy." *Thinkpeace* 9.39: 1–8.

Bugental, J. (1965). *The Search for Authenticity.* New York: Holt, Rinehart & Winston.

Campbell, J. (1964). *Occidental Mythology.* New York: Viking.

———. (1973). *Hero with a Thousand Faces.* Princeton: Princeton University Press.

Capra, F. (1982). *The Turning Point.* New York: Simon & Schuster.

———. (1993). "Bringing Forth a World." *Elmwood Quarterly* 9.3: 4–6.

Chinen, A. B. (1993). *Beyond the Hero: Classic Tales for Men in Search of Soul.* Los Angeles: Tarcher.

Cobb, J. B. (1990). "From Individualism to Persons in Community: A Postmodern Economic Theory." In D. R. Griffin, ed., *Postmodern Spirituality, Political Economy, and Art.* Albany, NY: SUNY Press.

Daly, H. (1977). *Steady State Economics.* San Francisco: W. H. Freeman.

Daly, H. E. (1988). "The Steady-State Economy: Postmodern Alternative to Growthmania." In D. R. Griffin, ed., *Spirituality and Society.* Albany, NY: SUNY Press.

Daly, H. E. and J. B. Cobb. (1989). *For the Common Good.* Boston: Beacon Press.

Deloria, V. (1993). "If You Think about It, You Will See That It is True." *Noetic Sciences Review* 27: 62–71.

Dreher, H. and B. McNeill. (1993). "Mind-Body Health: The Birth of a Movement." *Noetic Sciences Review* 27: 28–36.

Earley, J. (1990). *Inner Journeys: A Guide to Personal and Social Transformation.* York Beach, ME: Samuel Weiser.

———. (in press). *Interactive Group Therapy: Theory and Practice.*

Ehrlich, P. R. and A. H. Ehrlich (1991). *The Population Explosion.* New York: Simon & Schuster.

Eisler, R. (1987). *The Chalice and The Blade: Our History, Our Future.* San Francisco: Harper & Row.

Elbow, P. (1973). *Writing without Teachers.* New York: Oxford University Press.

Elgin, D. (1993). *Awakening Earth.* New York: Morrow.

Ellis, A. (1962). *Reason and Emotion in Psychotherapy.* Secaucus, NJ: Lyle Stuart.

Erikson, E. (1963). *Childhood and Society.* New York: Norton.

Etzioni, A. (1993). *The Spirit of Community: Rights, Responsibilities and the Communitarian Agenda.* New York: Crown.

Ferguson, M. (1980). *The Aquarian Conspiracy.* Los Angeles: Tarcher.

Feuerstein, G. (1987). *Structures of Consciousness.* Lower Lake, CA: Integral Publishing.

Fodor, I. E. (1996). "A Cognitive Perspective for Gestalt Therapy." *British Gestalt Journal.* 5.1: 31–42.

Fried, M. H. (1967). *The Evolution of Political Society.* New York: Random House.

Gardner, H. (1983). *Frames of Mind.* New York: Basic Books.

Gebser, J. (1986). *The Ever-Present Origin.* Athens, OH: Ohio University Press.

Gilligan, C. (1982). *In a Different Voice.* Cambridge, MA: Harvard University Press.

Gilman, R. (1993). "Looking Back from 2003." *In Context* 36: 56–60.

Glantz, K. and J. K. Pearce (1989). *Exiles from Eden.* New York: Norton.

Gleick, J. (1987). *Chaos: Making a New Science.* New York: Penguin.

Goldsmith, E. (1993). *The Way: An Ecological World-view.* Boston: Shambhala.

Greenberg, L. S. and J. Pascual-Leone (1994). In R. A. Neimeyer and M. J. Mahoney, eds., *Constructivism in Psychotherapy.* Washington, DC: American Psychological Association.

Grinde, R. A. (1991). "Iroquois Political Theory and the Roots of American Democracy." *Exiled in the Land of the Free.* Santa Fe: Clear Light.

Guidano, V. F. (1991). *The Self in Process.* New York: Guilford Press.

Halal, W. E. (1994). "Let's Turn Organizations into Markets." *The Futurist* 28.3: 9–14.

Halal, W. E., A. Geranmayeh, and J. Pourdehnad, eds. (1993). *Internal Markets: Bringing the Power of Free Enterprise Inside Your Organization.* New York: Wiley.

Hanh, T. N. (1993). *Touching Peace.* Berkeley: Parallax Press.

Harman, W. (1988). *Global Mind Change.* Indianapolis: Knowledge Systems.

Harris, M. (1978). *Cannibals and Kings.* New York: Vintage Books.

———. (1980). *Cultural Materialism: The Struggle for a Science of Culture.* New York: Vintage Books.

Hawken, P. (1993). "A Declaration of Sustainability." *Utne Reader* 59: 54–61.

———. (1993). *The Ecology of Commerce.* New York: HarperCollins.

Houston, J. (1987). *The Search for the Beloved: Journeys in Sacred Psychology.* Los Angeles: Tarcher.

Institute of Noetic Sciences. (1993). "How Do We Know What We Think We Know? Toward an Epistemology of Consciousness." *Noetic Sciences Review* 27: 72–76.

Jaynes, J. (1976). *The Origin of Consciousness in the Breakdown of the Bicameral Mind.* Boston: Houghton Mifflin.

Johnson, A. W. and T. Earle (1987). *The Evolution of Human Societies.* Stanford, CA: Stanford University Press.

Johnston, C. M. (1984). *The Creative Imperative.* Berkeley, CA: Celestial Arts.

———. (1991). *Necessary Wisdom: Meeting the Challenge of a New Cultural Maturity.* Seattle: ICD Press.

Kahler, E. (1956). *Man the Measure: A New Approach to History.* New York: Braziller.

Kegan, R. (1982). *The Evolving Self: Problem and Process in Human Development.* Cambridge, MA: Harvard University Press.

Kidder, R. M. (1994). *Shared Values for a Troubled World.* San Francisco: Jossey-Bass.

Koestler, A. (1978). *Janus.* New York: Random House.

Korten, D. C. (1993). "Coming Back to Life." *In Context* 36: 18–23.

———. (1995). *When Corporations Rule the World.* Hartford, CT: Kumarian Press.

Lappé, F. M. and P. DuBois (1994). *The Quickening of America.* San Francisco: Jossey-Bass.

Laszlo, E. (1987). *Evolution: The Grand Synthesis.* Boston: Shambhala.

Lenski, G. and J. Lenski (1987). *Human Societies: An Introduction to Macrosociology.* New York: McGraw-Hill.

Lewin, R. (1992). *Complexity: Life at the Edge of Chaos.* New York: Macmillan.

Liddon, S. C. (1989). *The Dual Brain, Religion, and the Unconscious.* Buffalo, NY: Prometheus Books.

Lovelock, J. (1982). *Gaia: A New Look at Life on Earth.* Oxford: Oxford University Press.

Lowen, A. (1975) *Bioenergetics.* New York: Penguin.

Macy, J. (1990). "The Ecological Self: Postmodern Ground for Right Action." In D. R. Griffin, ed., *Postmodern Spirituality, Political Economy, and Art.* Albany, NY: SUNY Press.

———. (1991). *World as Lover, World as Self.* Berkeley: Parallax Press.

Mahler, M., F. Pine and A. Bergman (1975). *The Psychological Birth of the Human Infant.* New York: Basic Books.

Maturana, H. R. and F. J. Varela (1987). *The Tree of Knowledge.* Boston: Shambhala.

McLaughlin, C. and G. Davidson (1990). *Builders of the Dawn.* Summertown, TN: The Book Publishing Co.

McNeill, W. (1976). *Plagues and People.* New York: Doubleday/Anchor.

Meadows, D. H., D. L. Meadows, and J. Randers (1992). *Beyond The Limits.* Port Mills, VT: Chelsea Green.

Milner, H. (1989). *Sweden: Social Democracy in Practice.* New York: Oxford University Press.

Mollison, B. (1990). *Permaculture: A Practical Guide for a Sustainable Future.* Conelo, CA: Island Press.

Moreno, J. L. (1956). *Psychodrama: Foundations of Psychotherapy,* vol. 2. Beacon, NY: Beacon House.

Morris, D. (1993). "A Globe of Villages." *In Context* 36: 28–32.

Morrison, R. (1991). *We Build the Road as We Travel.* Philadelphia: New Society Publishers.

Olson, R. L. (1991). "The Greening of High Tech." *The Futurist* (May–June) 28–34.

Ornstein, R. and P. Ehrlich (1989). *New World, New Mind.* New York: Simon & Schuster.

Parsons, T. (1966). *Societies: Evolutionary and Comparative Perspectives.* Englewood Cliffs, NJ: Prentice Hall.

Peavey, F. (1986). *Heart Politics.* Philadelphia: New Society Publishers.

Peck, S. (1987). *The Different Drum: Community-Making and Peace.* New York: Simon & Schuster.

Perls, F., R. F. Hefferline, and P. Goodman (1951). *Gestalt Therapy.* New York: Bantam.

Perry, J. W. (1987). *The Heart of History: Individuality in Evolution.* Albany, NY: SUNY Press.

Piaget, J. (1977). *The Essential Piaget.* New York: Basic Books.

Rifkin, J. (1981). *Entropy: A New World View.* Toronto: Bantam Books.

———. (1991). *Biosphere Politics.* New York: Crown Publishers, Inc.

———. (1994). *The End of Work.* New York: Putnam.

Robarchek, C. A. (1989). "Hobbesian and Rousseauan Images of Man: Autonomy and Individualism in a Peaceful Society." *Societies at Peace: Anthropological Perspectives.* New York: Routledge.

Robertson, J. (1990). *Future Wealth.* New York: Bootstrap Press.

Roszak, T. (1992). *The Voice of the Earth.* New York: Simon & Schuster.

Rozin, P. and C. Nemeroff (1990). "The Laws of Sympathetic Magic: A Psychological Analysis of Similarity and Contagion." *Cultural Psychology: Essays on Comparative Human Development.* Cambridge: Cambridge University Press.

Russell, P. (1983). *The Global Brain.* Los Angeles: Tarcher.

Sagan, E. (1985). *At the Dawn of Tyranny.* New York: Knopf.

Sahlins, M. (1962). *Moala: Culture and Nature on a Fijian Island.* Ann Arbor, MI: University of Michigan Press.

———. (1972). *Stone Age Economics.* Chicago: Aldine.

Sahlins, M. D. and E. R. Service, eds. (1988). *Evolution and Culture.* Ann Arbor, MI: University of Michigan Press.

Sale, K. (1991). *Dwellers in the Land.* Philadelphia: New Society Publishers.

Schaef, A. W. (1987). *When Society Becomes an Addict.* San Francisco: Harper & Row.

Schmookler, A. B. (1984). *The Parable of the Tribes.* Boston: Houghton Mifflin Co. Second edition, Albany, NY: SUNY Press, 1994.

———. (1988). *Out of Weakness: Healing the Wounds that Drive us to War.* New York: Bantam.

———. (1993). *The Illusion of Choice.* Albany, NY: SUNY Press.

Shaffer, C. R. and K. Anundsen (1993). *Creating Community Anywhere.*

New York: Tarcher.

Spretnak, C. (1993). *States of Grace.* San Francisco: Harper & Row.

Stern, D. (1985). *The Interpersonal World of the Infant.* New York: Basic Books.

Swimme, B. and T. Berry (1992). *The Universe Story.* San Francisco: Harper & Row.

Tarnas, R. (1991). *The Passion of the Western Mind.* New York: Harmony Books.

Taylor, E. (1993). "Our Roots: The American Visionary Tradition." *Noetic Sciences Review* 27: 6–17.

Teilhard de Chardin (1965). *The Phenomenon of Man.* New York: Harper & Row.

Tibbs, H. B. C. (1992). "Industrial Ecology: An Environmental Agenda for Industry." *Whole Earth Review* 77: 4–19.

Todd, J. and N. J. Todd (1993). *From Ecocities to Living Machines.* Berkeley, CA: North Atlantic Books.

Turner, V. (1974). "Passages, Margins, and Poverty: Religious Symbols of Communitas." In *Dramas, Fields, and Metaphors: Symbolic Action in Human Society.* Ithaca, NY: Cornell University Press.

van Gelder, S. (1994). *In Context,* 38 (Spring 1994).

von Bertalanffy, L. (1968). *General System Theory.* New York: Braziller.

Waldrop, M. M. (1992). *Complexity: The Emerging Science at the Edge of Order and Chaos.* New York: Simon & Schuster.

Washburn, M. (1988). *The Ego and the Dynamic Ground.* Albany, NY: SUNY Press. Second edition, Albany, NY: SUNY Press, 1995.

———. (1994). *Transpersonal Psychology in Psychoanalytic Perspective.* Albany, NY: SUNY Press.

Whyte, L. L. (1948). *The Next Development in Man.* New York: Henry Holt.

Wilber, K. (1977). *The Spectrum of Consciousness.* Wheaton, IL: Quest Books.

———. (1980). *The Atman Project.* Wheaton, IL: Quest Books.

———. (1983). *Up from Eden: A Transpersonal View of Human Evolution.* Boulder, CO: Shambhala.

———. (1986). *Transformations of Consciousness.* Boston: Shambhala.

———. (1995). *Sex, Ecology, Spirituality.* Boston: Shambhala.

Wilson, E. O. and S. R. Kellert (1993). *The Biophilia Hypothesis.* Washington, DC: Shearwater Books.

Index